Chi's Sweet Home

チーズ スイートホーム

10

Konami Kanata

contents
homemade 165~182 + 🐾

165 a cat guides 3

166 a cat feels certain 11

167 a cat is watched 19

168 a cat is concerning 27

169 a cat communicates 35

170 a cat is misread 43

171 a cat has signals crossed 51

172 a cat is told 59

173 a cat goes to see 67

174 a cat ponders 75

175 a cat realizes 83

176 a cat queries 91

177 a cat is briefed 99

178 a cat trains 107

179 a cat holds 115

180 a cat masters 123

181 a cat joins up 131

182 a cat begins to change 139

🐾 extras 147

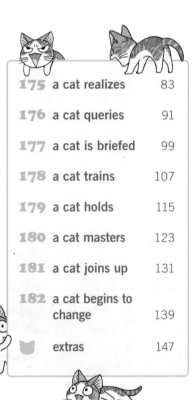

homemade 165: a cat guides

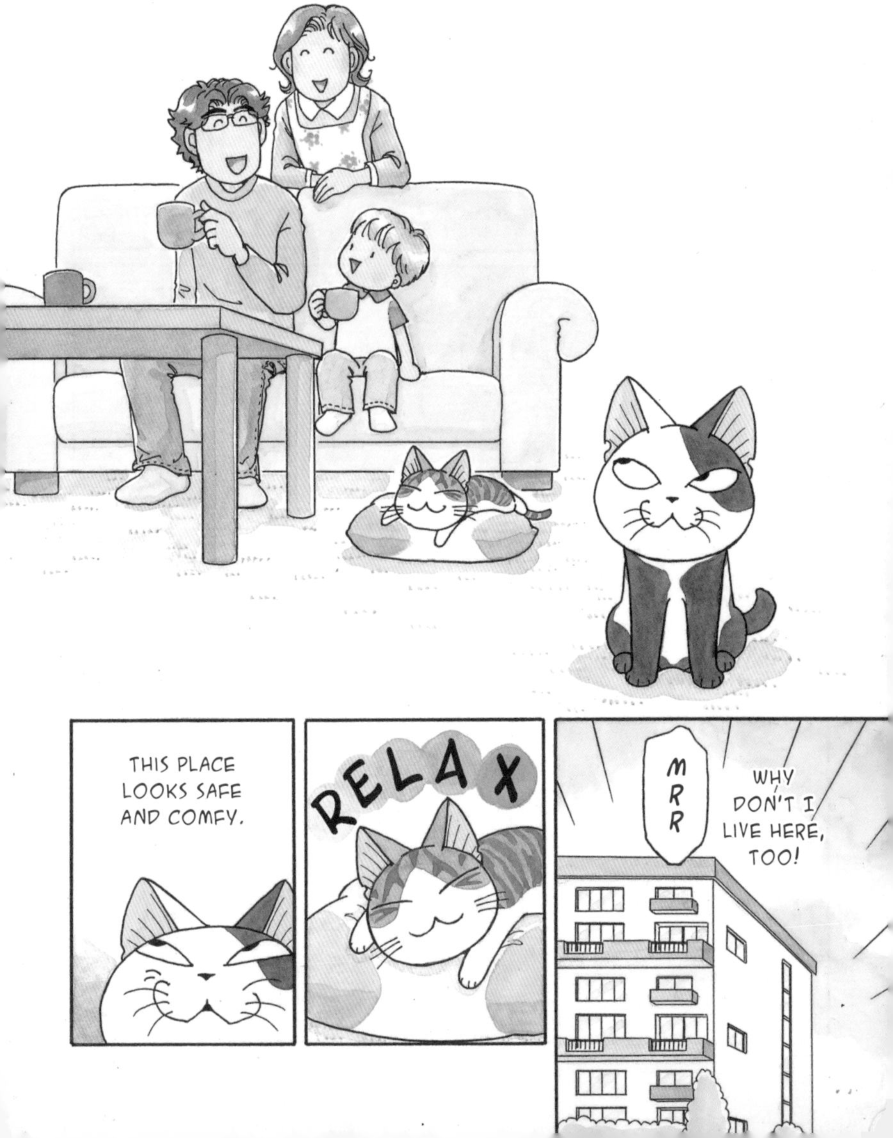
THIS PLACE LOOKS SAFE AND COMFY.
RELAX
MRR
WHY DON'T I LIVE HERE, TOO!

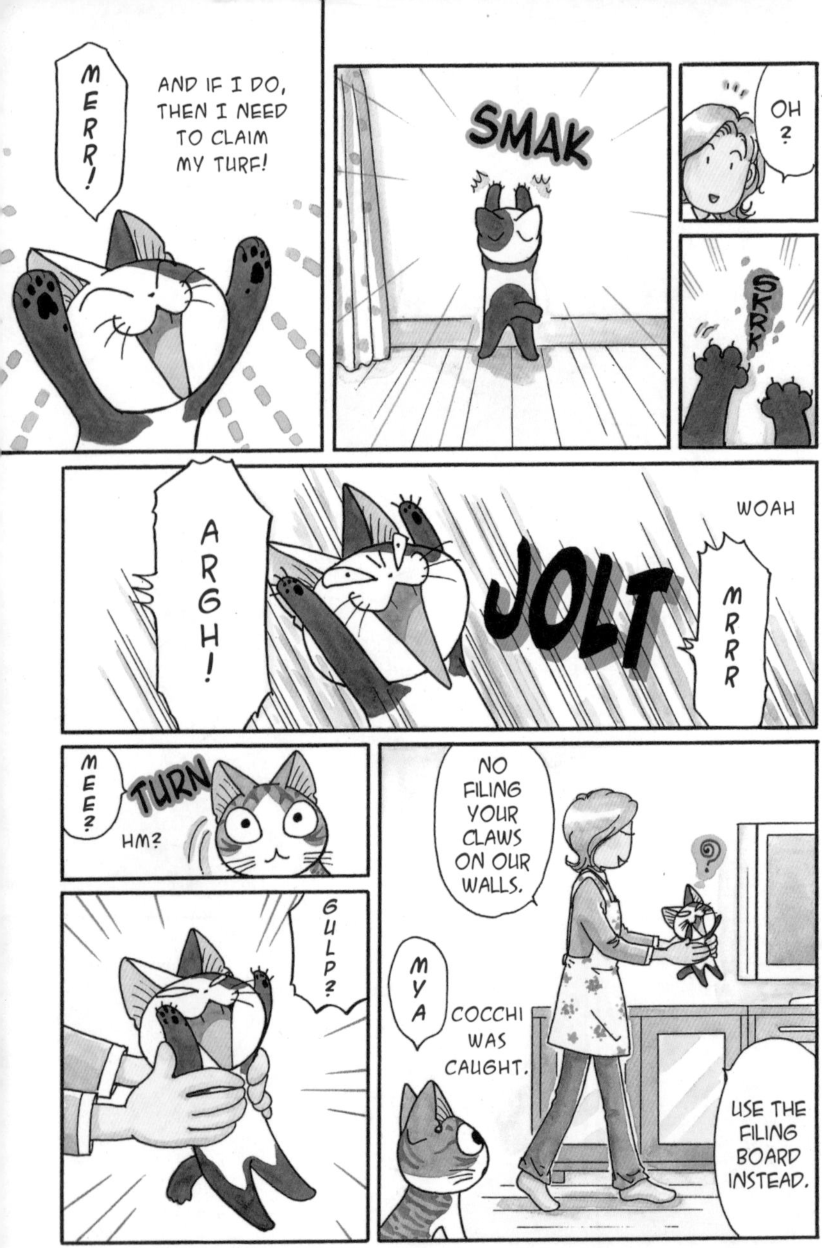
MERR!
AND IF I DO, THEN I NEED TO CLAIM MY TURF!
SMAK
OH?
SKRK
ARGH!
JOLT
WOAH
MRRR
MEE?
TURN
HM?
NO FILING YOUR CLAWS ON OUR WALLS.
MYA
COCCHI WAS CAUGHT.
USE THE FILING BOARD INSTEAD.
GULP?

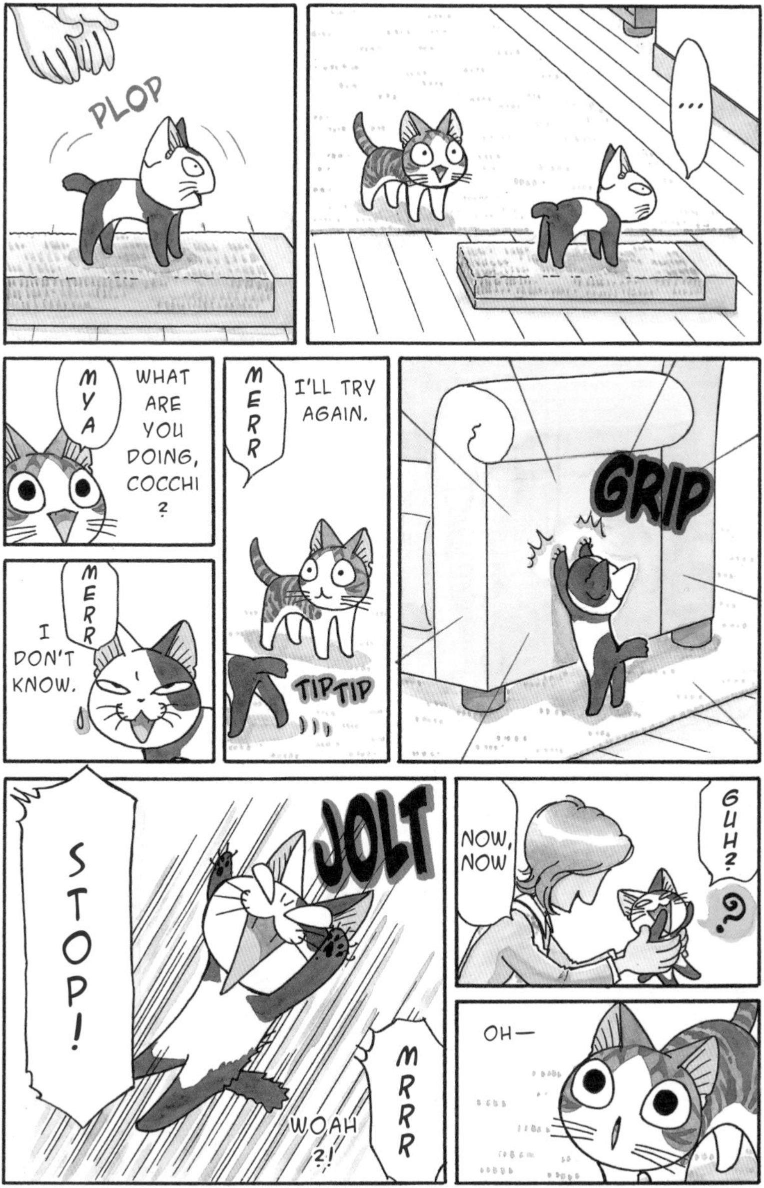
PLOP
...
MYA
WHAT ARE YOU DOING, COCCHI?
MERR
I DON'T KNOW.
MERR
I'LL TRY AGAIN.
TIPTIP
GRIP
STOP!
JOLT
WOAH?!
MRRR
NOW, NOW
GUH?
?
OH—

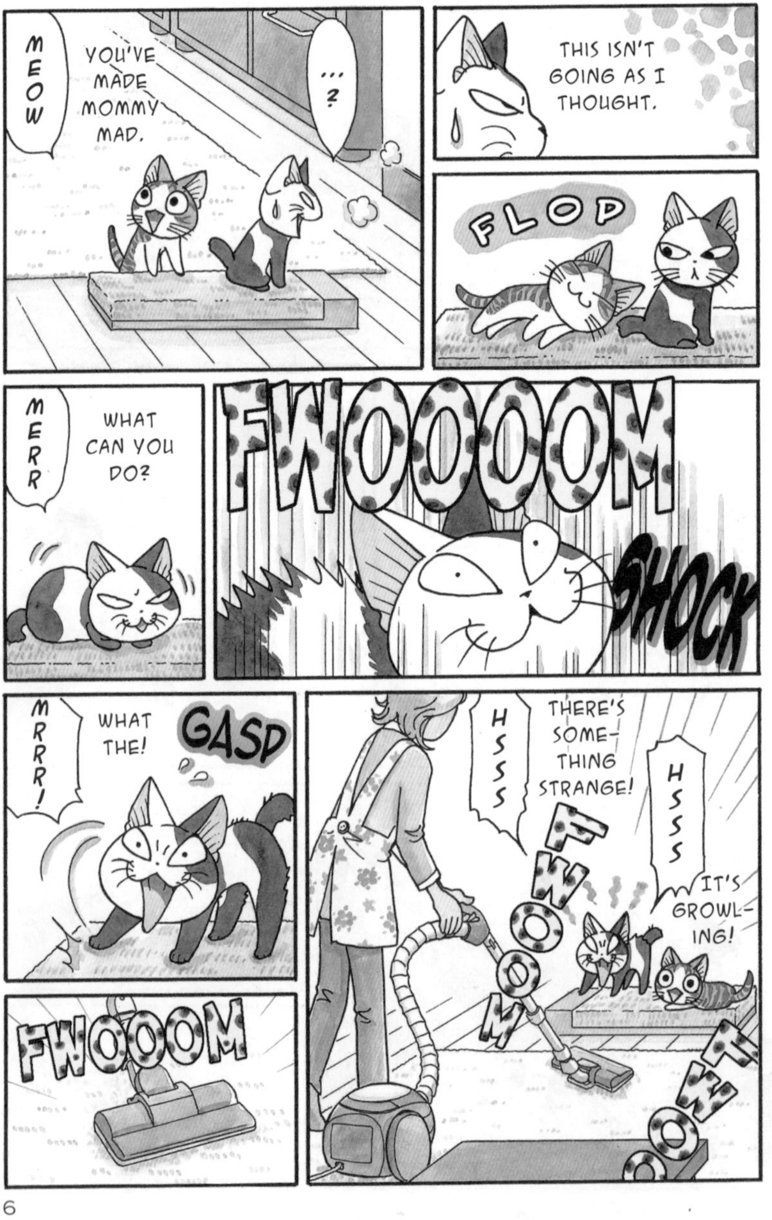
MEOW
YOU'VE MADE MOMMY MAD.
...?
THIS ISN'T GOING AS I THOUGHT.
FLOP
MERR
WHAT CAN YOU DO?
FWOOOOM
SHOCK
MRRR!
WHAT THE!
GASP
FWOOOM
HSSS
THERE'S SOME-THING STRANGE!
HSSS
FWOOOM
IT'S GROWL-ING!

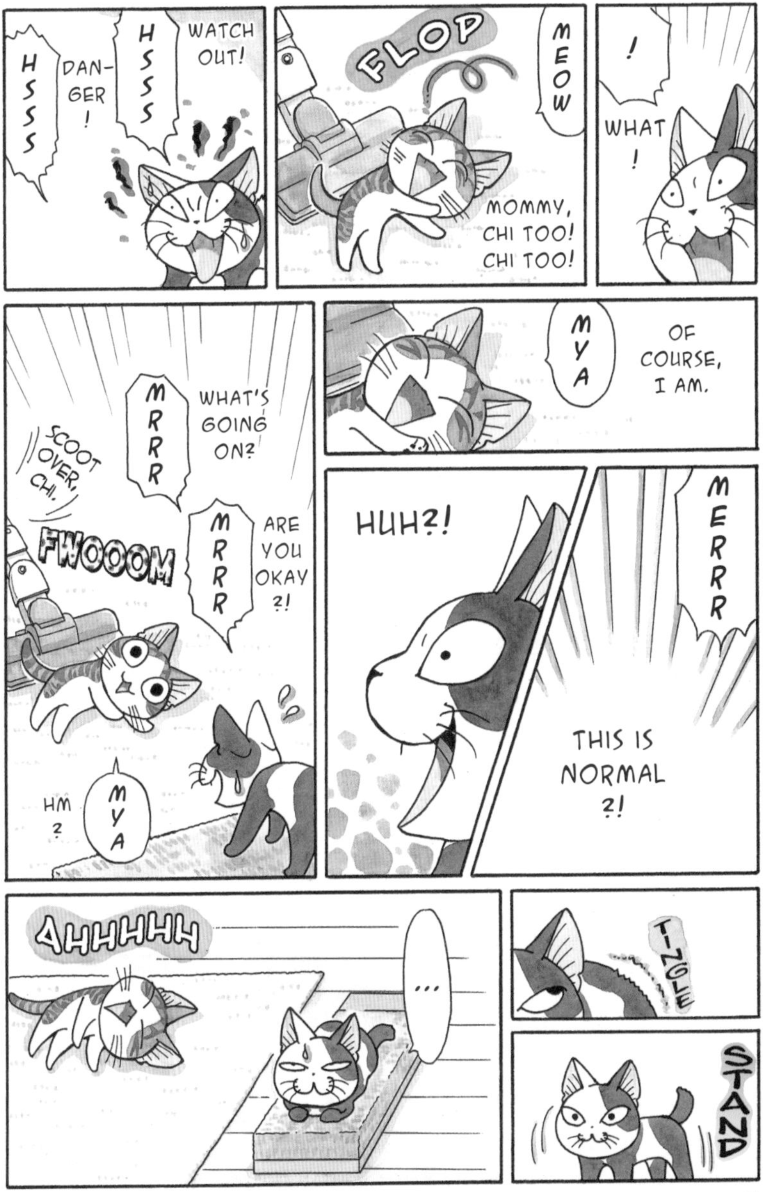
HSSS
DAN-GER!
HSSS
WATCH OUT!
FLOP
MEOW
MOMMY, CHI TOO! CHI TOO!
!
WHAT!
SCOOT OVER, CHI.
FWOOOM
MRRR
WHAT'S GOING ON?
MRRR
ARE YOU OKAY?!
HM?
MYA
MYA
OF COURSE, I AM.
HUH?!
MERRR
THIS IS NORMAL?!
AHHHHH
...
TINGLE
STAND

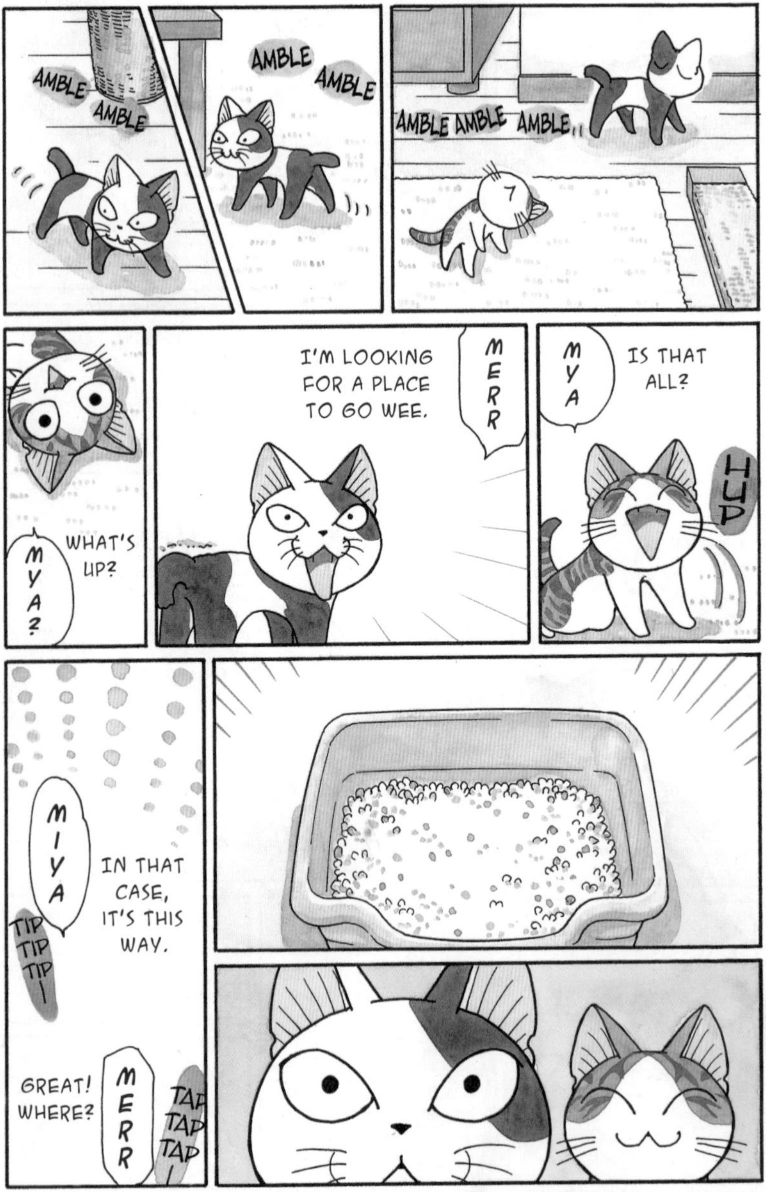
AMBLE
AMBLE
AMBLE
AMBLE
AMBLE AMBLE AMBLE..
MYA?
WHAT'S UP?
MERR
I'M LOOKING FOR A PLACE TO GO WEE.
MYA
IS THAT ALL?
HUP
MIYA
IN THAT CASE, IT'S THIS WAY.
TIP TIP TIP
MERR
GREAT! WHERE?
TAP TAP TAP

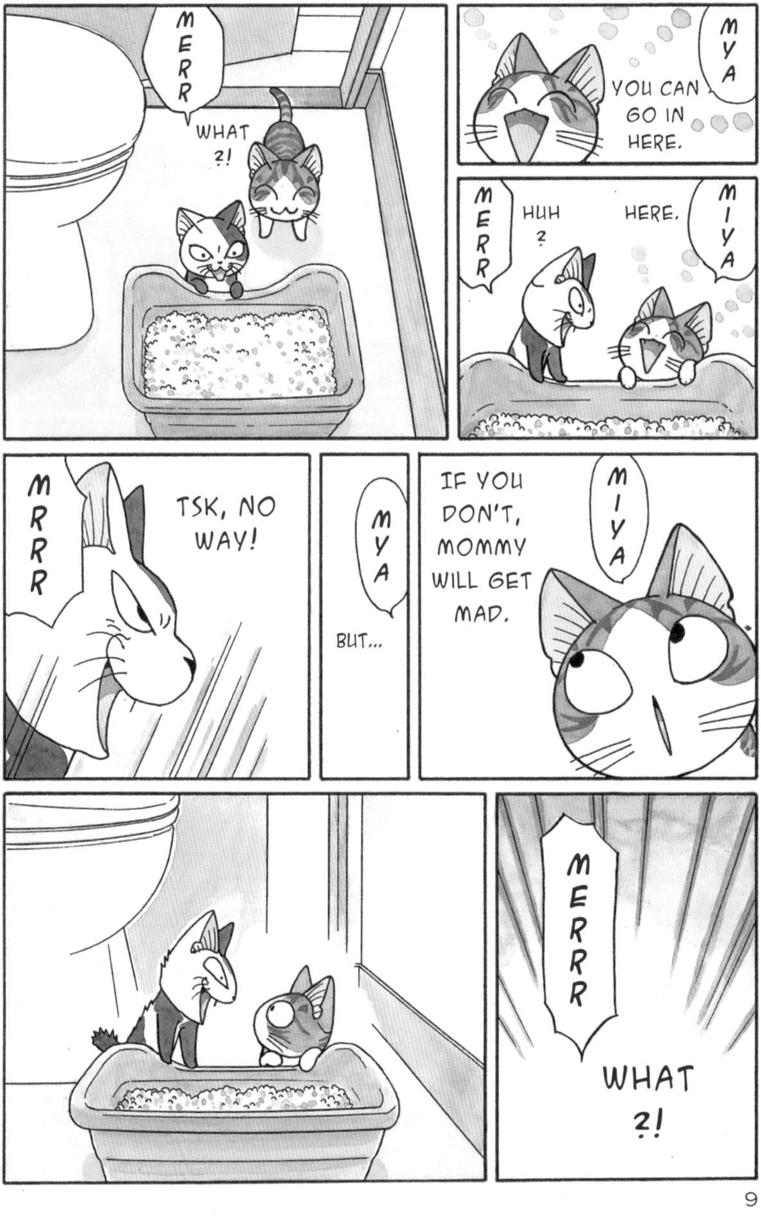

MERR
WHAT ?!
MYA
YOU CAN GO IN HERE.
MERR
HUH ?
HERE.
MIYA
MRRR
TSK, NO WAY!
MYA
BUT...
IF YOU DON'T, MOMMY WILL GET MAD.
MIYA
MERRR
WHAT ?!

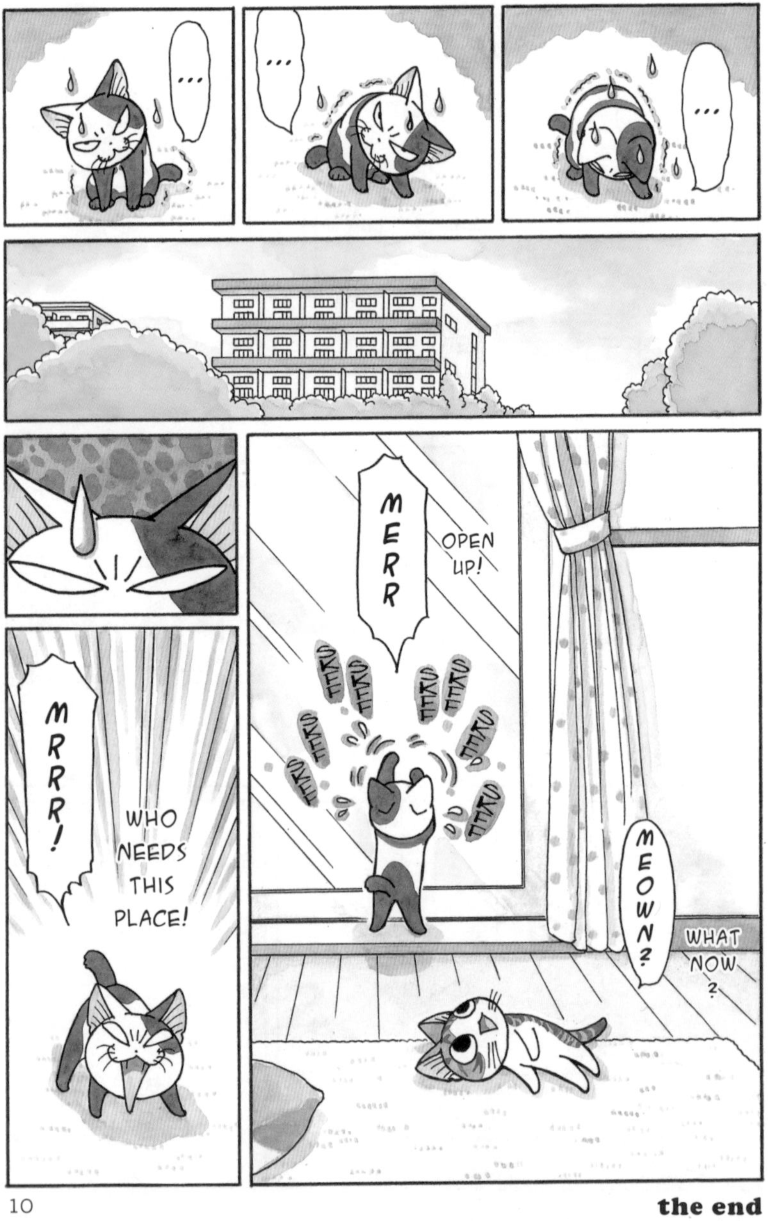
...
...
...
MRRR!
WHO NEEDS THIS PLACE!
MERR
OPEN UP!
SKEE
SKEE
SKEE
SKEE
SKEE
SKEE
SKEE
SKEE
MEOWN?
WHAT NOW?

the end

homemade 166: a cat feels certain

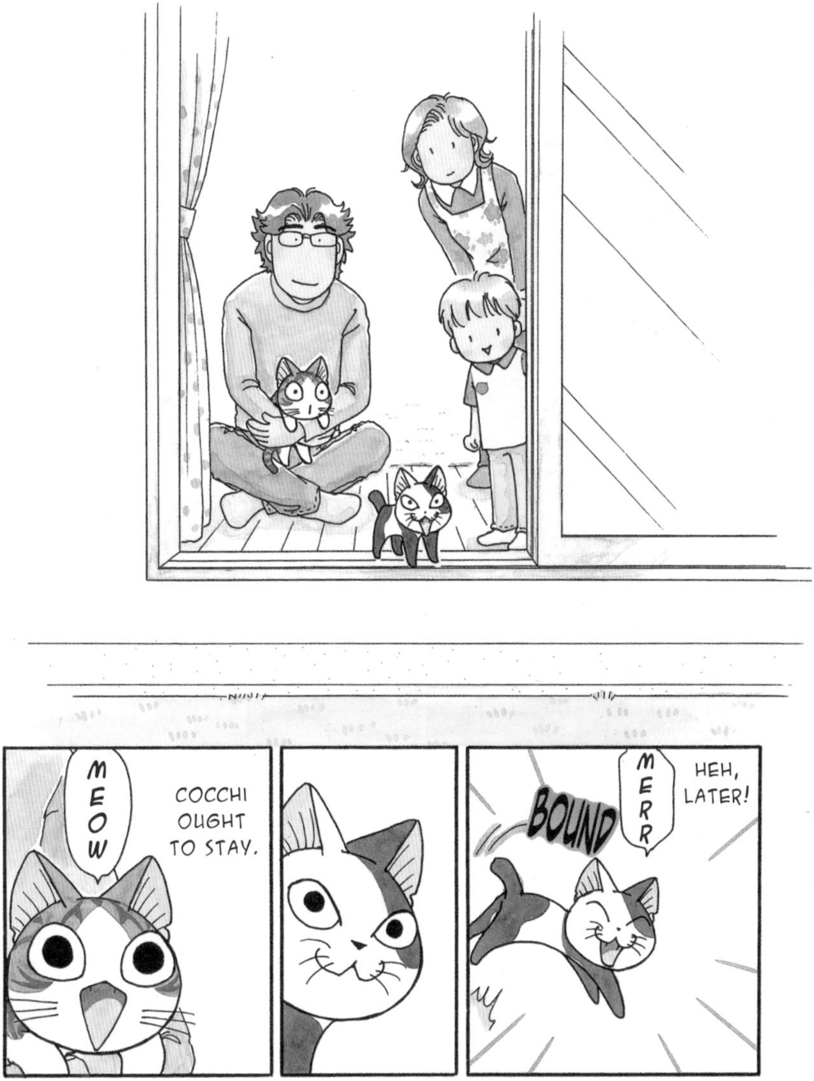
MEOW
COCCHI OUGHT TO STAY.
BOUND
MERR
HEH, LATER!

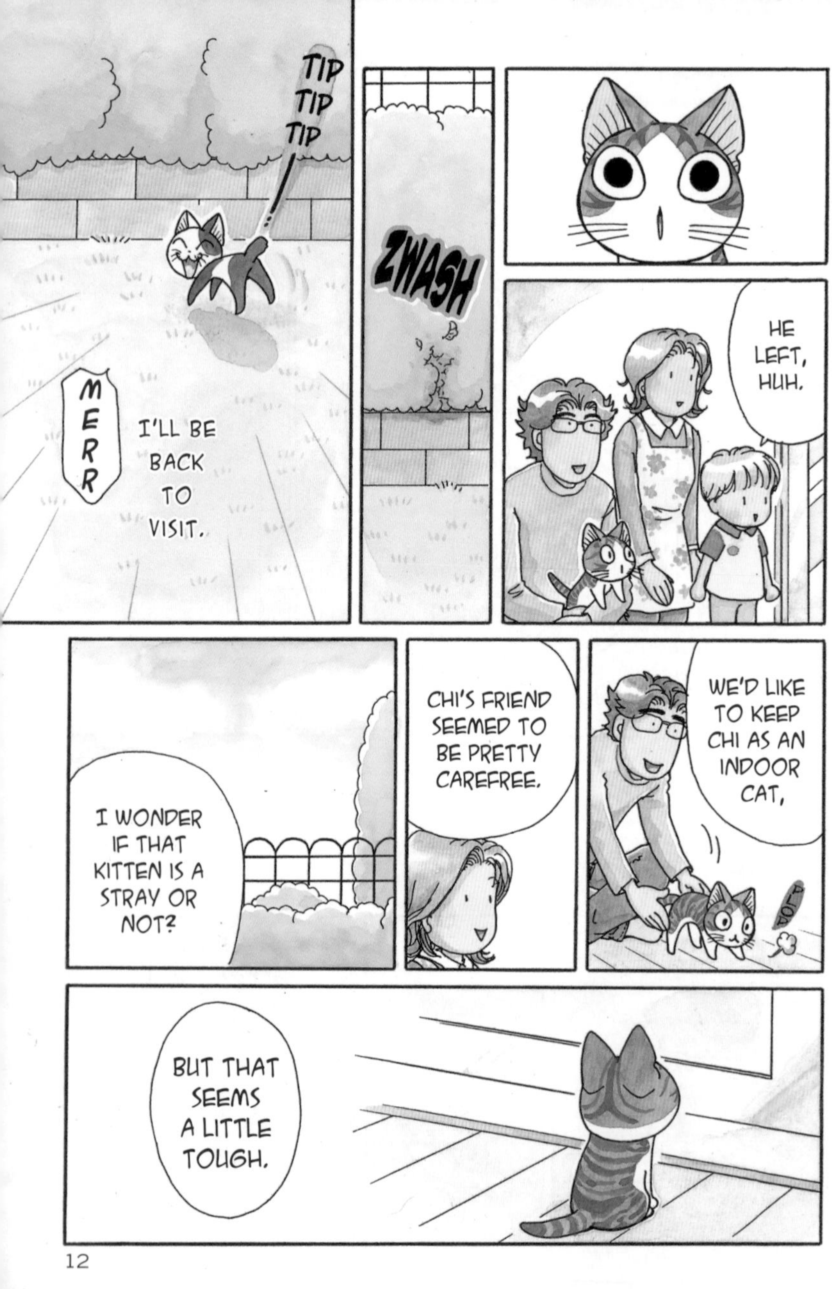
TIP
TIP
TIP
MERR
I'LL BE BACK TO VISIT.
ZWASH
HE LEFT, HUH.
I WONDER IF THAT KITTEN IS A STRAY OR NOT?
CHI'S FRIEND SEEMED TO BE PRETTY CAREFREE.
WE'D LIKE TO KEEP CHI AS AN INDOOR CAT,
BUT THAT SEEMS A LITTLE TOUGH.

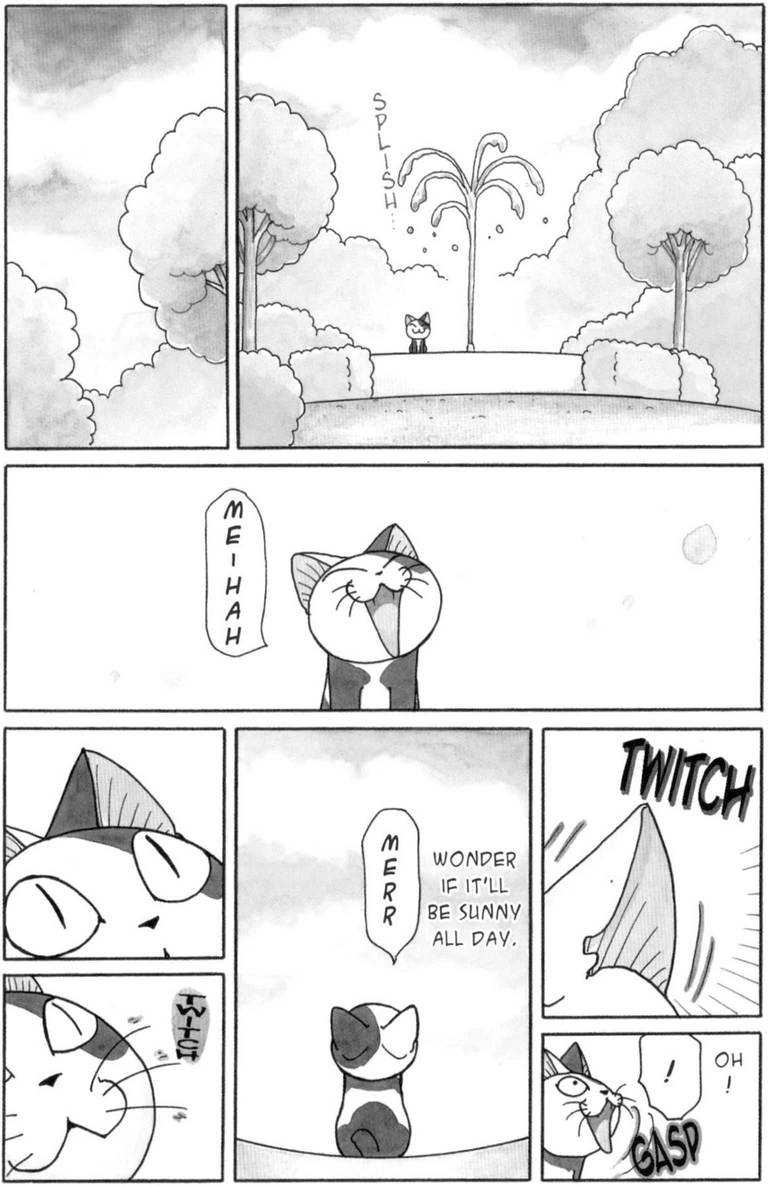
SPLISH..
MEIHAH
TWITCH
MERR
WONDER IF IT'LL BE SUNNY ALL DAY.
TWITCH
!
OH!
GASP

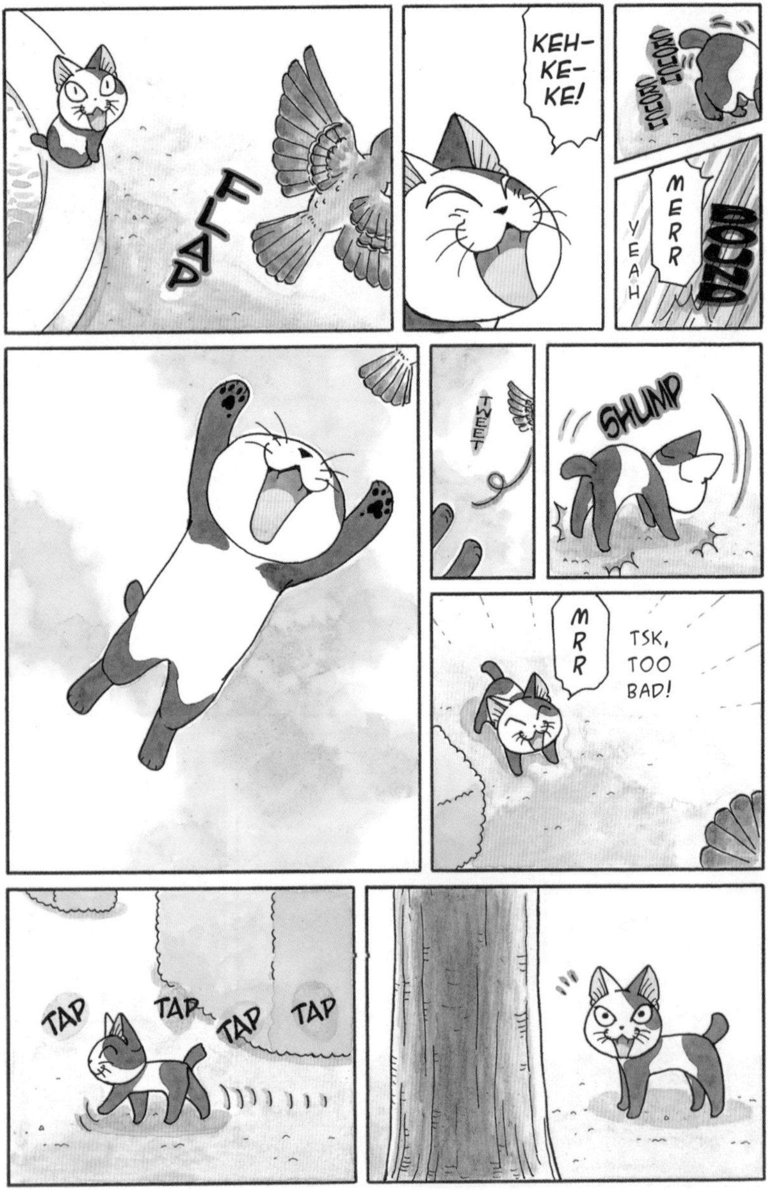
FLAP
KEH-KE-KE!
CROUCH CROUCH
MERR
YEAH
BOING
TWEET
SHUMP
MRR
TSK, TOO BAD!
TAP TAP TAP TAP

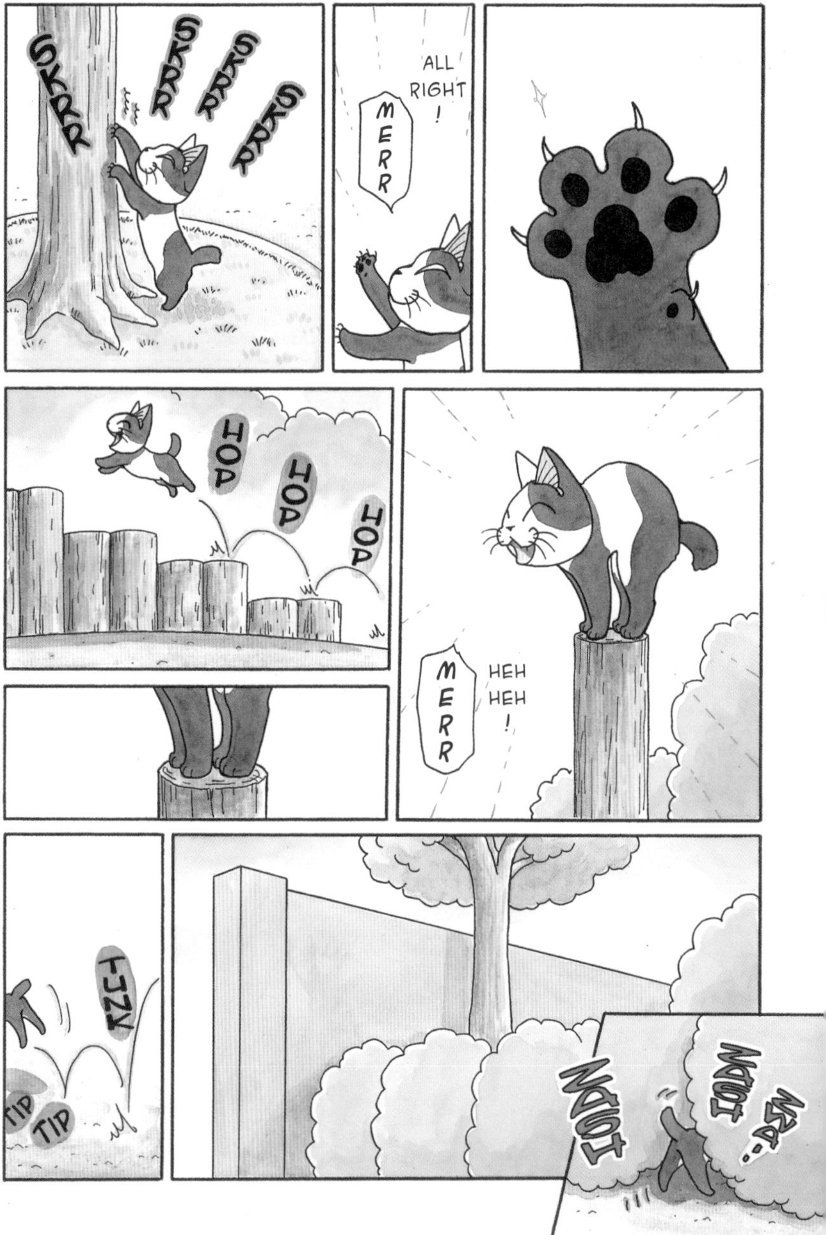
SKRR
SKRR
SKRR
SKRR
MERR
ALL RIGHT!
HOP
HOP
HOP
MERR
HEH HEH!
TIP
TIP

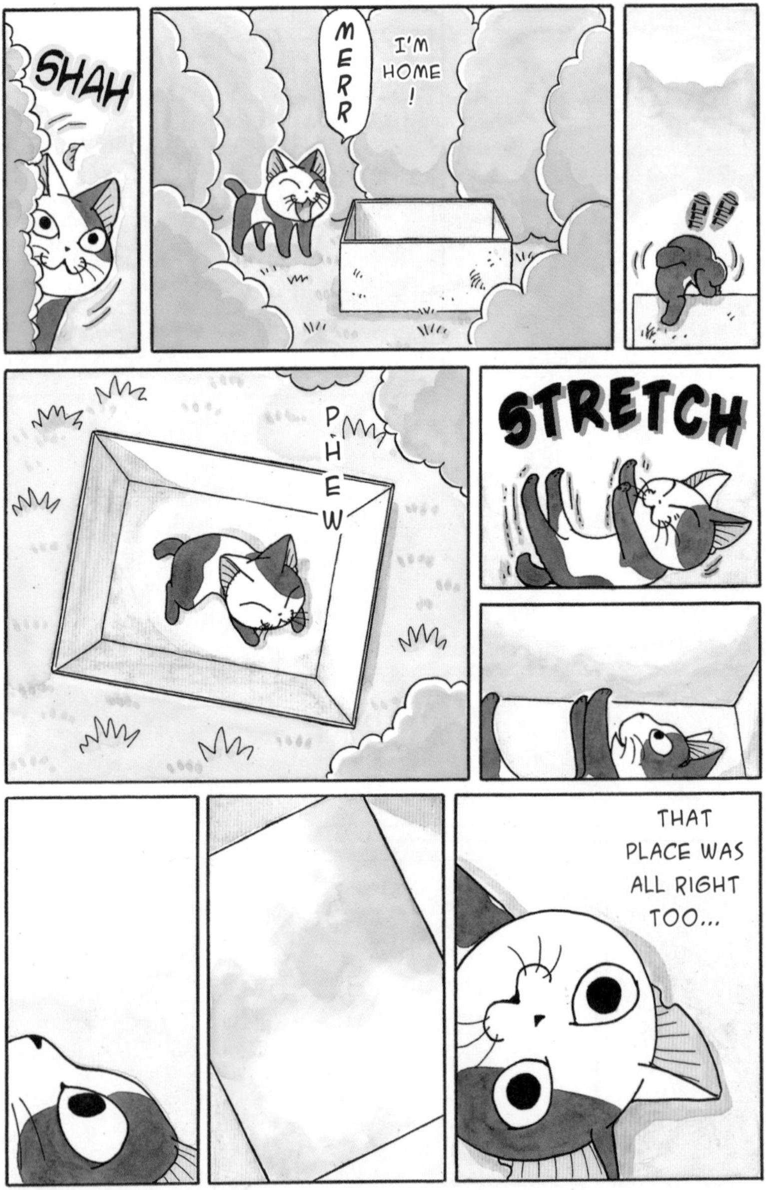
SHAH
MERR
I'M HOME!
PHEW
STRETCH
THAT PLACE WAS ALL RIGHT TOO...

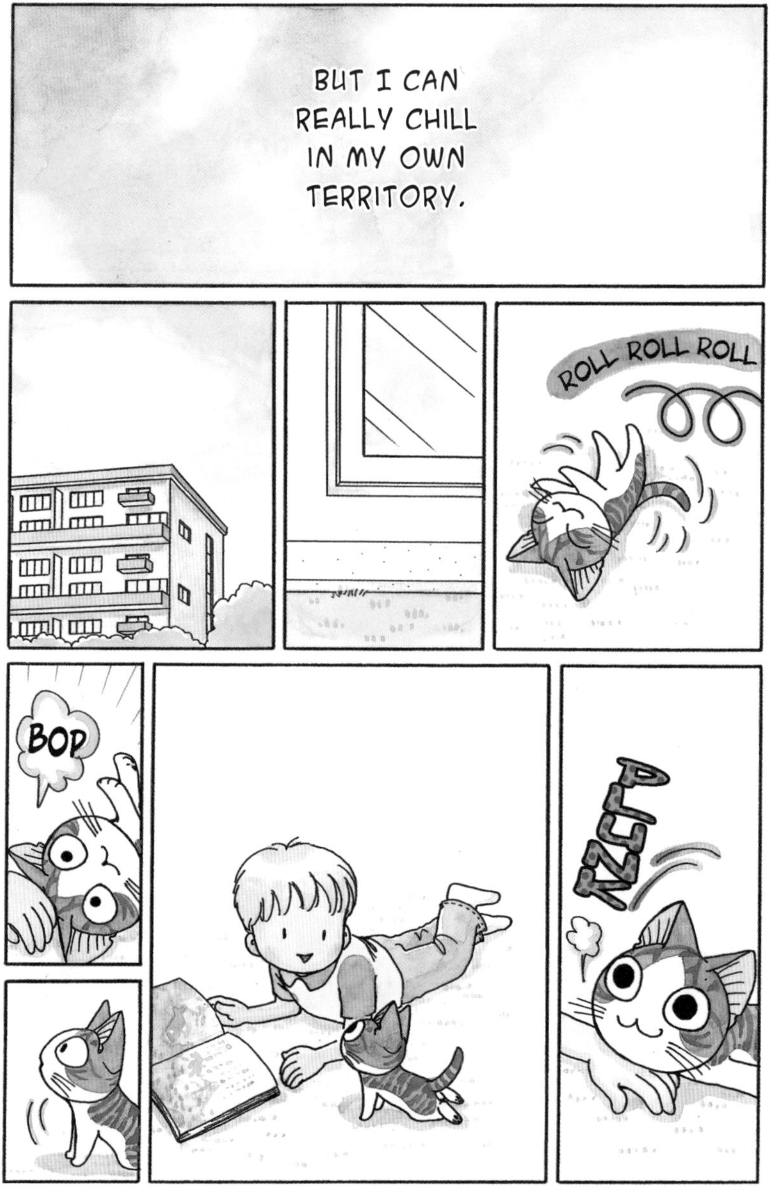
BUT I CAN REALLY CHILL IN MY OWN TERRITORY.
ROLL ROLL ROLL
BOP

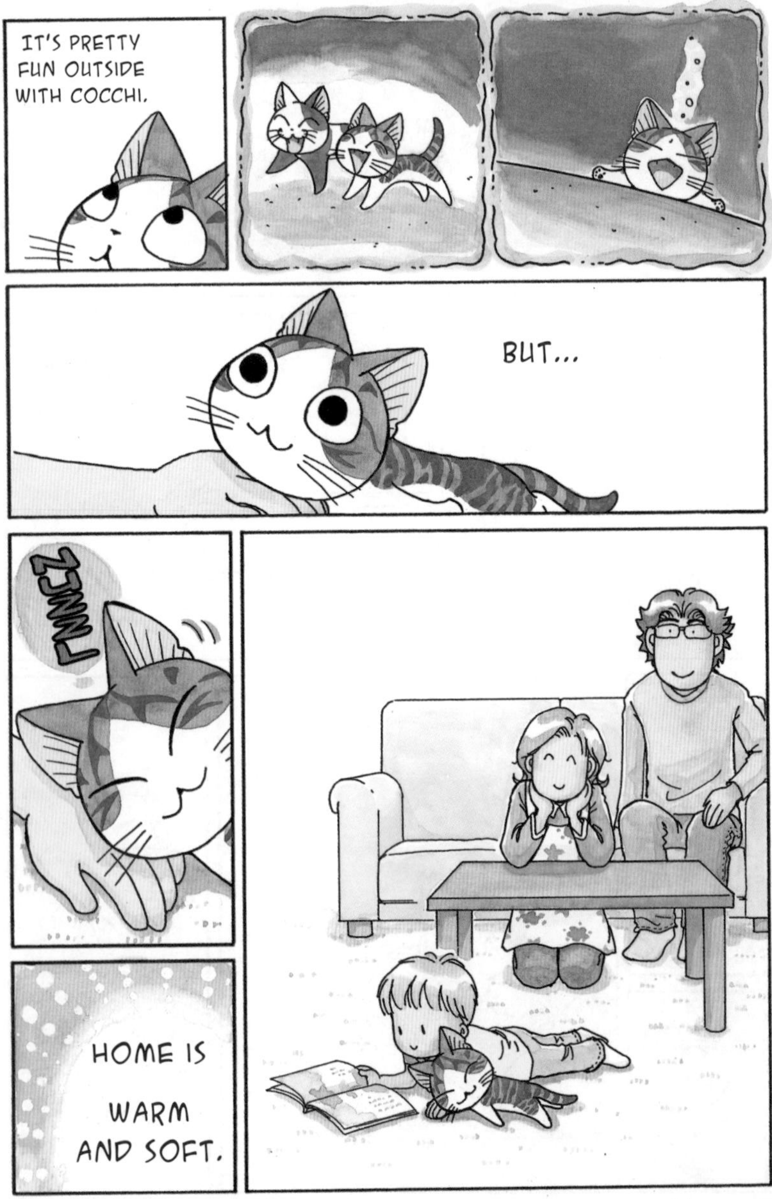
IT'S PRETTY FUN OUTSIDE WITH COCCHI.
BUT...
HOME IS
WARM AND SOFT.

the end

homemade 167: a cat is watched

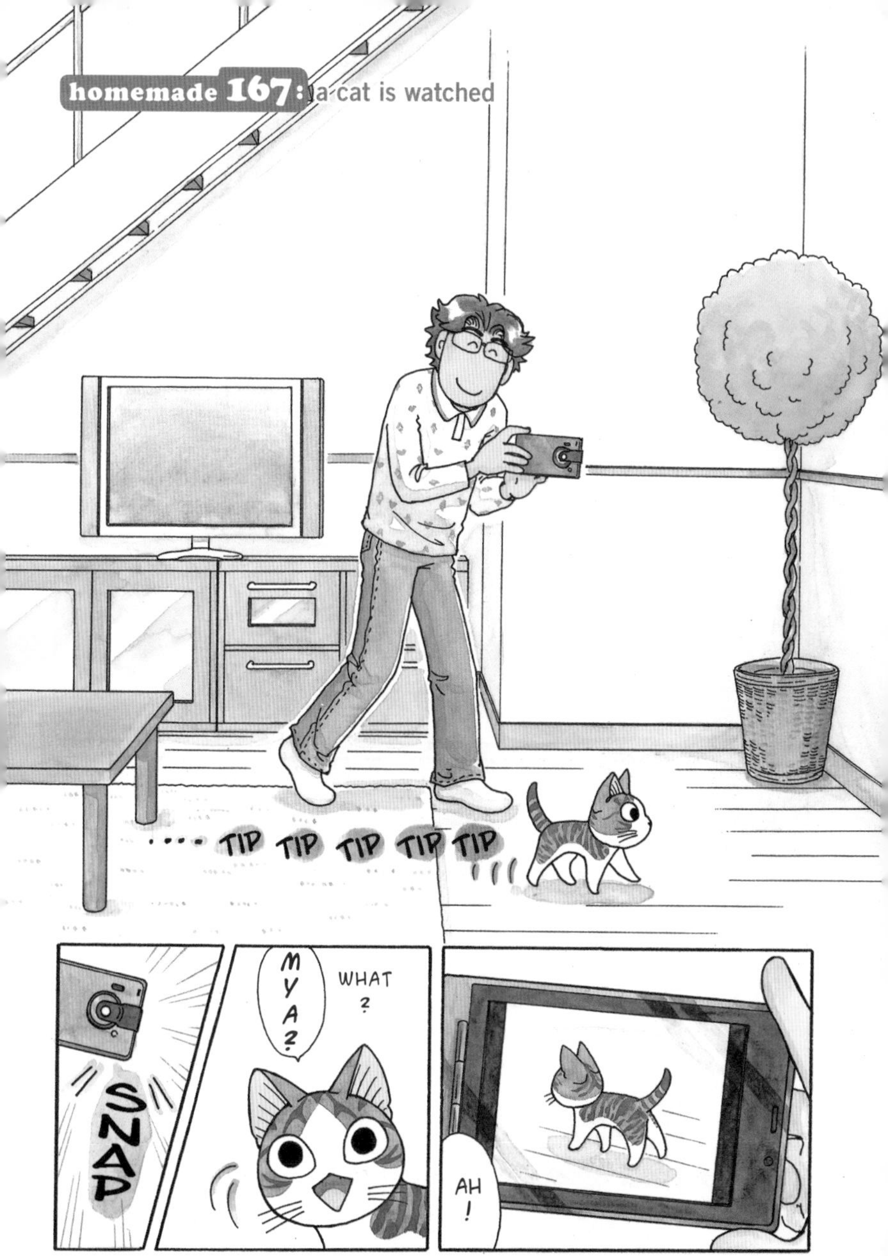

.... TIP TIP TIP TIP TIP
SNAP
MYA?
WHAT?
AH!

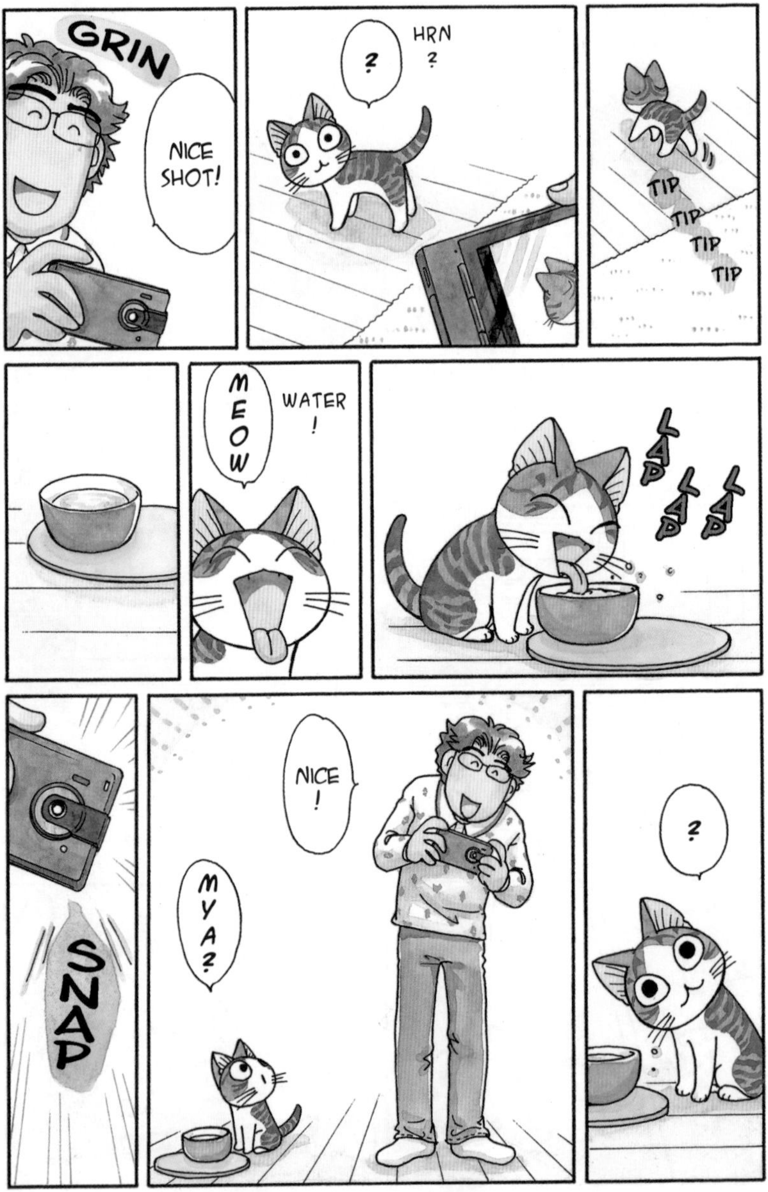
GRIN
NICE SHOT!
?
HRN ?
TIP TIP TIP TIP
MEOW
WATER !
LAP LAP LAP
SNAP
NICE !
MYA?
?

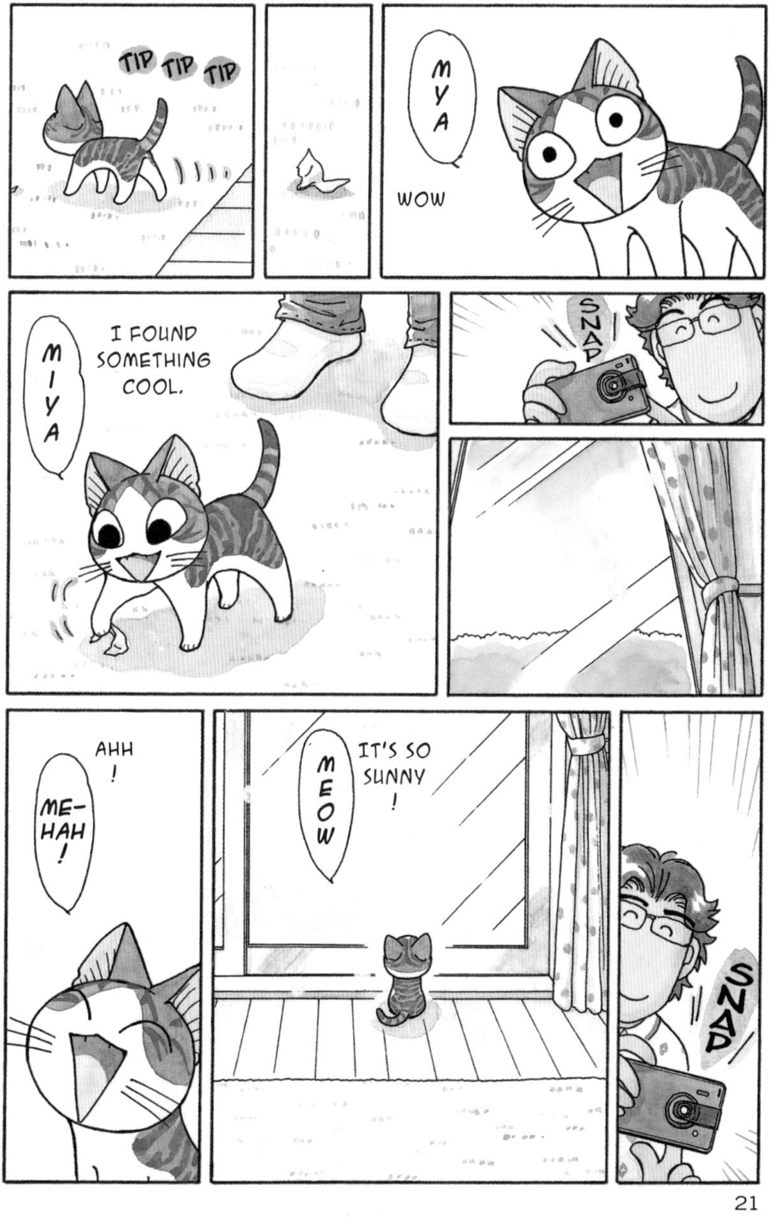
TIP TIP TIP
MYA
WOW
MIYA
I FOUND SOMETHING COOL.
SNAP
AHH!
ME-HAH!
MEOW
IT'S SO SUNNY!
SNAP

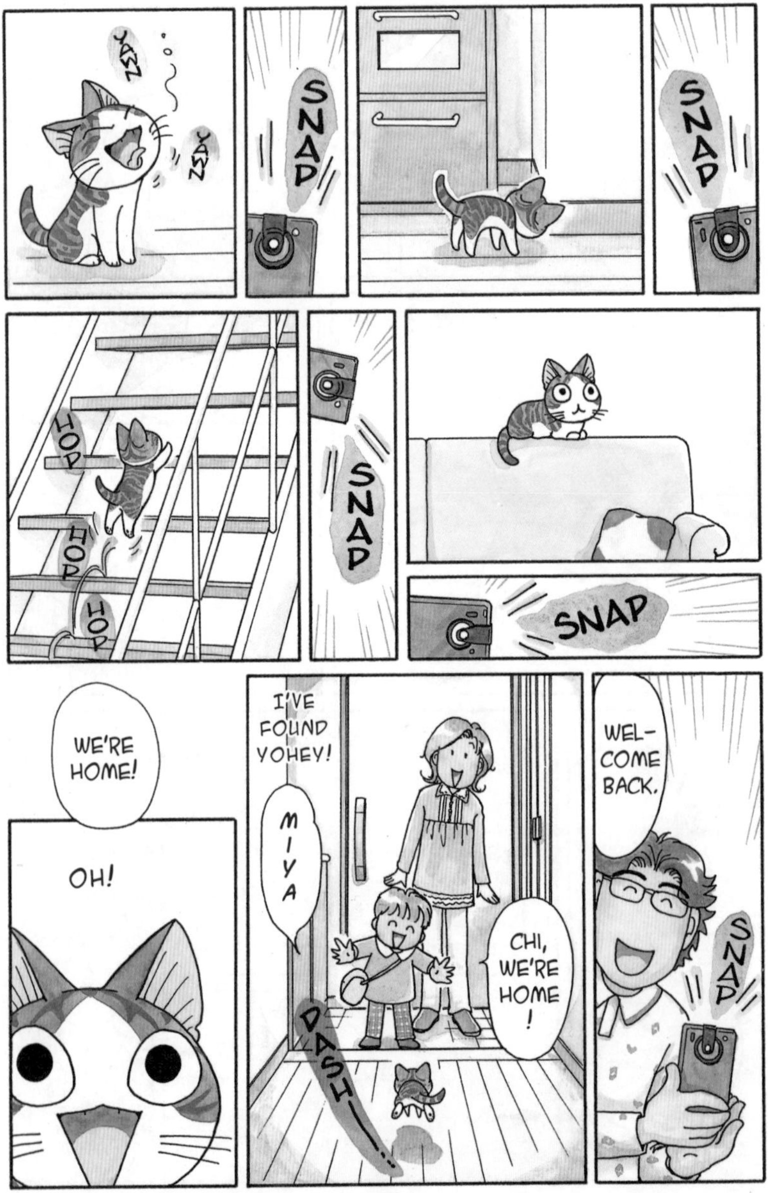
YAWN
YAWN
SNAP
SNAP
HOP
HOP
HOP
SNAP
SNAP
WE'RE HOME!
OH!
I'VE FOUND YOHEY!
MIYA
CHI, WE'RE HOME!
DASH
WEL-COME BACK.
SNAP

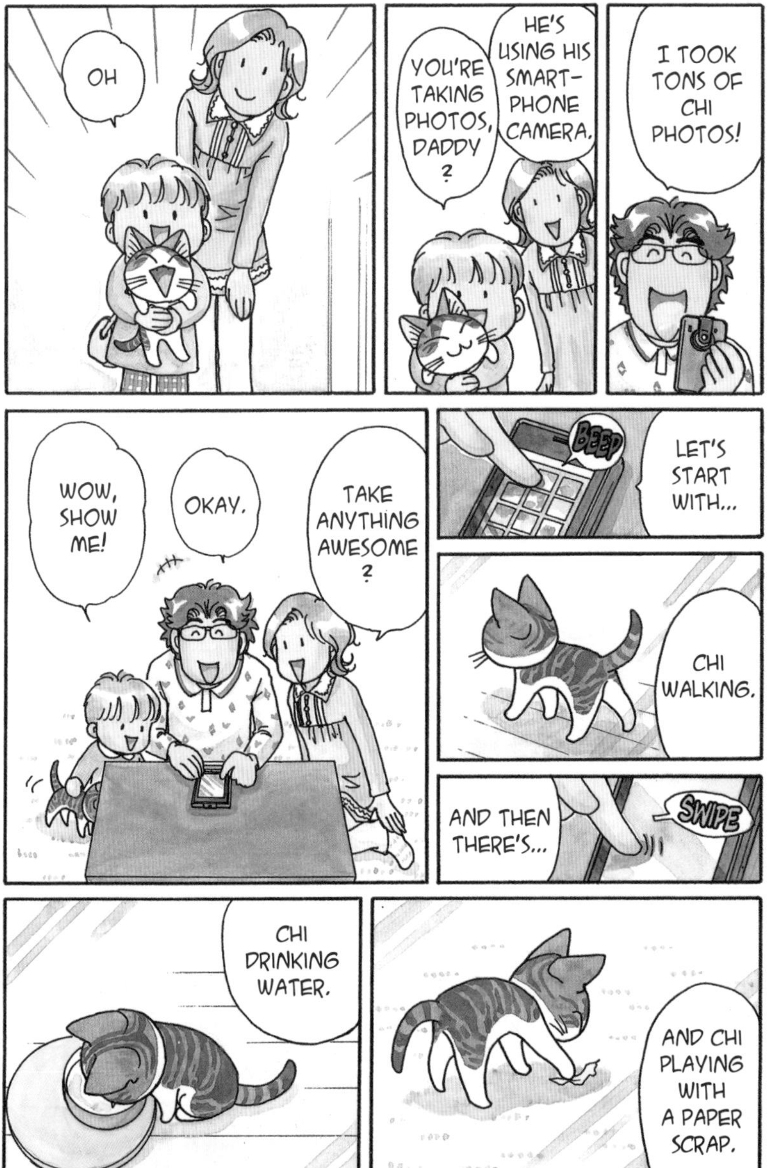
OH
YOU'RE TAKING PHOTOS, DADDY?
HE'S USING HIS SMART-PHONE CAMERA.
I TOOK TONS OF CHI PHOTOS!
WOW, SHOW ME!
OKAY.
TAKE ANYTHING AWESOME?
BEEP
LET'S START WITH...
CHI WALKING.
AND THEN THERE'S...
SWIPE
CHI DRINKING WATER.
AND CHI PLAYING WITH A PAPER SCRAP.

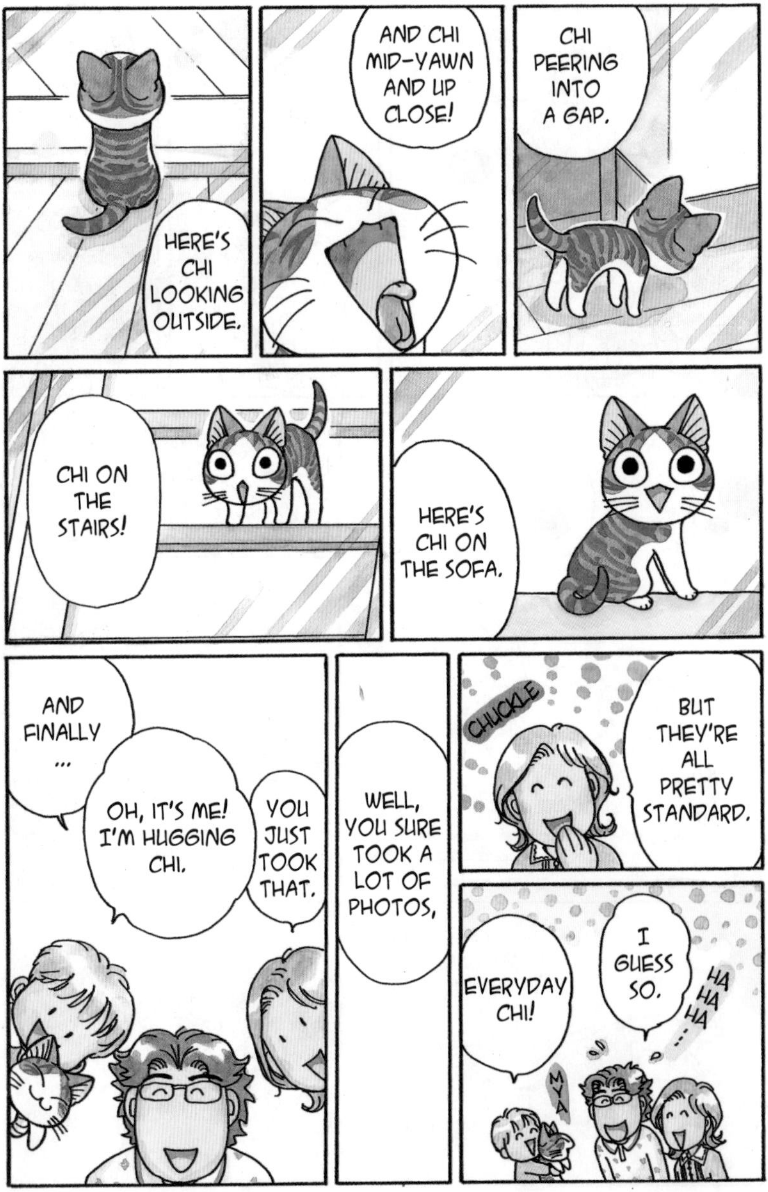
HERE'S CHI LOOKING OUTSIDE.
AND CHI MID-YAWN AND UP CLOSE!
CHI PEERING INTO A GAP.
CHI ON THE STAIRS!
HERE'S CHI ON THE SOFA.
AND FINALLY ...
OH, IT'S ME! I'M HUGGING CHI.
YOU JUST TOOK THAT.
WELL, YOU SURE TOOK A LOT OF PHOTOS,
CHUCKLE
BUT THEY'RE ALL PRETTY STANDARD.
EVERYDAY CHI!
I GUESS SO.
HA HA HA ...
MYA

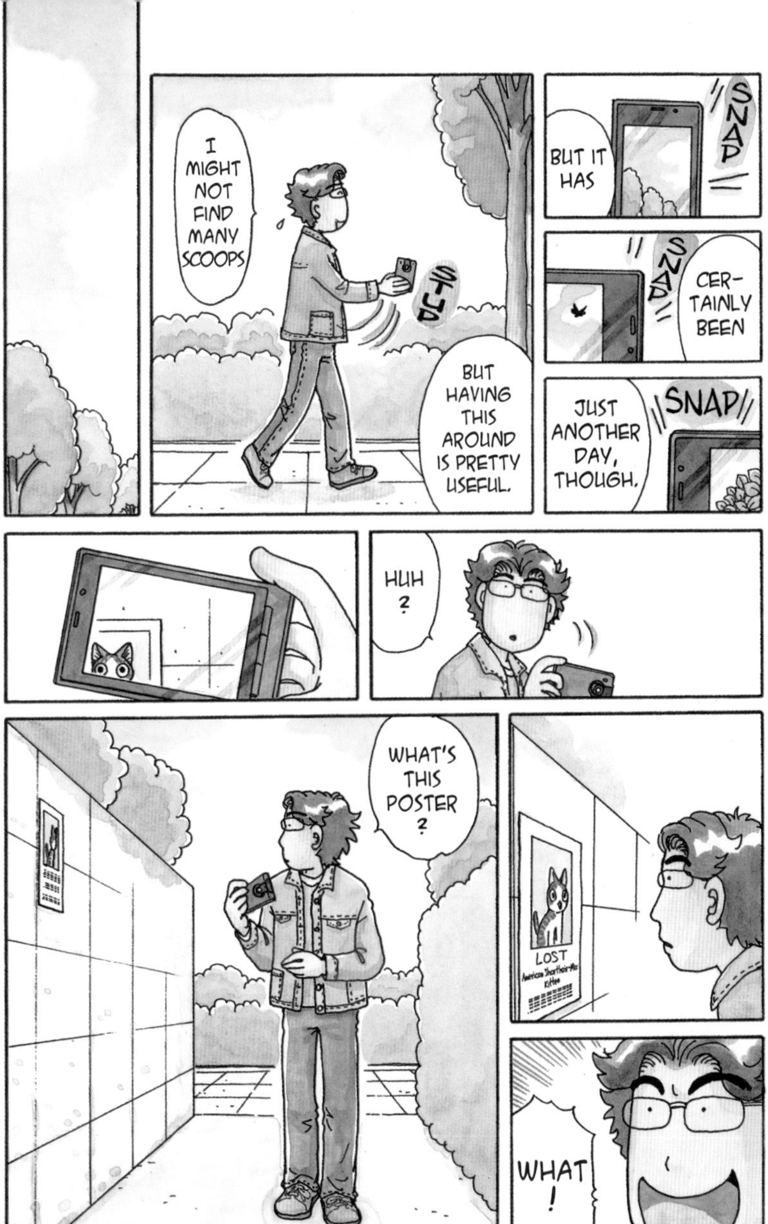
I MIGHT NOT FIND MANY SCOOPS
STUD
BUT HAVING THIS AROUND IS PRETTY USEFUL.
BUT IT HAS
SNAP
SNAP
CER-TAINLY BEEN
JUST ANOTHER DAY, THOUGH.
SNAP
HUH?
WHAT'S THIS POSTER?
LOST
American Shorthair-Mix Kitten
WHAT!

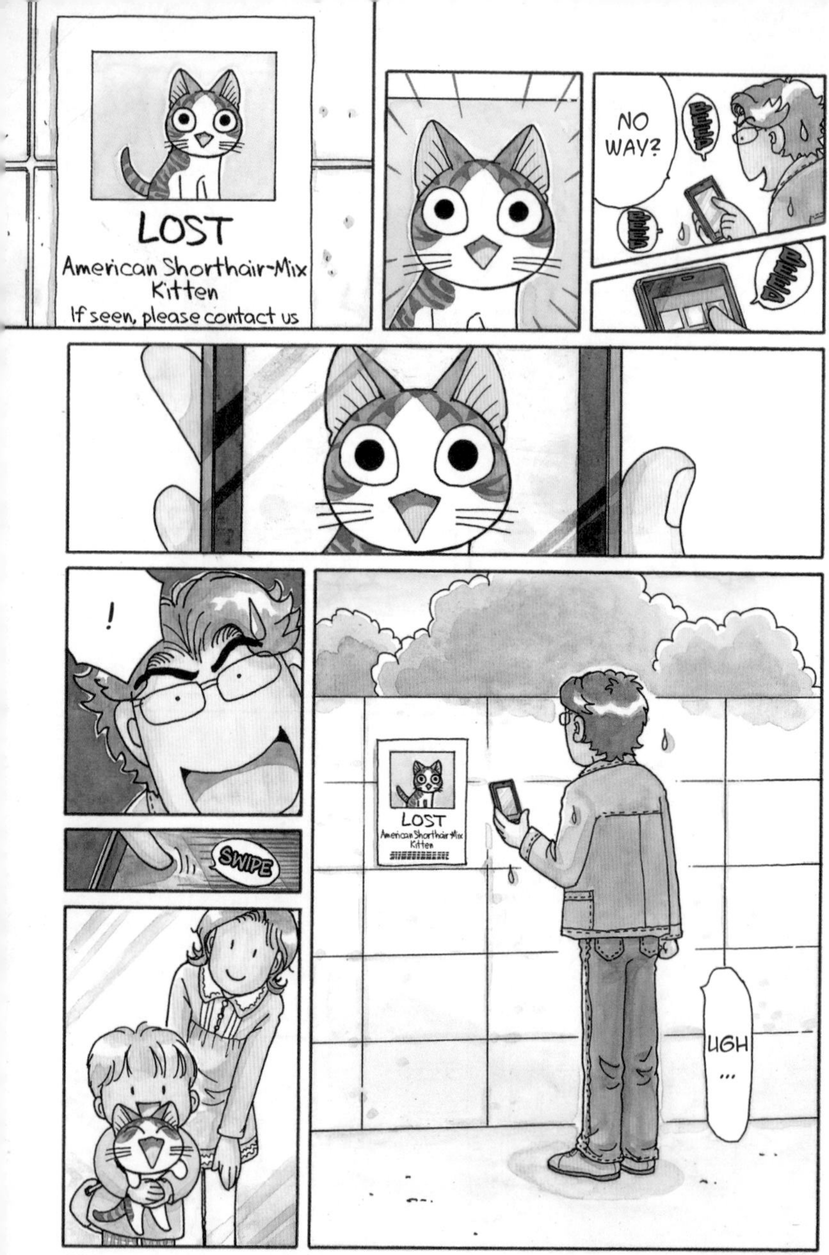
LOST
American Shorthair-Mix Kitten
If seen, please contact us
NO WAY?
!
SWIPE
LOST
American Shorthair-Mix Kitten
UGH ...

the end

homemade 168: a cat is concerning

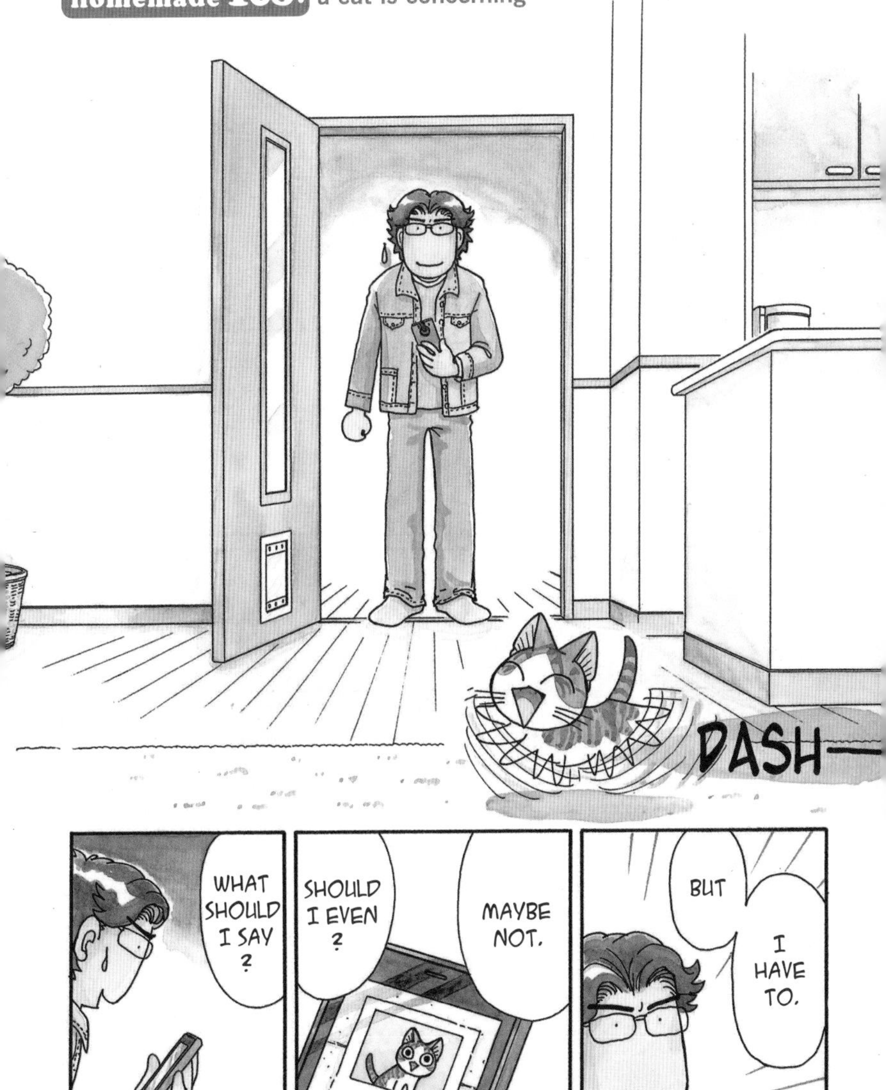
DASH—
WHAT SHOULD I SAY?
SHOULD I EVEN?
LOST
American Shorthair Mix
Kitten
MAYBE NOT.
BUT
I HAVE TO.

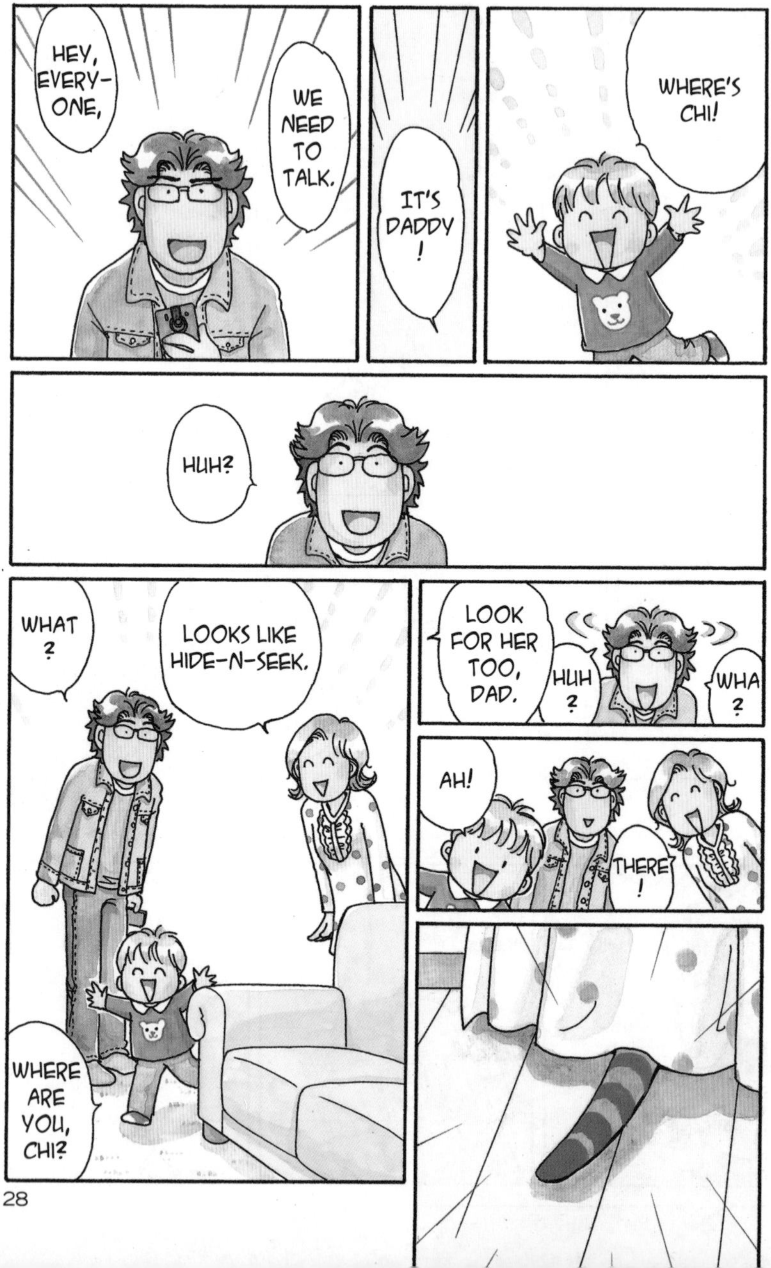
HEY, EVERY-ONE,
WE NEED TO TALK.
IT'S DADDY!
WHERE'S CHI!
HUH?
WHAT?
LOOKS LIKE HIDE-N-SEEK.
WHERE ARE YOU, CHI?
LOOK FOR HER TOO, DAD.
HUH?
WHA?
AH!
THERE!

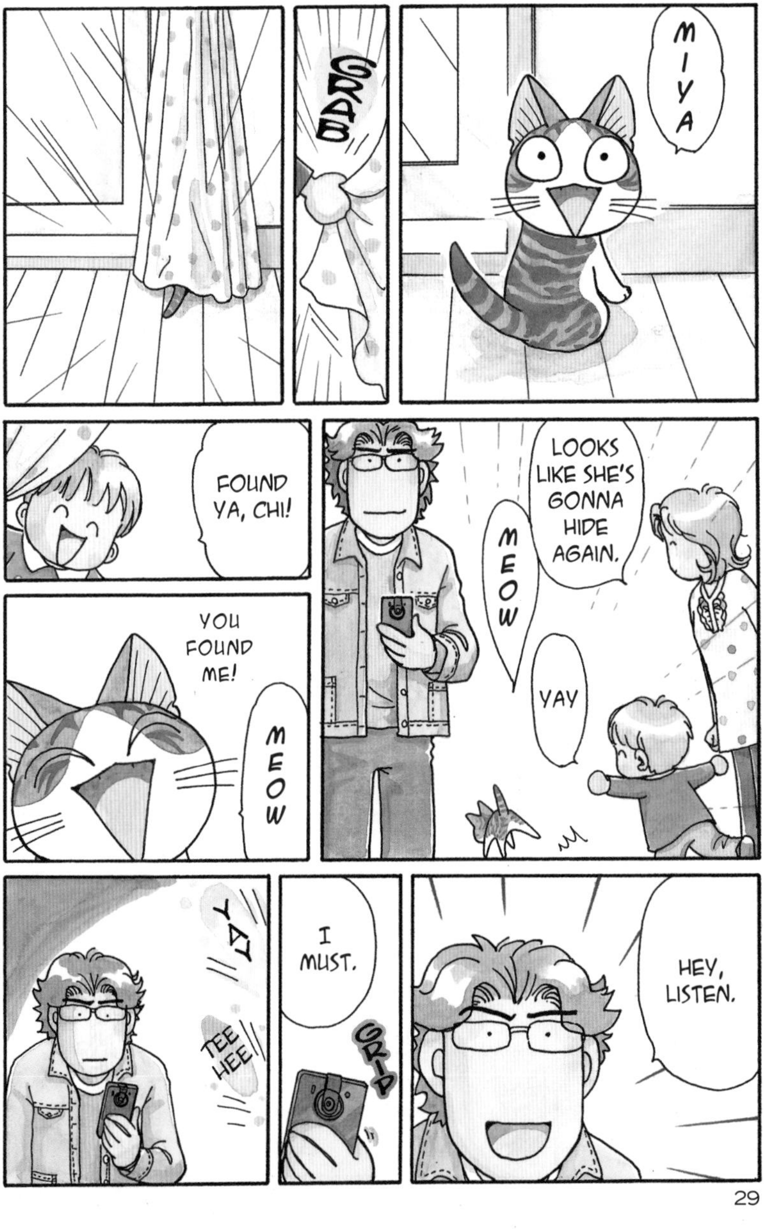
GRAB
MIYA
FOUND YA, CHI!
YOU FOUND ME!
MEOW
LOOKS LIKE SHE'S GONNA HIDE AGAIN.
MEOW
YAY
YAY
TEE HEE
I MUST.
GRIP
HEY, LISTEN.

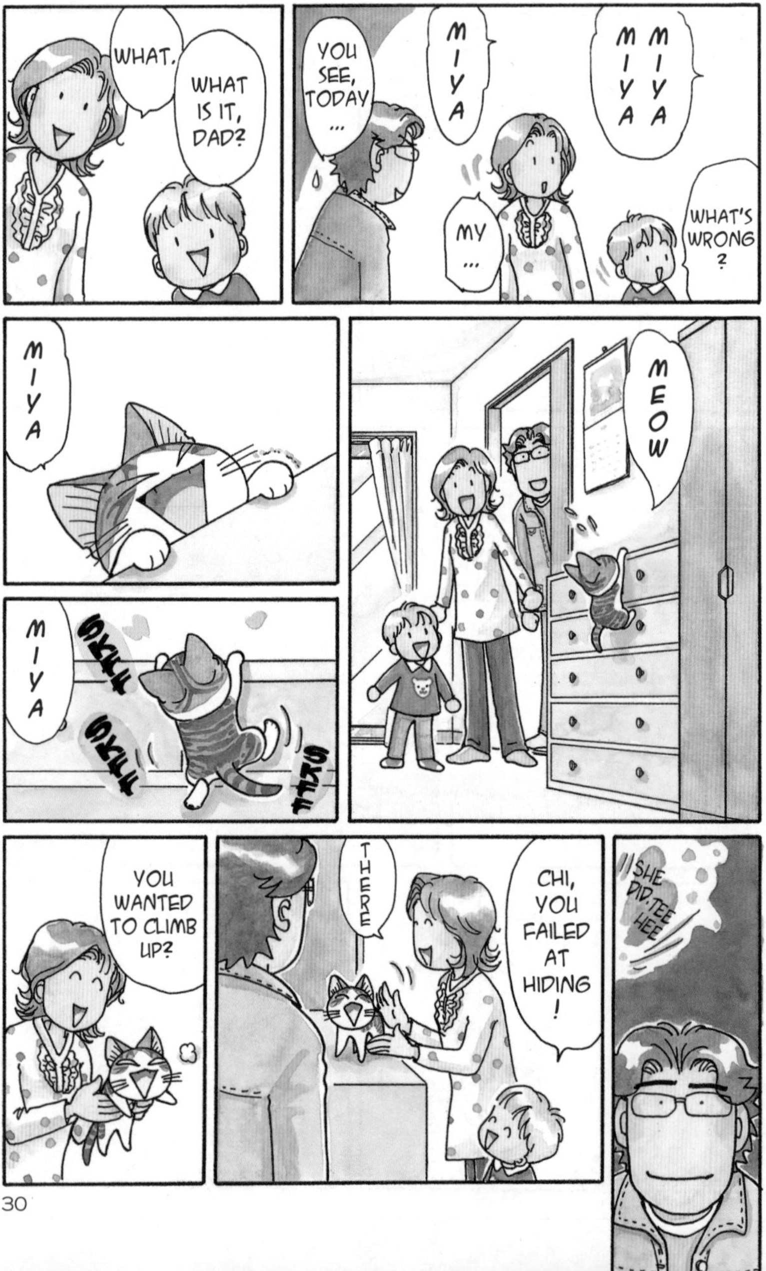
WHAT.
WHAT IS IT, DAD?
YOU SEE, TODAY ...
MIYA
MIYA MIYA
MY ...
WHAT'S WRONG?
MIYA
MIYA
SKFF
SKFF
SKFF
MEOW
YOU WANTED TO CLIMB UP?
THERE
CHI, YOU FAILED AT HIDING!
SHE DID. TEE HEE

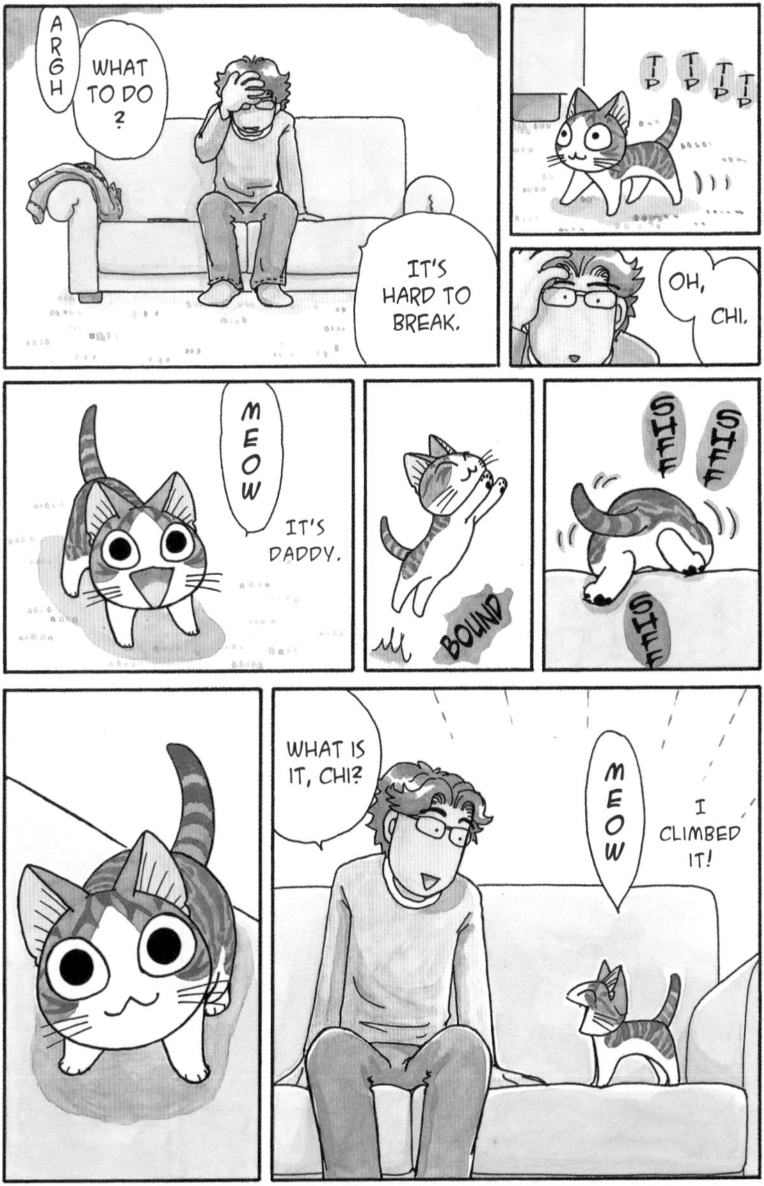
ARGH
WHAT TO DO ?
IT'S HARD TO BREAK.
TIP TIP TIP TIP
OH, CHI.
MEOW
IT'S DADDY.
BOUND
SHFF SHFF
SHFF
WHAT IS IT, CHI?
MEOW
I CLIMBED IT!

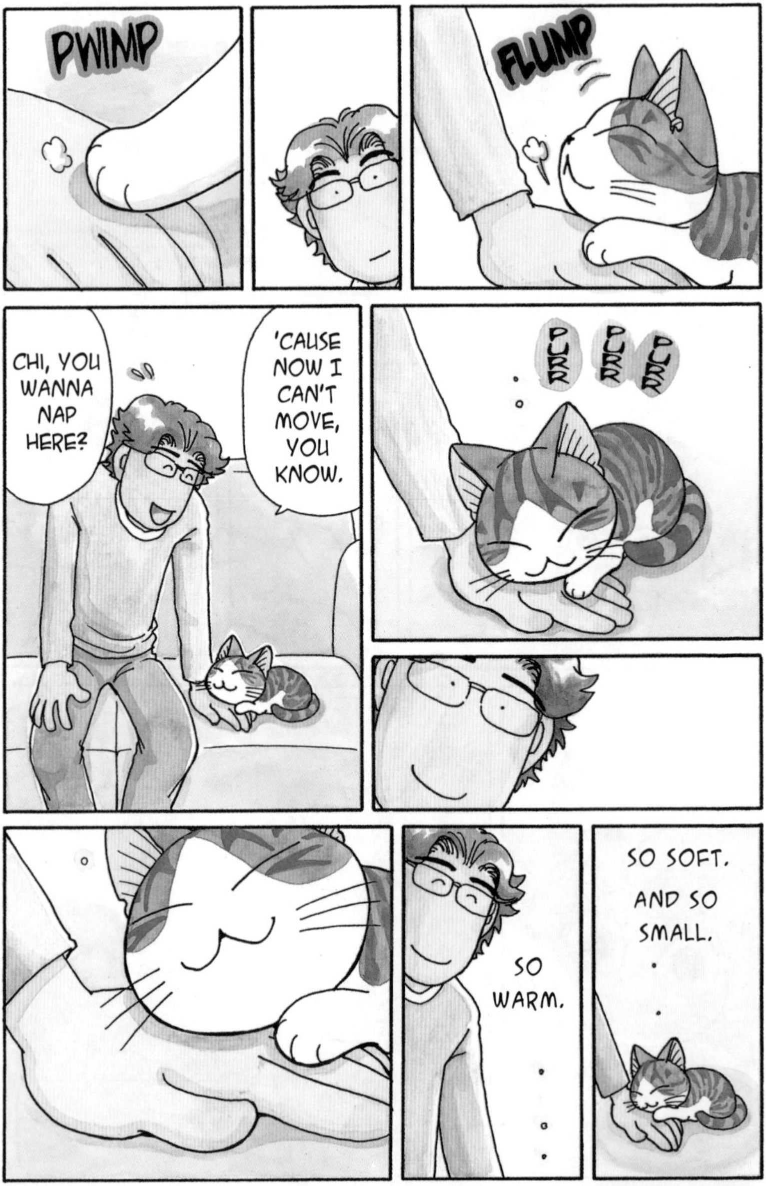
PWIMP
FLUMP
CHI, YOU WANNA NAP HERE?
'CAUSE NOW I CAN'T MOVE, YOU KNOW.
PURR
PURR
PURR
SO WARM.
SO SOFT.
AND SO SMALL.

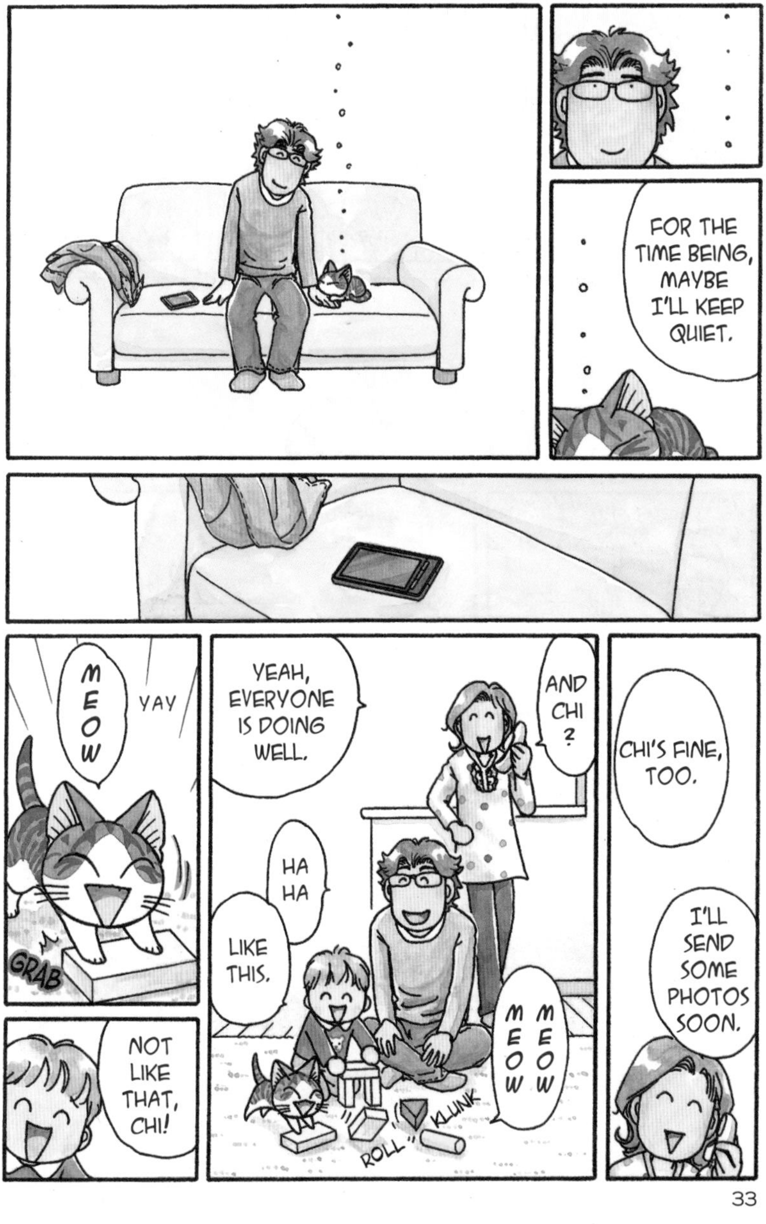

FOR THE TIME BEING, MAYBE I'LL KEEP QUIET.
MEOW
YAY
GRAB
NOT LIKE THAT, CHI!
YEAH, EVERYONE IS DOING WELL.
AND CHI?
HA HA
LIKE THIS.
MEOW MEOW
ROLL
KLUNK
CHI'S FINE, TOO.
I'LL SEND SOME PHOTOS SOON.

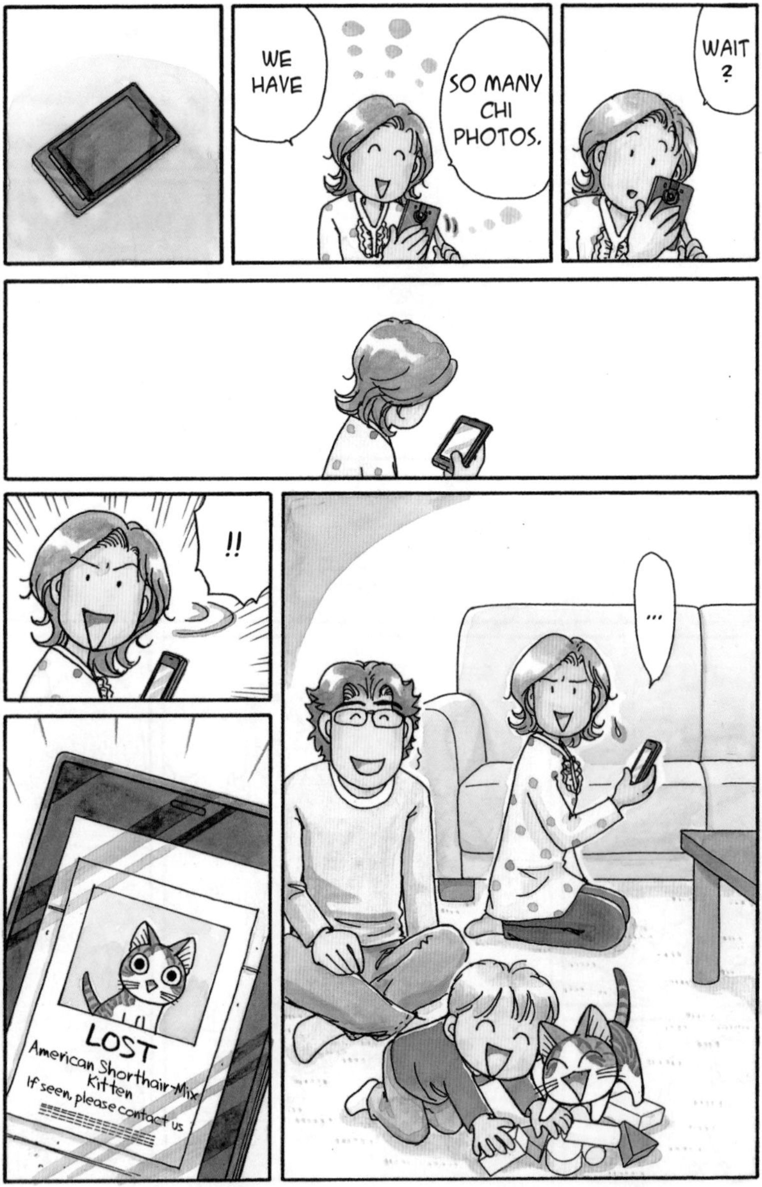
WE HAVE
SO MANY CHI PHOTOS.
WAIT ?
!!
LOST
American Shorthair-Mix Kitten
If seen, please contact us
...

the end

homemade 169: a cat communicates

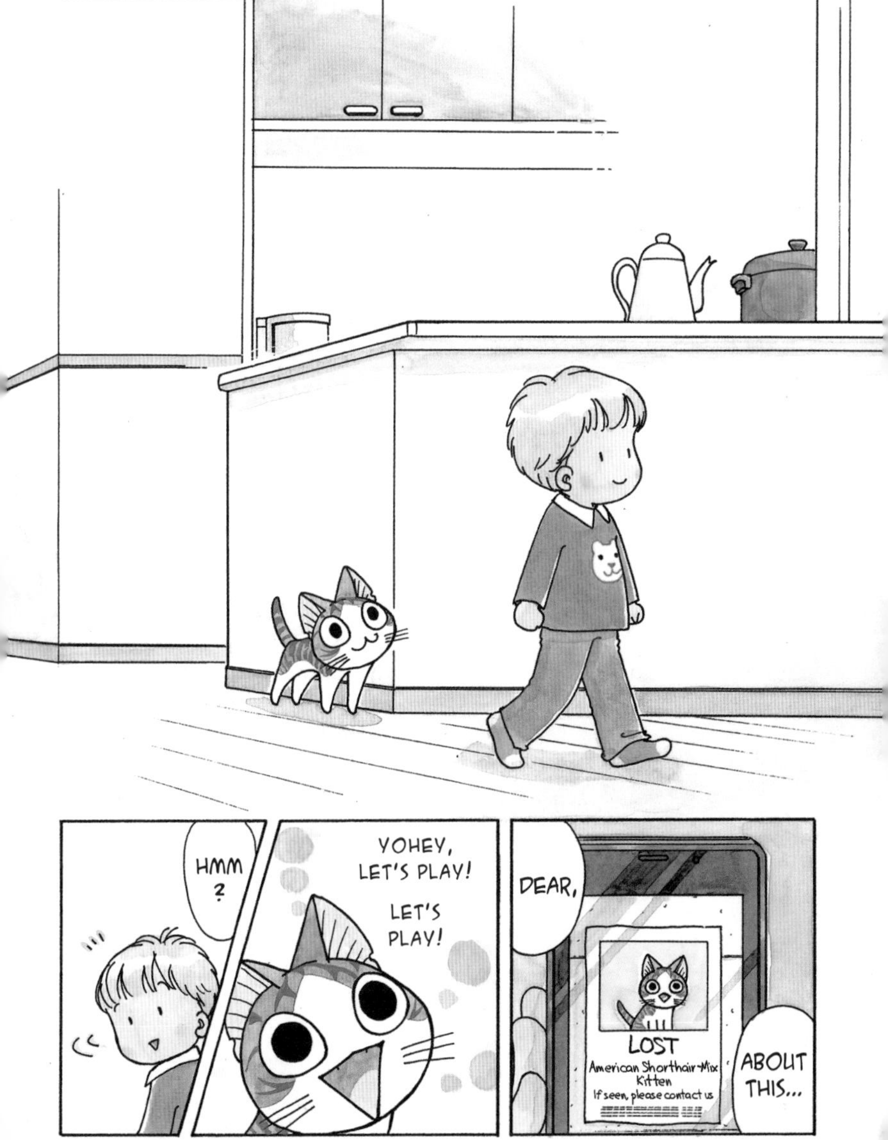
HMM ?
YOHEY, LET'S PLAY!
LET'S PLAY!
DEAR,
LOST
American Shorthair-Mix Kitten
If seen, please contact us
ABOUT THIS...

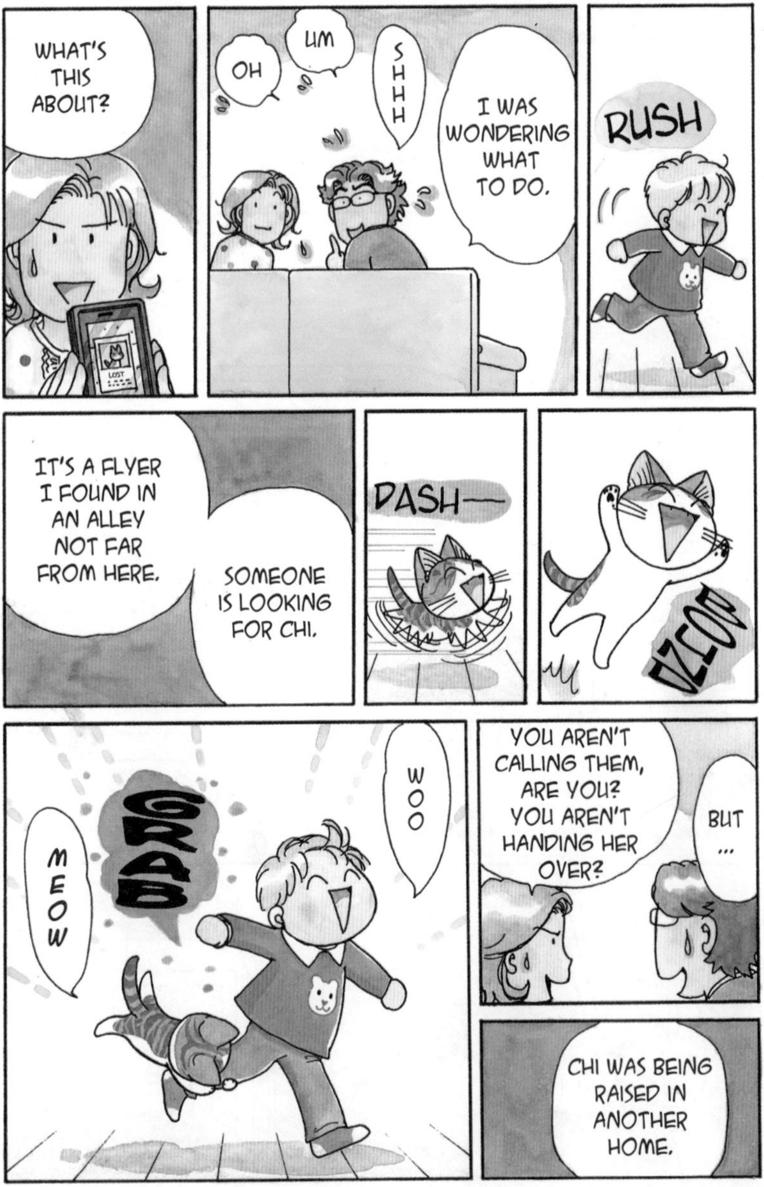
WHAT'S THIS ABOUT?
LOST
OH
UM
SHHH
I WAS WONDERING WHAT TO DO.
RUSH
IT'S A FLYER I FOUND IN AN ALLEY NOT FAR FROM HERE.
SOMEONE IS LOOKING FOR CHI.
DASH—
ZOOM
GRAB
WOO
MEOW
YOU AREN'T CALLING THEM, ARE YOU? YOU AREN'T HANDING HER OVER?
BUT ...
CHI WAS BEING RAISED IN ANOTHER HOME.

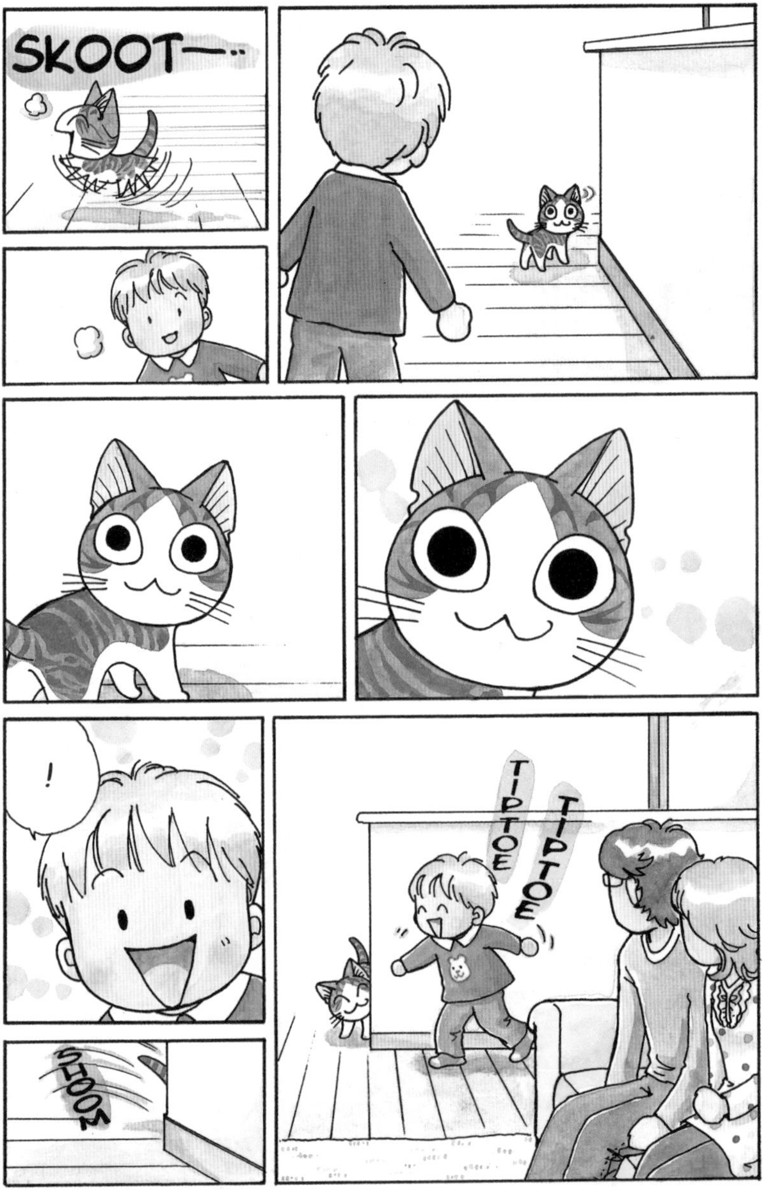
SKOOT—..
!
TIPTOE
TIPTOE
SHOOM

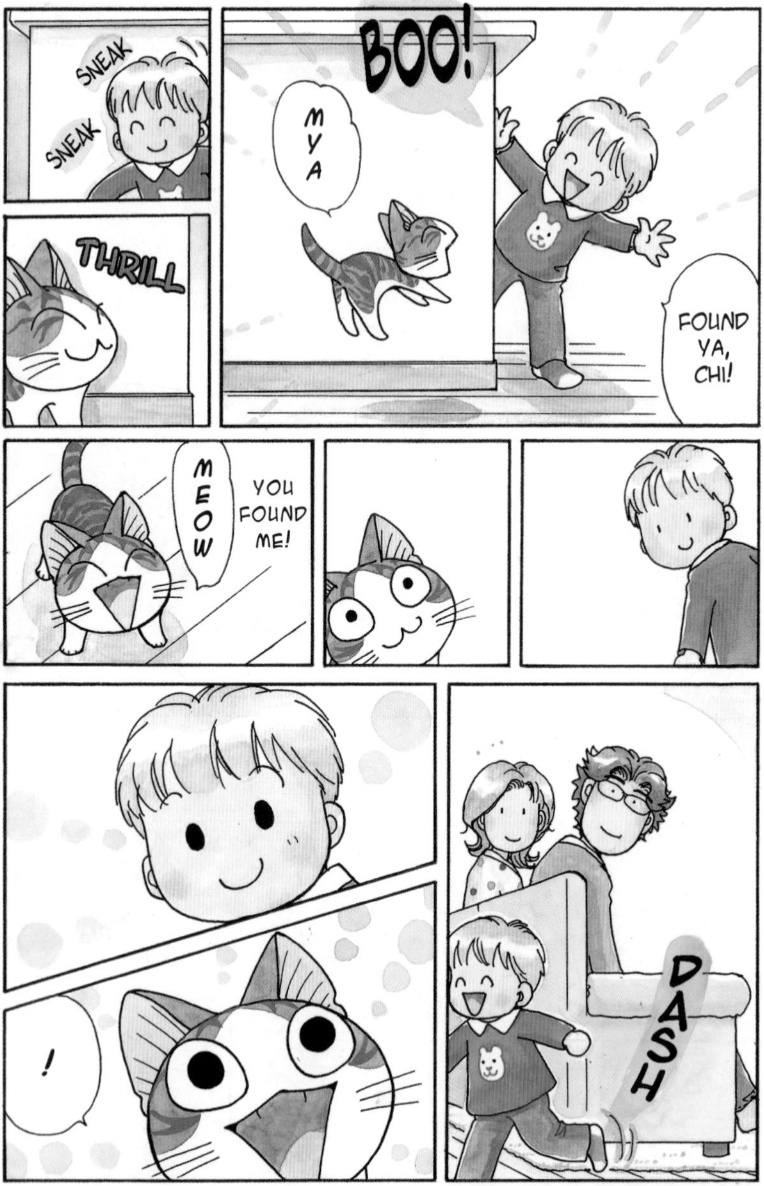
SNEAK
SNEAK
BOO!
MYA
THRILL
FOUND YA, CHI!
MEOW
YOU FOUND ME!
!
DASH

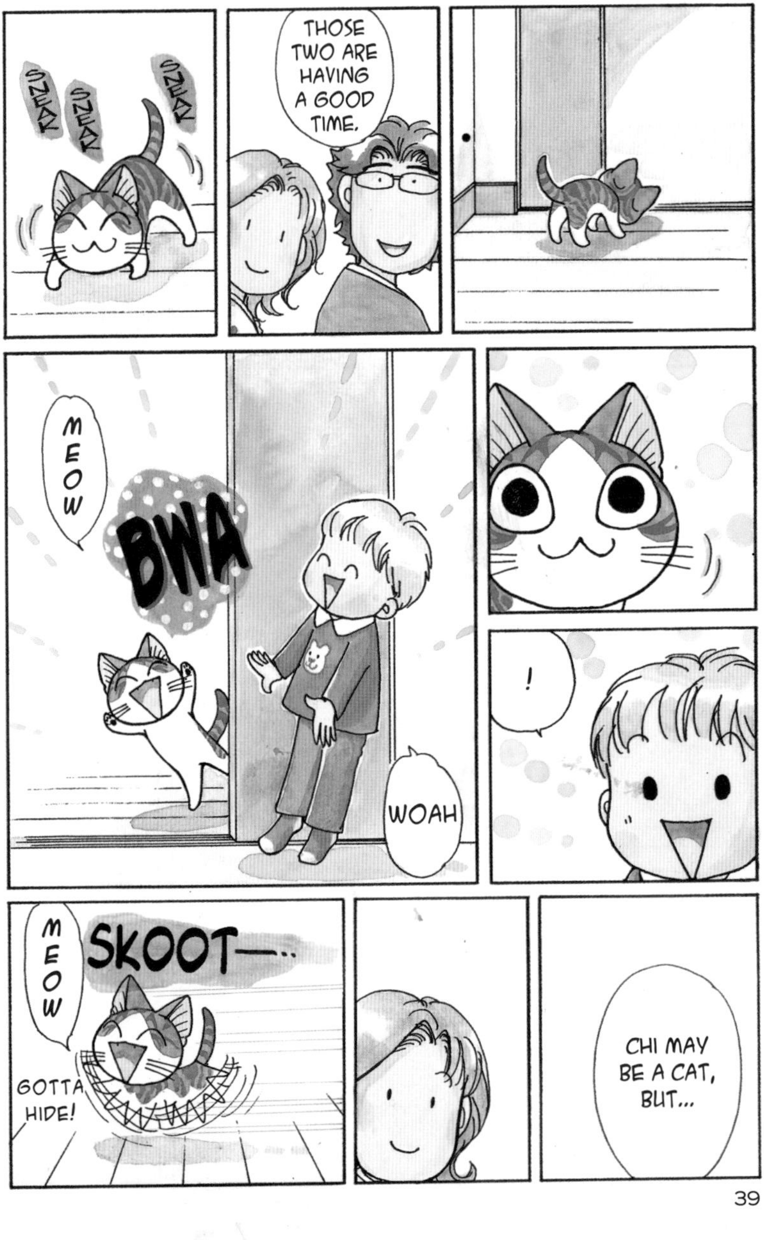
SNEAK SNEAK SNEAK
THOSE TWO ARE HAVING A GOOD TIME.
MEOW
BWA
WOAH
!
MEOW
SKOOT—..
GOTTA HIDE!
CHI MAY BE A CAT, BUT...

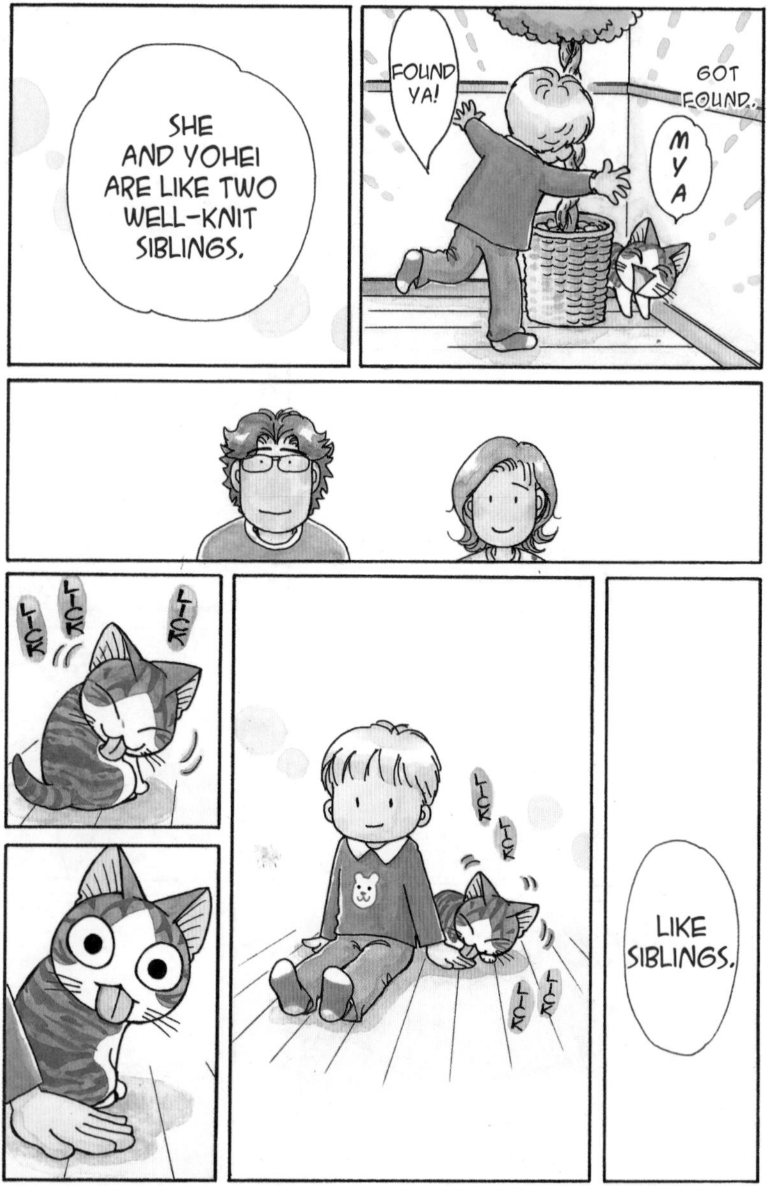
SHE AND YOHEI ARE LIKE TWO WELL-KNIT SIBLINGS.
FOUND YA!
GOT FOUND..
MYA
LICK
LICK
LICK
LICK
LICK
LICK
LICK
LIKE SIBLINGS.

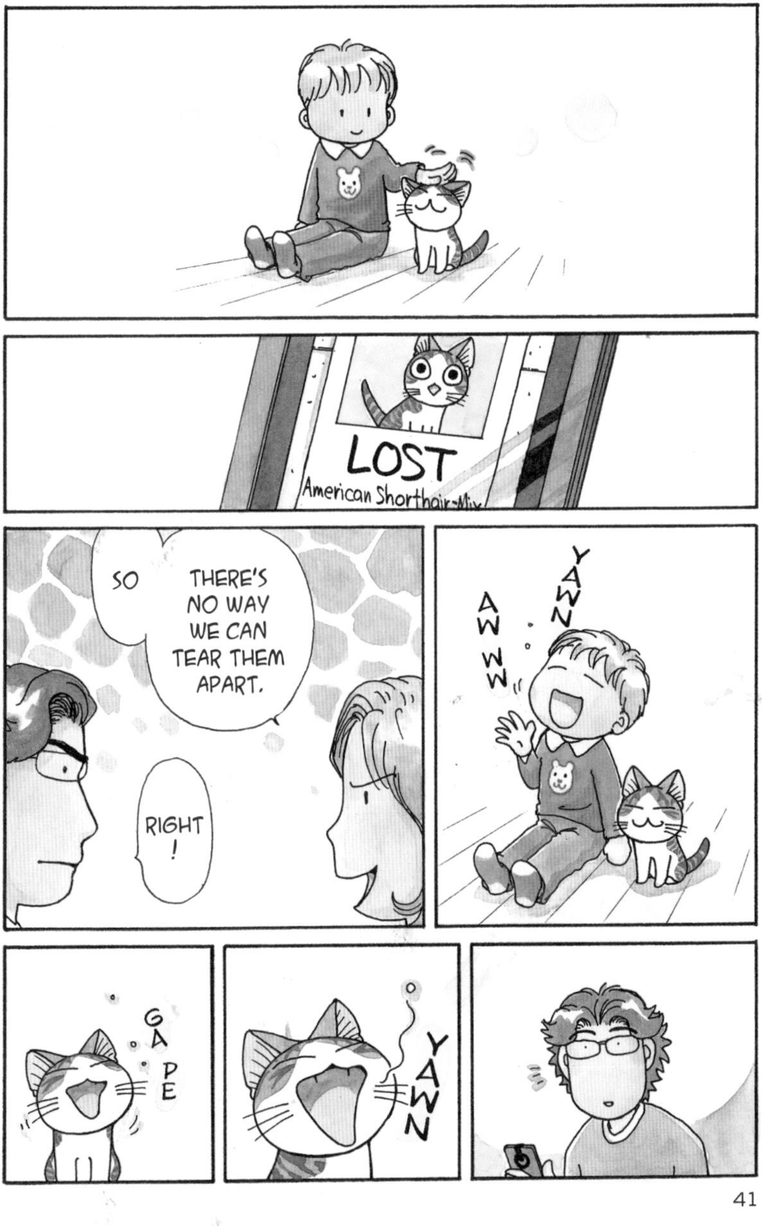
LOST
American Shorthair-Mix
SO
THERE'S NO WAY WE CAN TEAR THEM APART.
RIGHT!
AWWW
YAWN
GAPE
YAWN

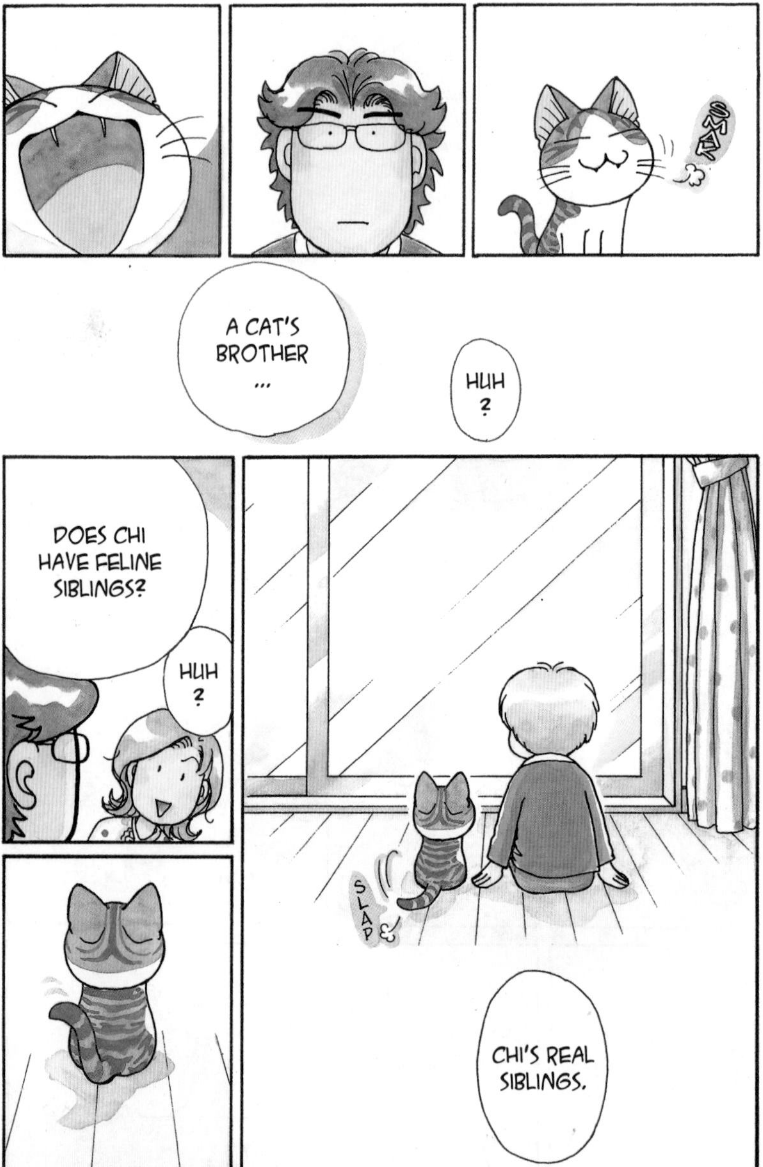
SWAY
A CAT'S BROTHER ...
HUH ?
DOES CHI HAVE FELINE SIBLINGS?
HUH ?
SLAP
CHI'S REAL SIBLINGS.

the end

homemade 170: a cat is misread

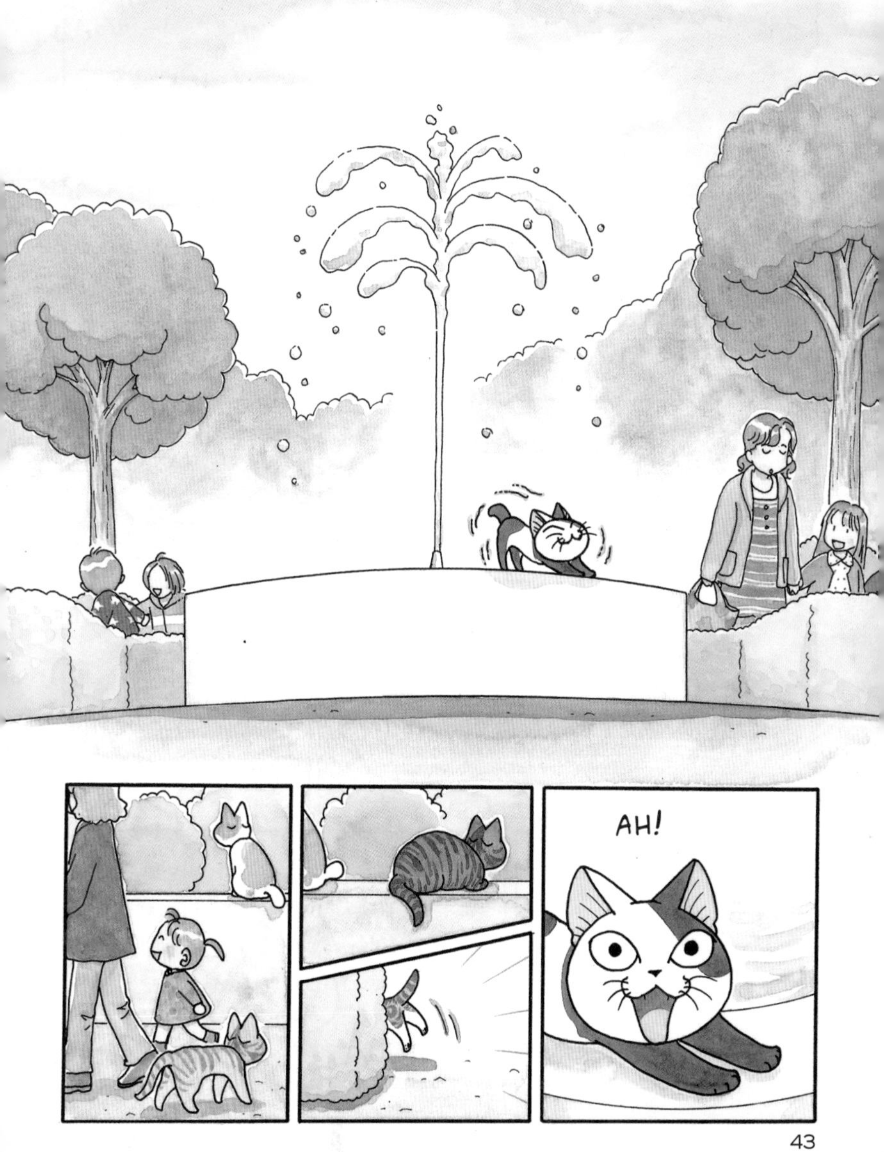
AH!

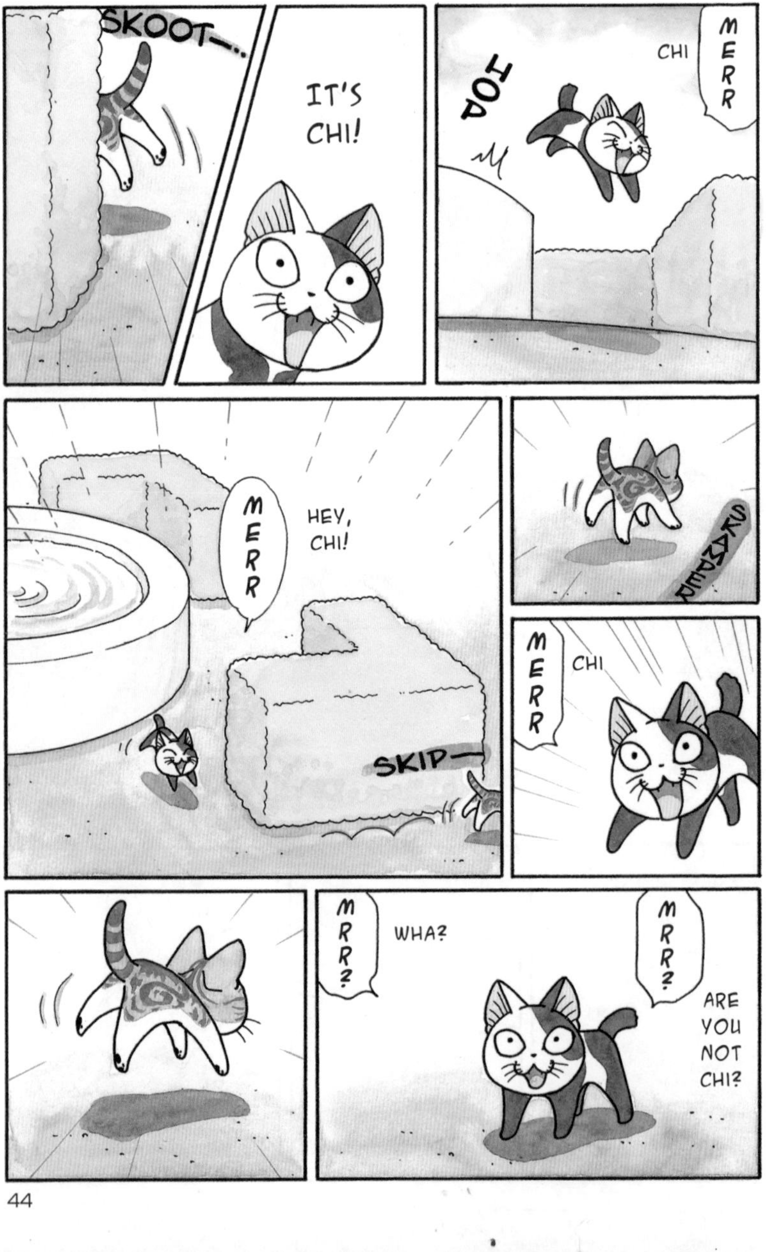
SKOOT—...
IT'S CHI!
HOP
MERR
CHI
MERR
HEY, CHI!
SKIP—
SKAMPER
MERR
CHI
MRR?
WHA?
MRR?
ARE YOU NOT CHI?

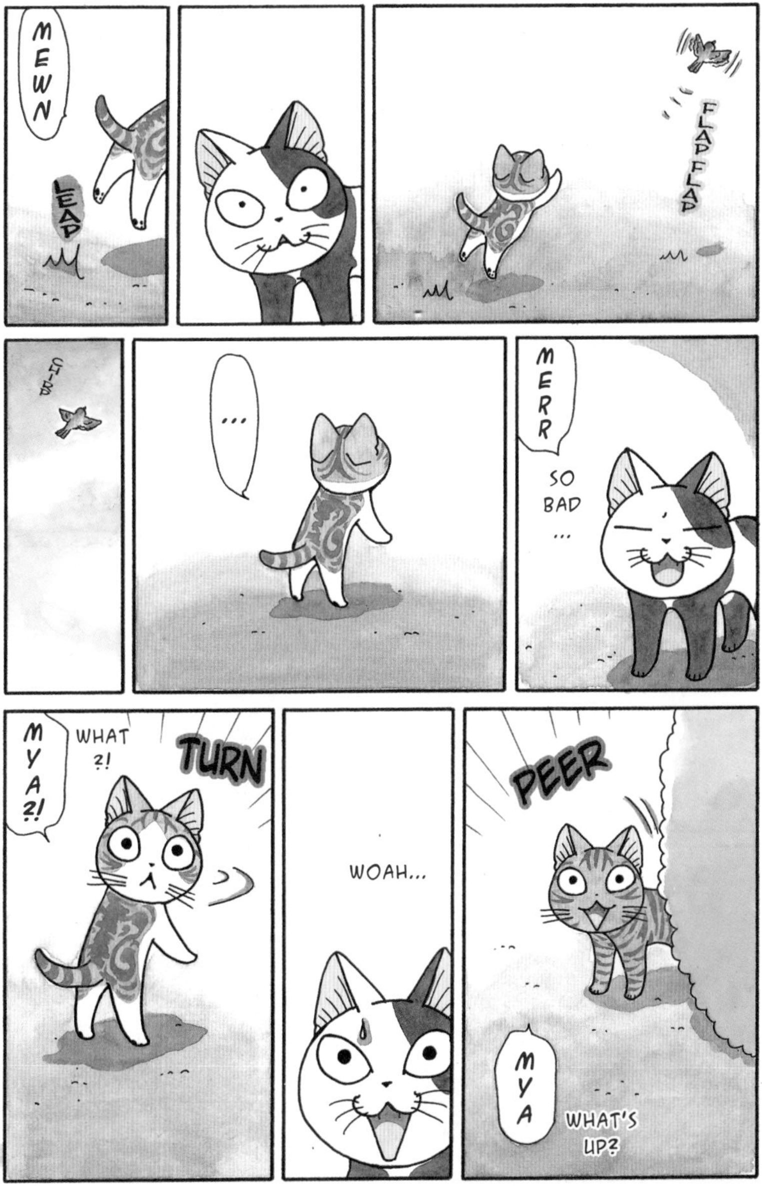
MEWN
LEAP
FLAP FLAP
CHIP
...
MERR
SO BAD ...
MYA?!
WHAT?!
TURN
WOAH...
PEER
MYA
WHAT'S UP?

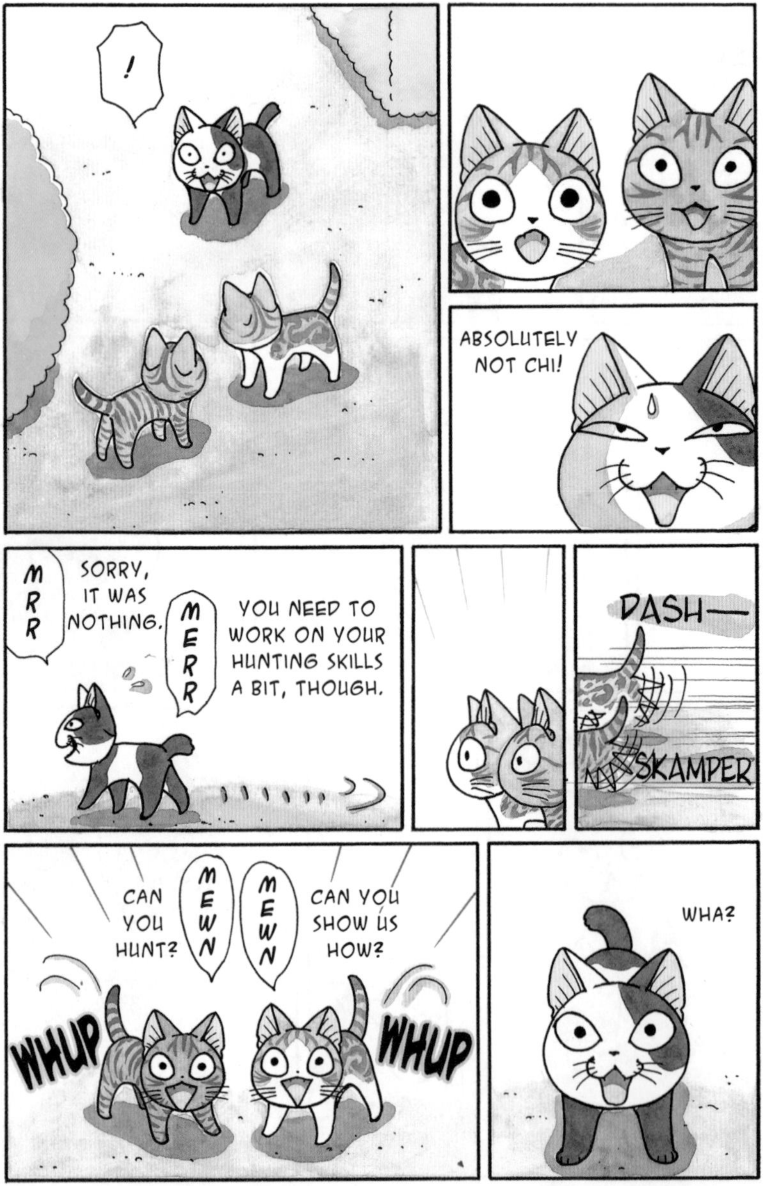
!
ABSOLUTELY NOT CHI!
MRR
SORRY, IT WAS NOTHING.
MERR
YOU NEED TO WORK ON YOUR HUNTING SKILLS A BIT, THOUGH.
DASH—
SKAMPER
CAN YOU HUNT?
MEWN
MEWN
CAN YOU SHOW US HOW?
WHUP
WHUP
WHA?

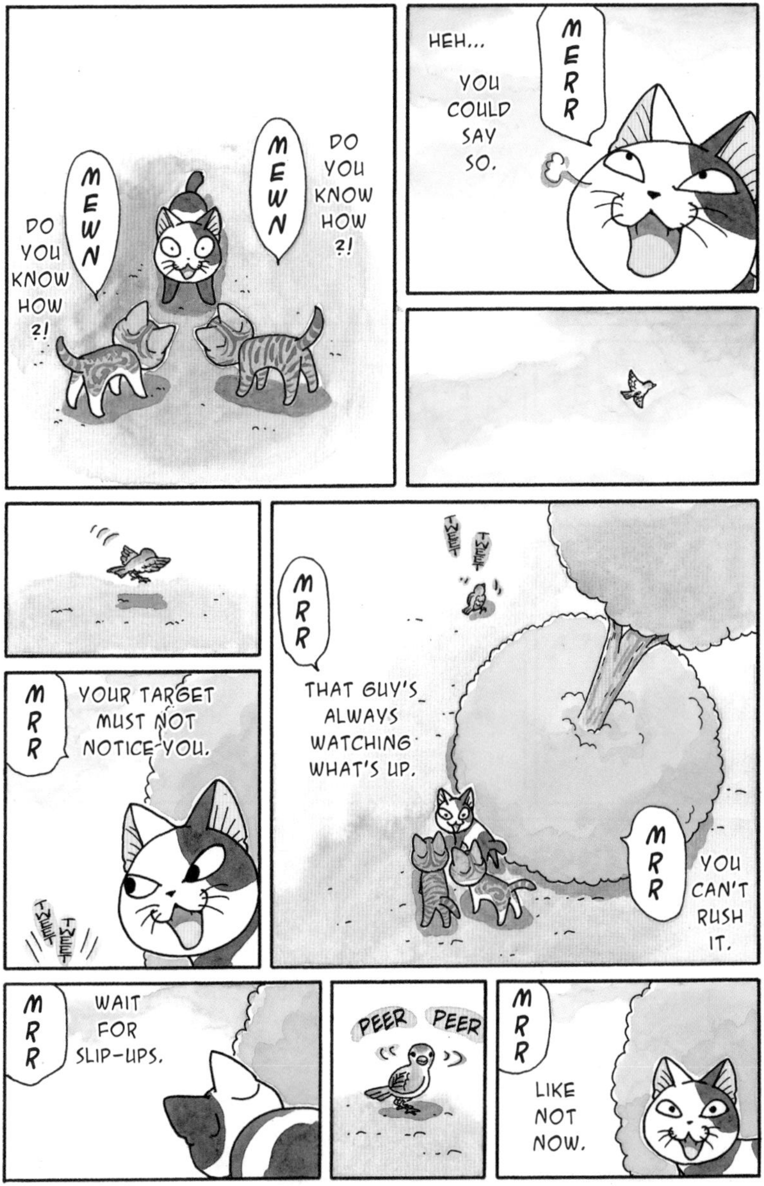
MEWN
DO YOU KNOW HOW ?!
MEWN
DO YOU KNOW HOW ?!
MERR
HEH...
YOU COULD SAY SO.
MRR
YOUR TARGET MUST NOT NOTICE YOU.
TWEET TWEET
TWEET TWEET
MRR
THAT GUY'S ALWAYS WATCHING WHAT'S UP.
MRR
YOU CAN'T RUSH IT.
MRR
WAIT FOR SLIP-UPS.
PEER PEER
MRR
LIKE NOT NOW.

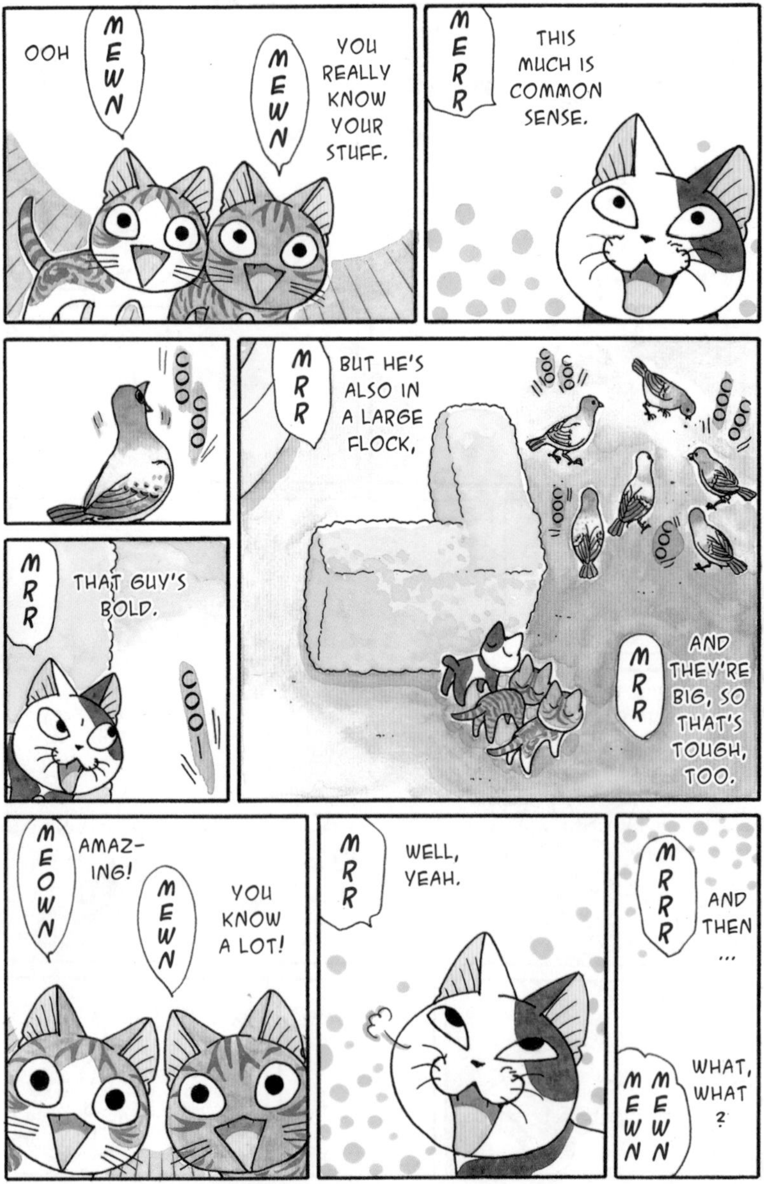
OOH
MEWN
MEWN
YOU REALLY KNOW YOUR STUFF.
MERR
THIS MUCH IS COMMON SENSE.
OOO
OOO
MRR
THAT GUY'S BOLD.
OOO
MRR
BUT HE'S ALSO IN A LARGE FLOCK,
OOO
OOO
OOO
OOO
OOO
MRR
AND THEY'RE BIG, SO THAT'S TOUGH, TOO.
MEOWN
AMAZ-ING!
MEWN
YOU KNOW A LOT!
MRR
WELL, YEAH.
MRRR
AND THEN ...
MEWN MEWN
WHAT, WHAT?

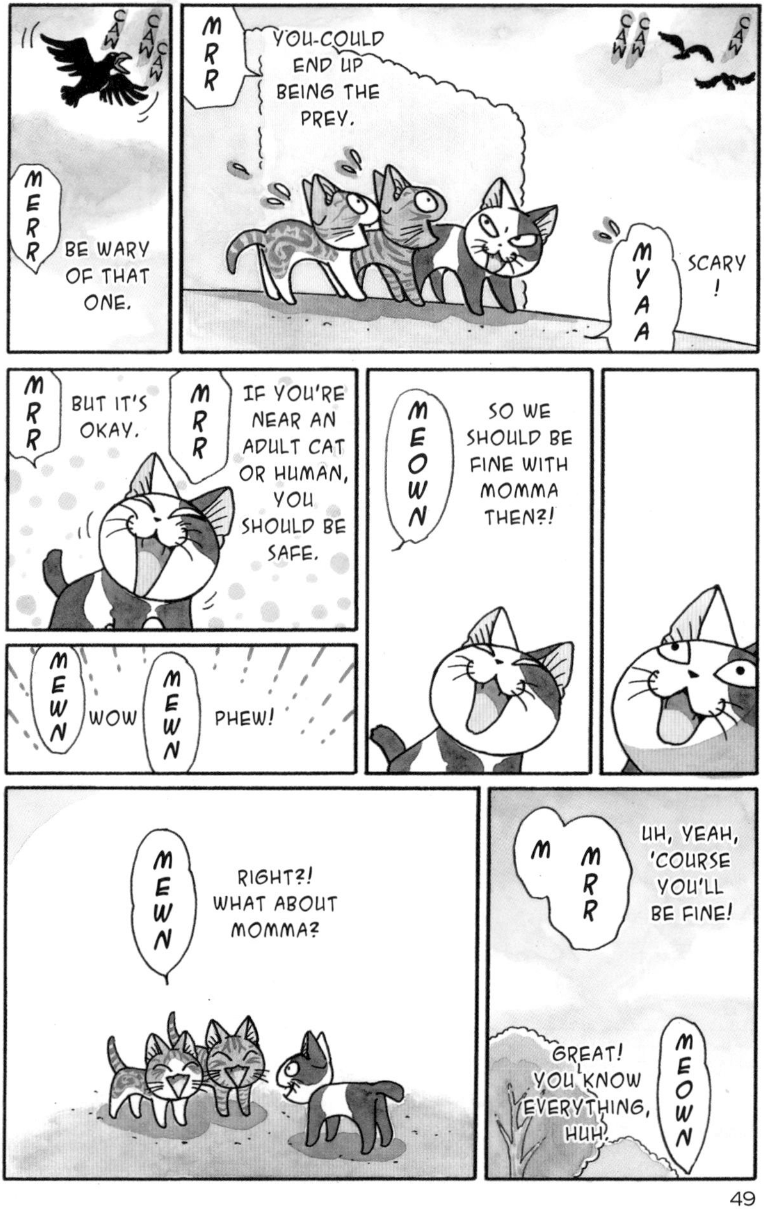
CAW
CAW
CAW
MERR
BE WARY OF THAT ONE.
MRR
YOU-COULD END UP BEING THE PREY.
CAW
CAW
CAW
MYAA
SCARY!
MRR
BUT IT'S OKAY.
MRR
IF YOU'RE NEAR AN ADULT CAT OR HUMAN, YOU SHOULD BE SAFE.
MEWN
WOW
MEWN
PHEW!
MEOWN
SO WE SHOULD BE FINE WITH MOMMA THEN?!
MEWN
RIGHT?! WHAT ABOUT MOMMA?
M
MRR
UH, YEAH, 'COURSE YOU'LL BE FINE!
GREAT! YOU KNOW EVERYTHING, HUH.
MEOWN

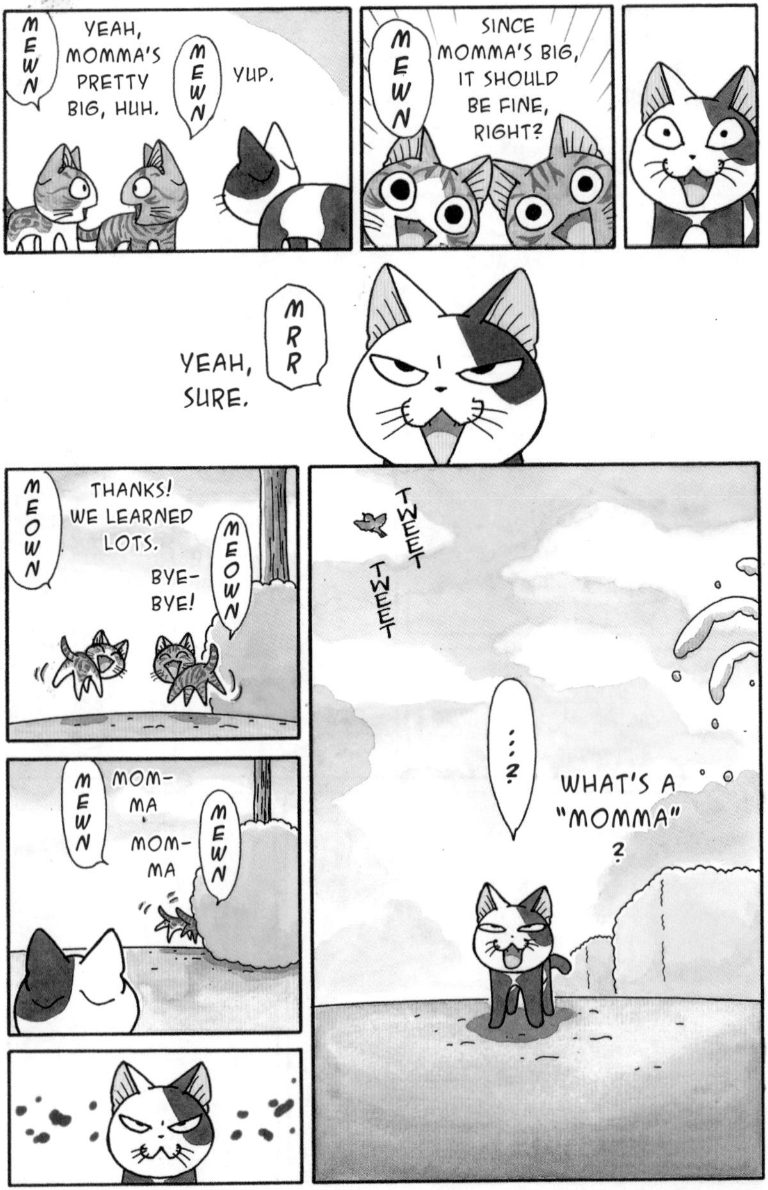

MEWN
YEAH, MOMMA'S PRETTY BIG, HUH.
MEWN
YUP.
MEWN
SINCE MOMMA'S BIG, IT SHOULD BE FINE, RIGHT?
MRR
YEAH, SURE.
MEOWN
THANKS! WE LEARNED LOTS.
BYE-BYE!
MEOWN
MEWN
MOM-MA
MOM-MA
MEWN
TWEET
TWEET
...?
WHAT'S A "MOMMA"?

the end

homemade 171: a cat has signals crossed

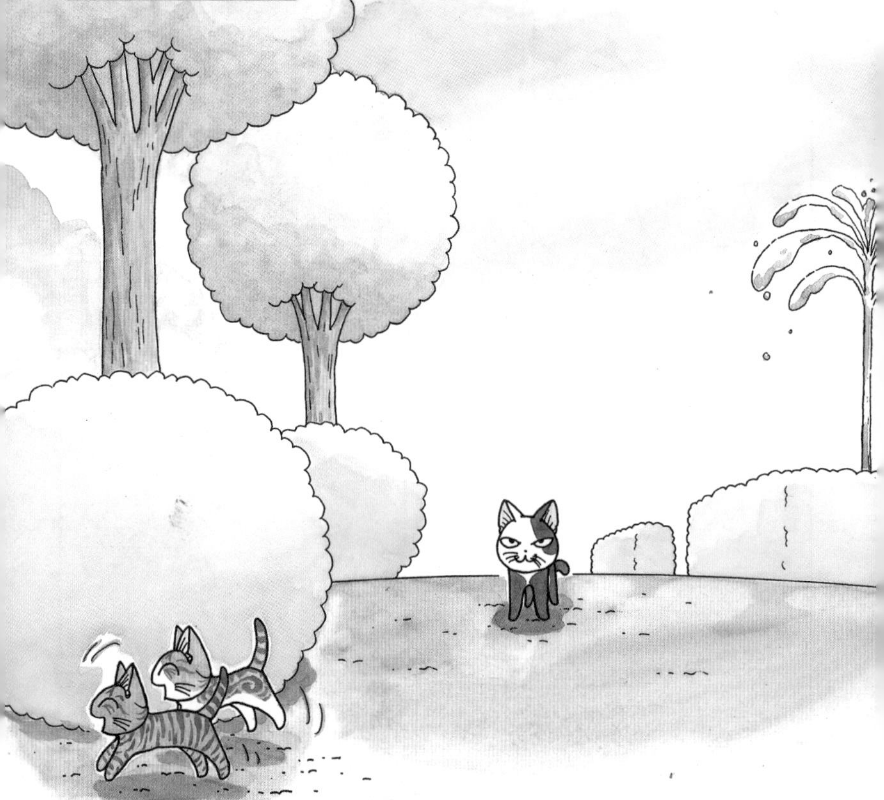

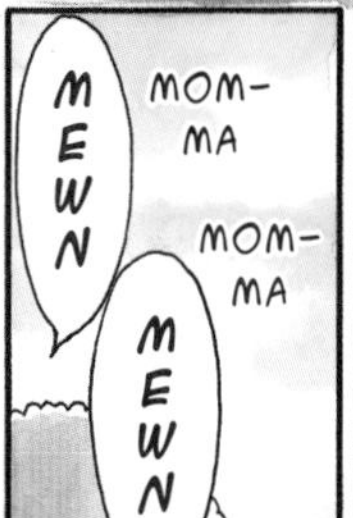
MEWN
MOM-MA
MOM-MA
MEWN

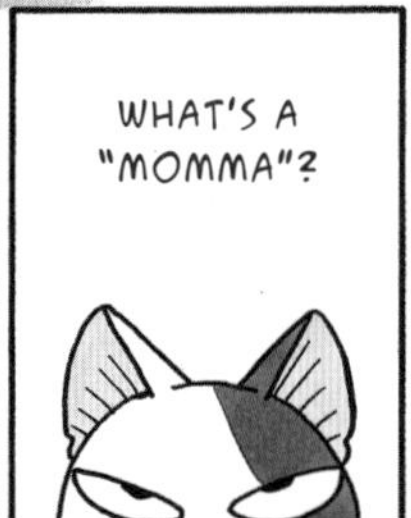
WHAT'S A "MOMMA"?

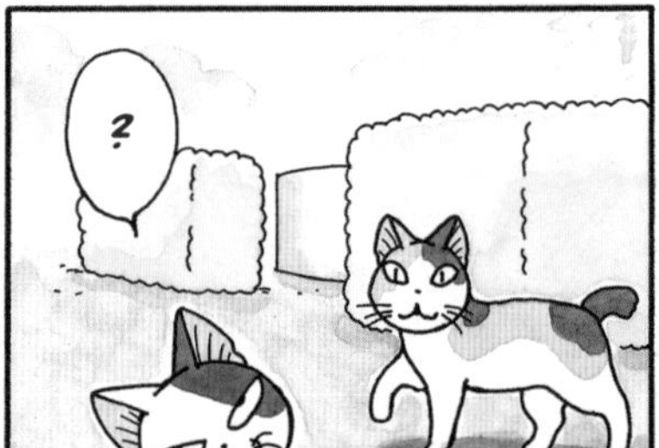
?

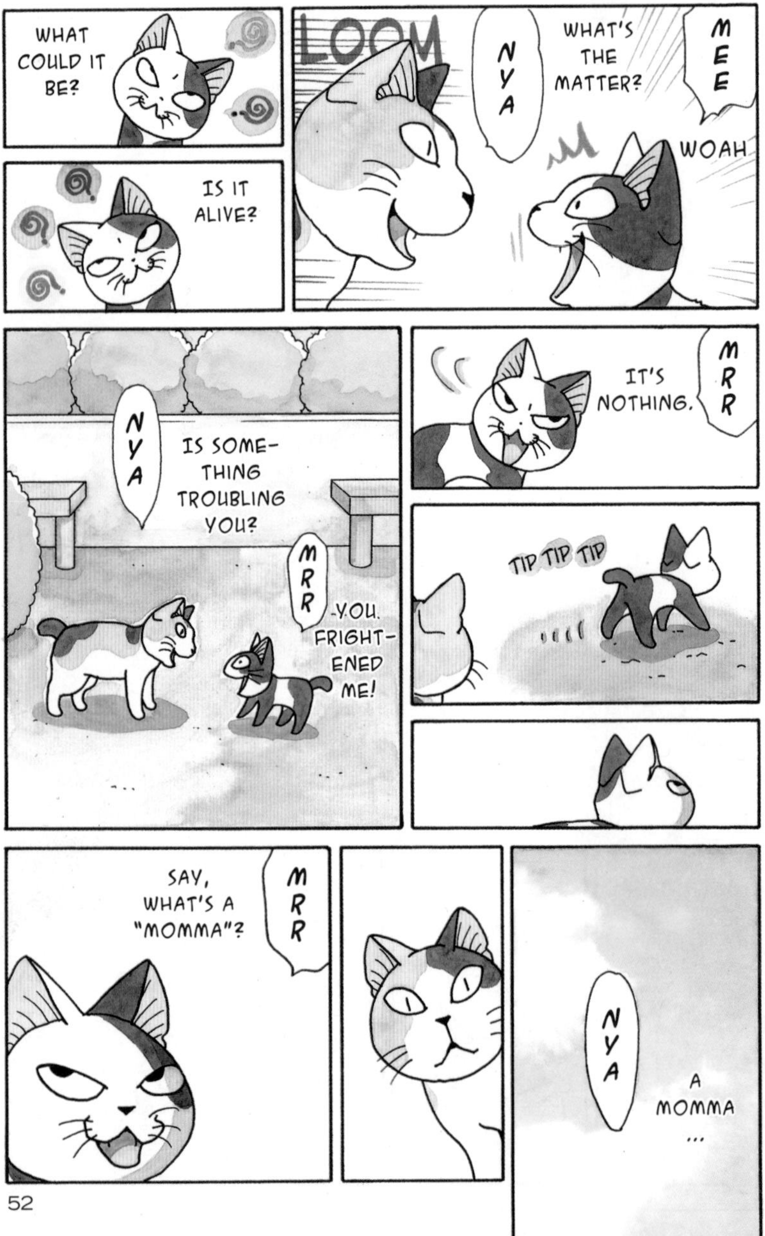
WHAT COULD IT BE?
IS IT ALIVE?
LOOM
NYA
WHAT'S THE MATTER?
MEE
WOAH
NYA
IS SOME-THING TROUBLING YOU?
MRR
-YOU. FRIGHT-ENED ME!
IT'S NOTHING.
MRR
TIP TIP TIP
SAY, WHAT'S A "MOMMA"?
MRR
NYA
A MOMMA ...

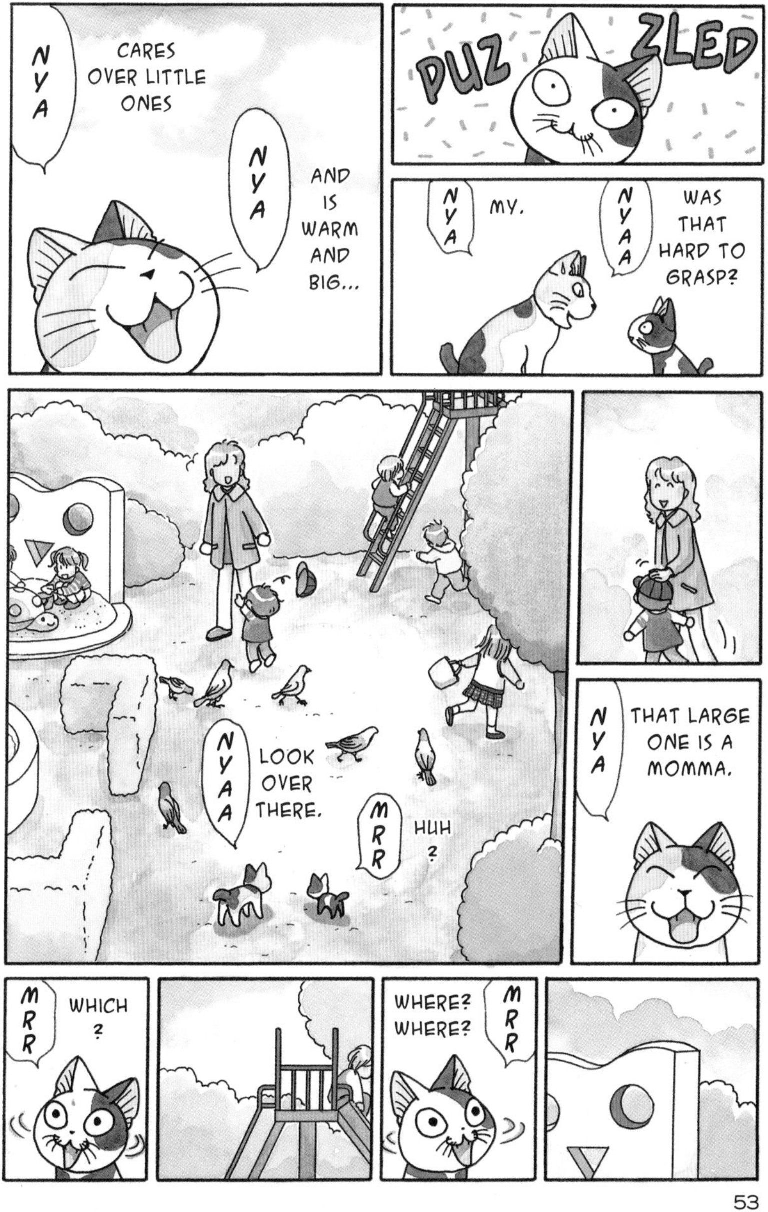

NYA
CARES OVER LITTLE ONES
NYA
AND IS WARM AND BIG...
PUZZLED
NYA
MY.
NYAA
WAS THAT HARD TO GRASP?
NYAA
LOOK OVER THERE.
MRR
HUH?
NYA
THAT LARGE ONE IS A MOMMA.
MRR
WHICH?
WHERE? WHERE?
MRR

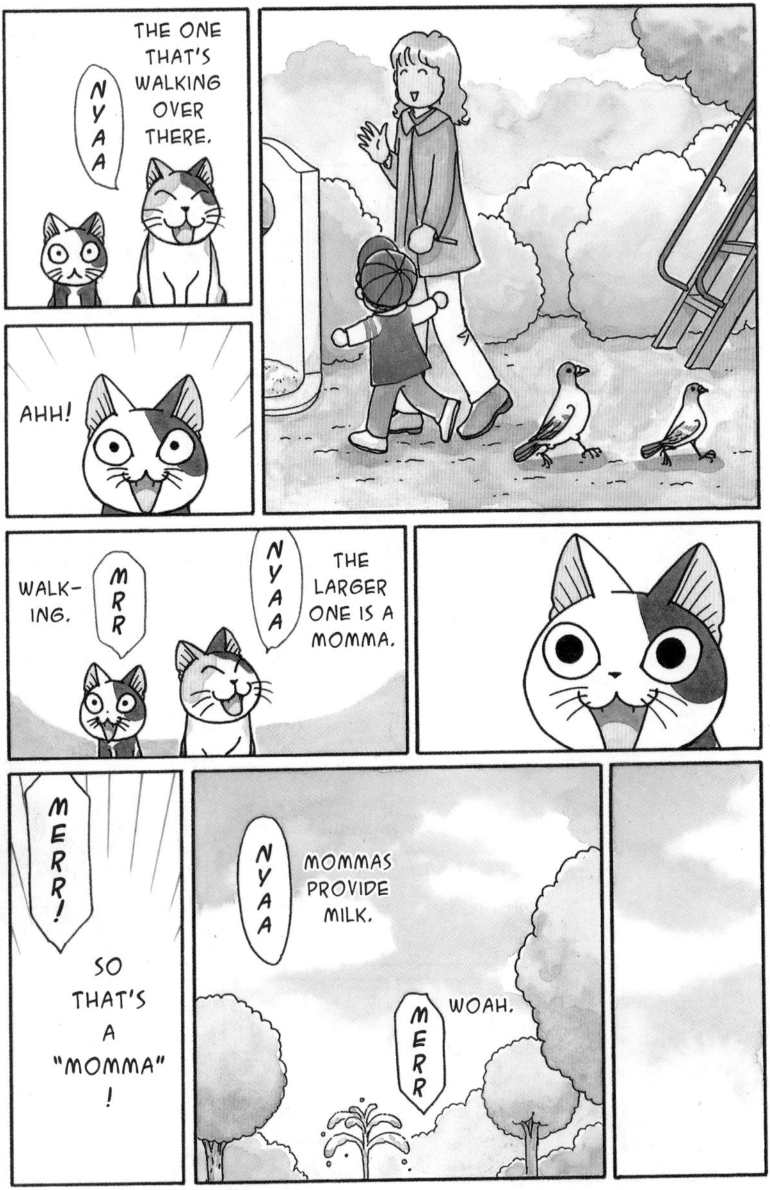
NYAA
THE ONE THAT'S WALKING OVER THERE.
AHH!
WALK-ING.
MRR
NYAA
THE LARGER ONE IS A MOMMA.
MERR!
SO THAT'S A "MOMMA"!
NYAA
MOMMAS PROVIDE MILK.
MERR
WOAH.

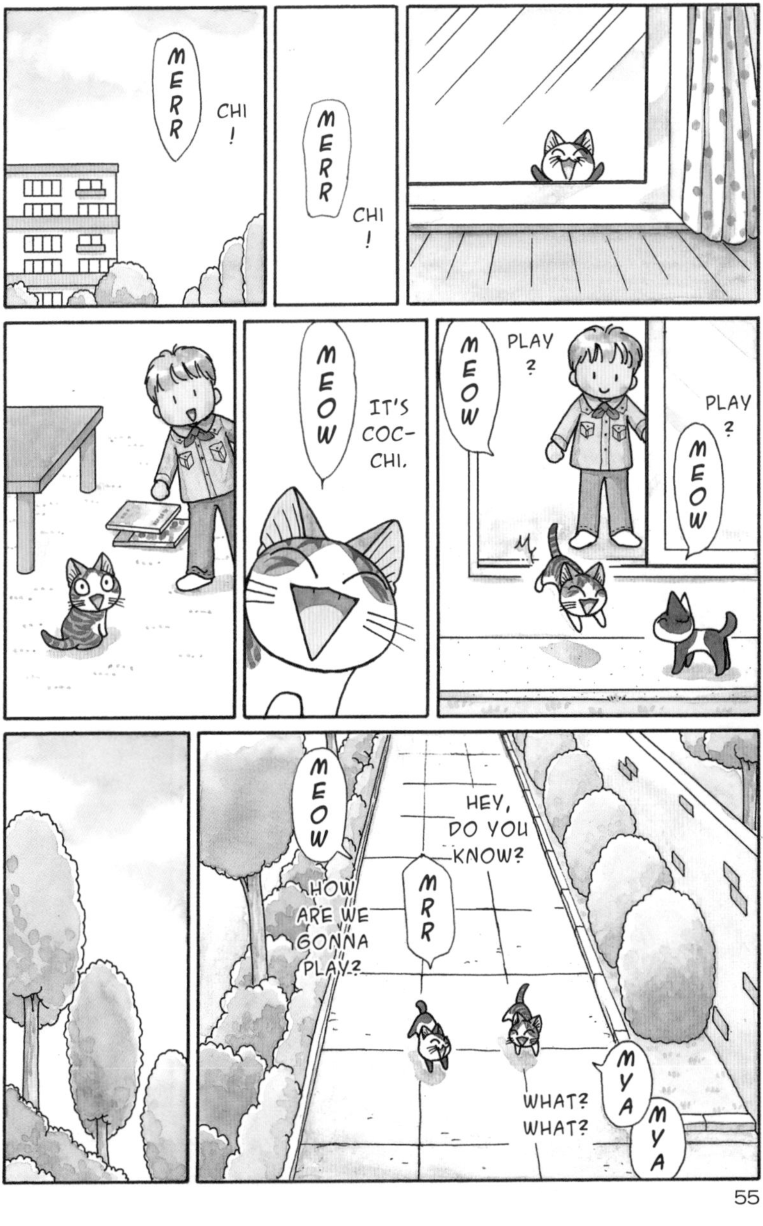
MERR
CHI!
MERR
CHI!
MEOW
IT'S COC-CHI.
MEOW
PLAY?
PLAY?
MEOW
MEOW
HOW ARE WE GONNA PLAY?
MRR
HEY, DO YOU KNOW?
MYA
WHAT? WHAT?
MYA

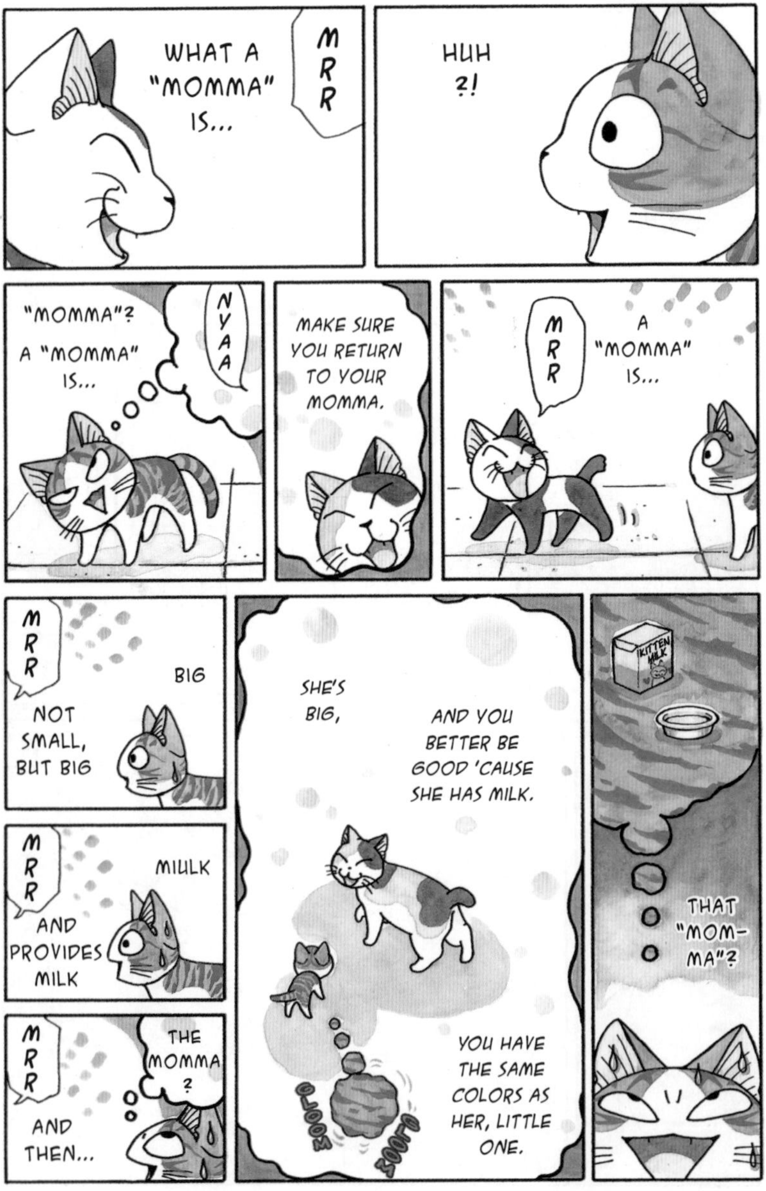
WHAT A "MOMMA" IS...
MRR
HUH ?!
"MOMMA"? A "MOMMA" IS...
NYAA
MAKE SURE YOU RETURN TO YOUR MOMMA.
MRR
A "MOMMA" IS...
MRR
BIG
NOT SMALL, BUT BIG
MRR
MIULK
AND PROVIDES MILK
MRR
THE MOMMA ?
AND THEN...
SHE'S BIG,
AND YOU BETTER BE GOOD 'CAUSE SHE HAS MILK.
GLOOM
GLOOM
YOU HAVE THE SAME COLORS AS HER, LITTLE ONE.
KITTEN MILK
THAT "MOM-MA"?

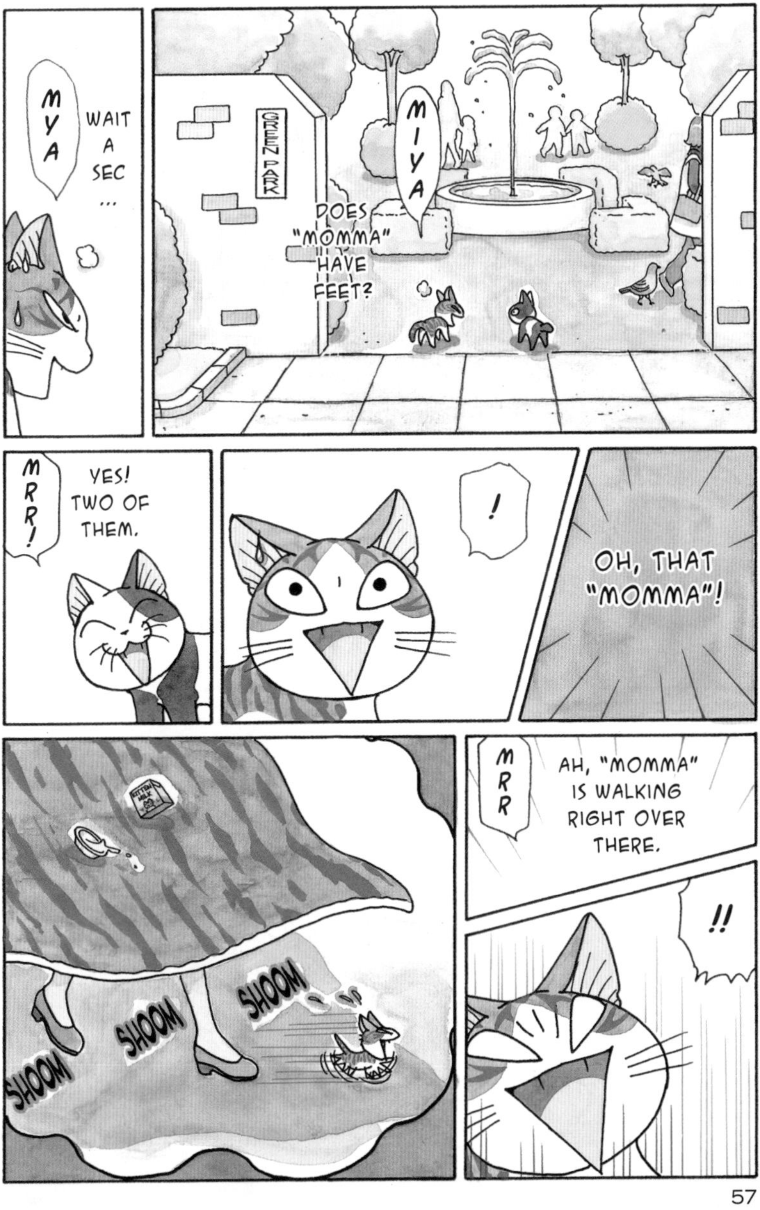

MYA
WAIT A SEC ...
GREEN PARK
MIYA
DOES "MOMMA" HAVE FEET?
MRR!
YES! TWO OF THEM.
!
OH, THAT "MOMMA"!
KITTEN MILK
SHOOM
SHOOM
SHOOM
MRR
AH, "MOMMA" IS WALKING RIGHT OVER THERE.
!!

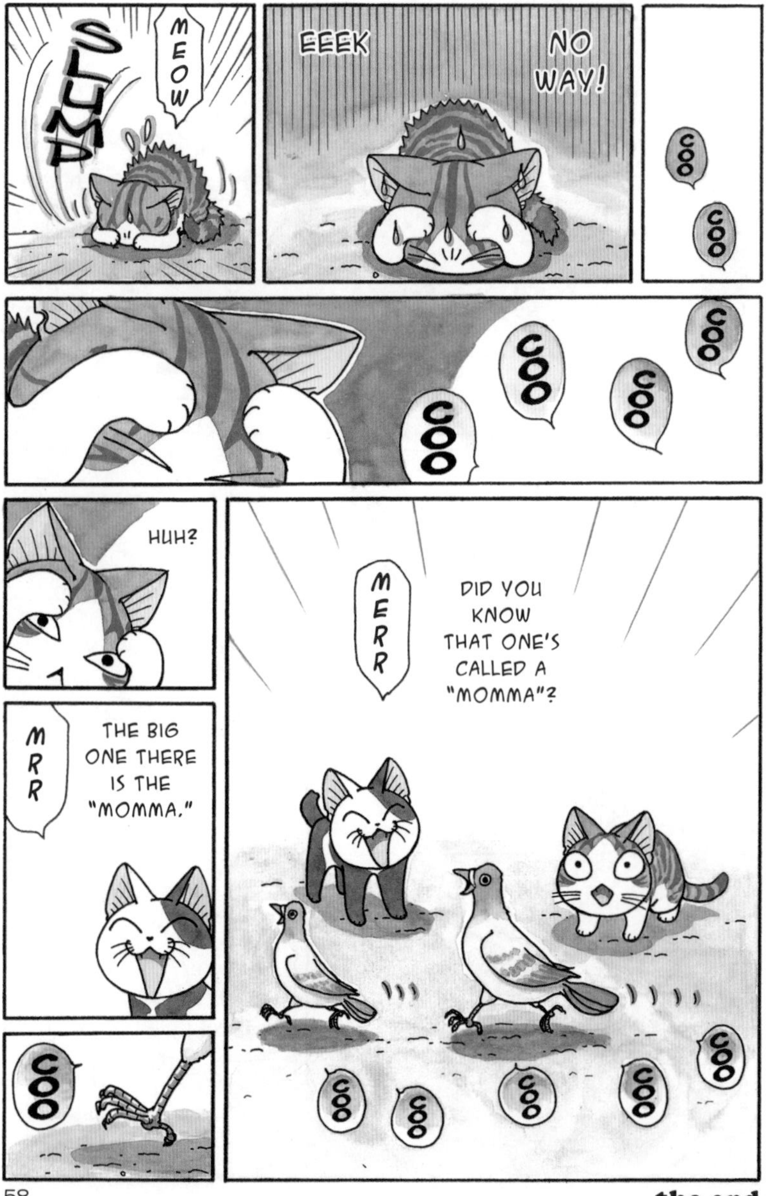
SLUMP
MEOW
EEEK
NO WAY!
COO
COO
COO
COO
COO
COO
HUH?
MRR
THE BIG ONE THERE IS THE "MOMMA."
COO
MERR
DID YOU KNOW THAT ONE'S CALLED A "MOMMA"?
COO
COO
COO
COO
COO
COO

the end

homemade 172: a cat is told

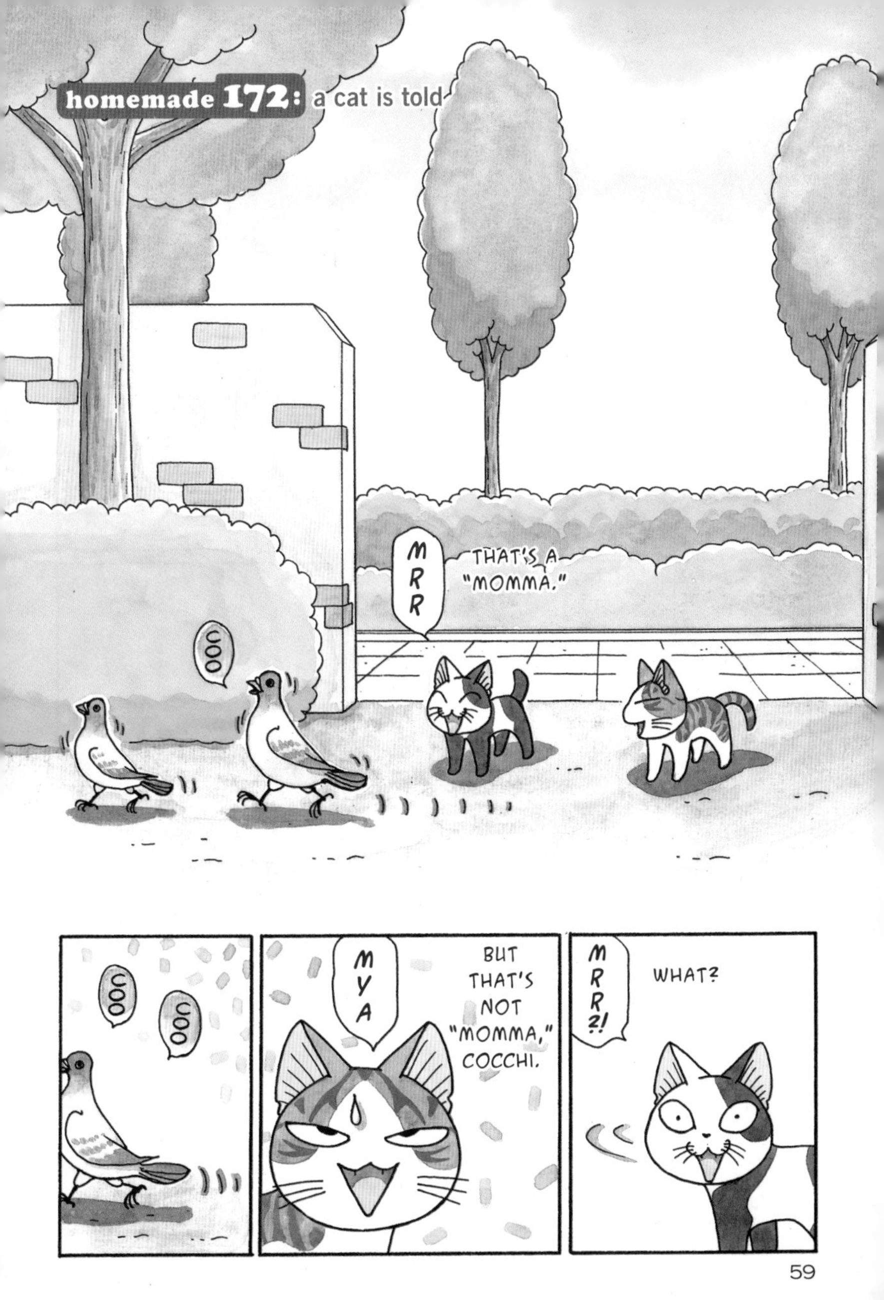
MRR
THAT'S A "MOMMA."
OOO
OOO
OOO
MYA
BUT THAT'S NOT "MOMMA," COCCHI.
MRR?!
WHAT?

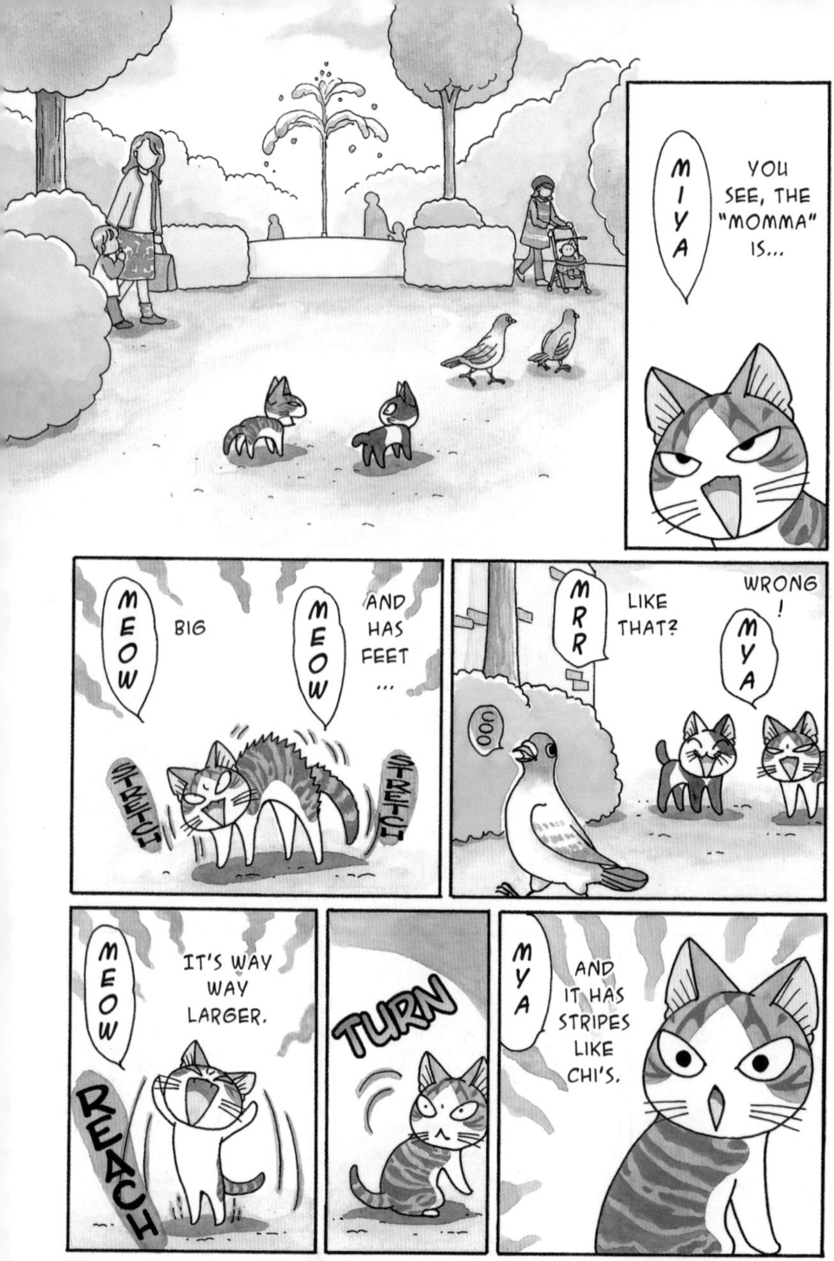
MIYA
YOU SEE, THE "MOMMA" IS...
MEOW
BIG
MEOW
AND HAS FEET ...
STRETCH
STRETCH
MRR
LIKE THAT?
COO
WRONG!
MYA
MEOW
IT'S WAY WAY LARGER.
REACH
TURN
MYA
AND IT HAS STRIPES LIKE CHI'S.

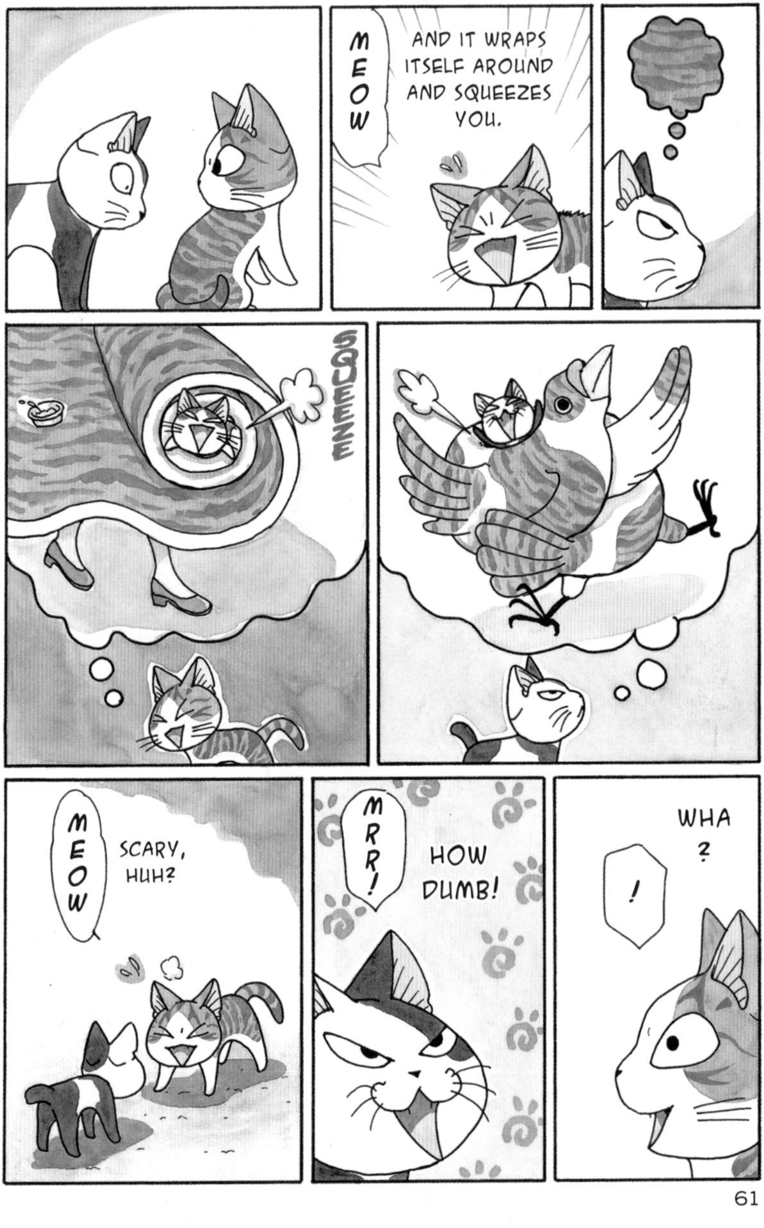
MEOW
AND IT WRAPS ITSELF AROUND AND SQUEEZES YOU.
SQUEEZE
MEOW
SCARY, HUH?
MRR!
HOW DUMB!
WHA?
!

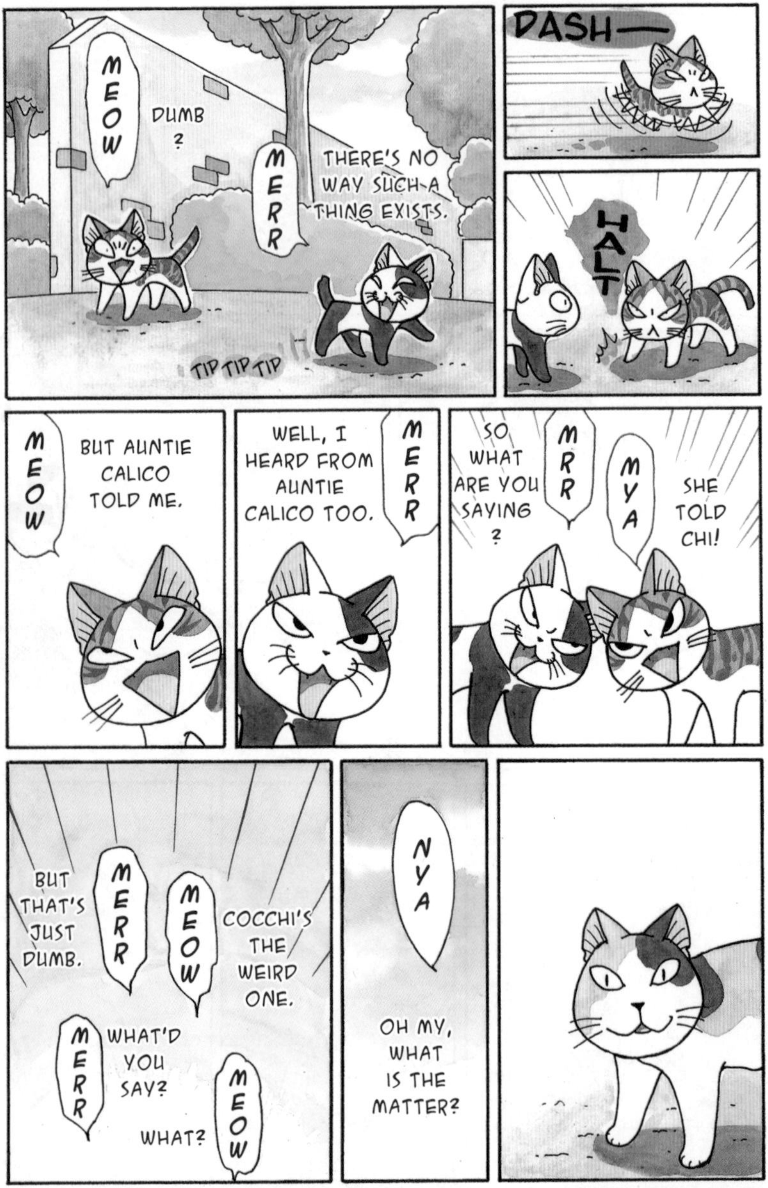
MEOW
DUMB?
MERR
THERE'S NO WAY SUCH A THING EXISTS.
TIP TIP TIP
DASH—
HALT
MEOW
BUT AUNTIE CALICO TOLD ME.
WELL, I HEARD FROM AUNTIE CALICO TOO.
MERR
SO WHAT ARE YOU SAYING?
MRR
MYA
SHE TOLD CHI!
BUT THAT'S JUST DUMB.
MERR
MEOW
COCCHI'S THE WEIRD ONE.
MERR
WHAT'D YOU SAY?
WHAT?
MEOW
NYA
OH MY, WHAT IS THE MATTER?

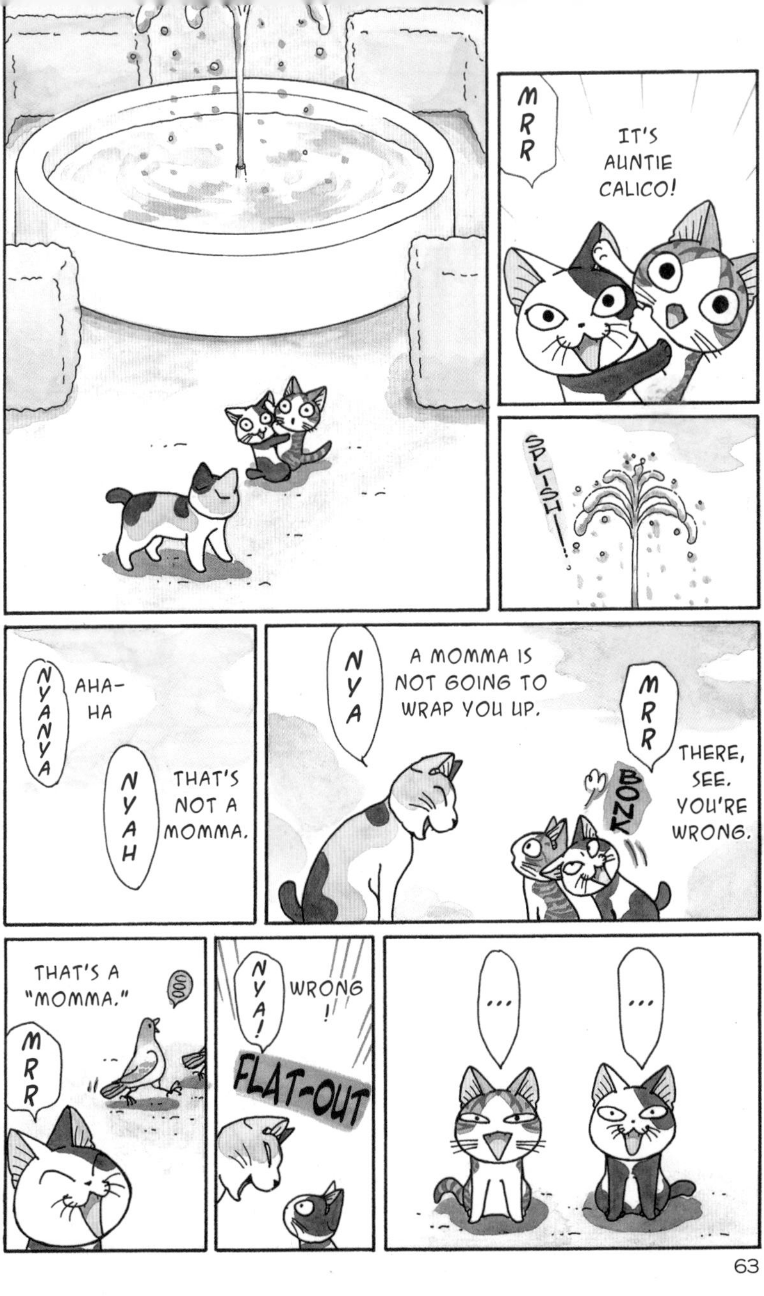

MRR
IT'S AUNTIE CALICO!
SPLISH
NYANYA
AHA-HA
NYAH
THAT'S NOT A MOMMA.
NYA
A MOMMA IS NOT GOING TO WRAP YOU UP.
MRR
BONK
THERE, SEE. YOU'RE WRONG.
THAT'S A "MOMMA."
MRR
NYA!
WRONG!
FLAT-OUT
...
...

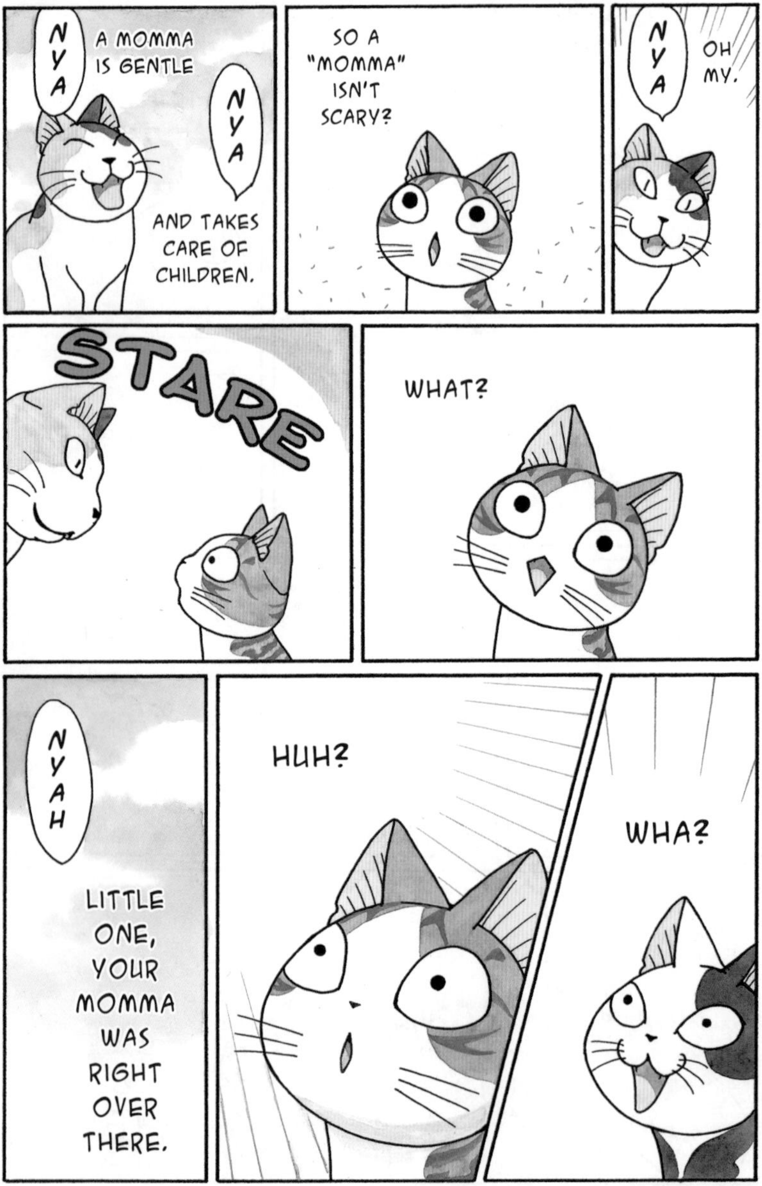

NYA
A MOMMA IS GENTLE
NYA
AND TAKES CARE OF CHILDREN.
SO A "MOMMA" ISN'T SCARY?
NYA
OH MY.
STARE
WHAT?
NYAH
LITTLE ONE, YOUR MOMMA WAS RIGHT OVER THERE.
HUH?
WHA?

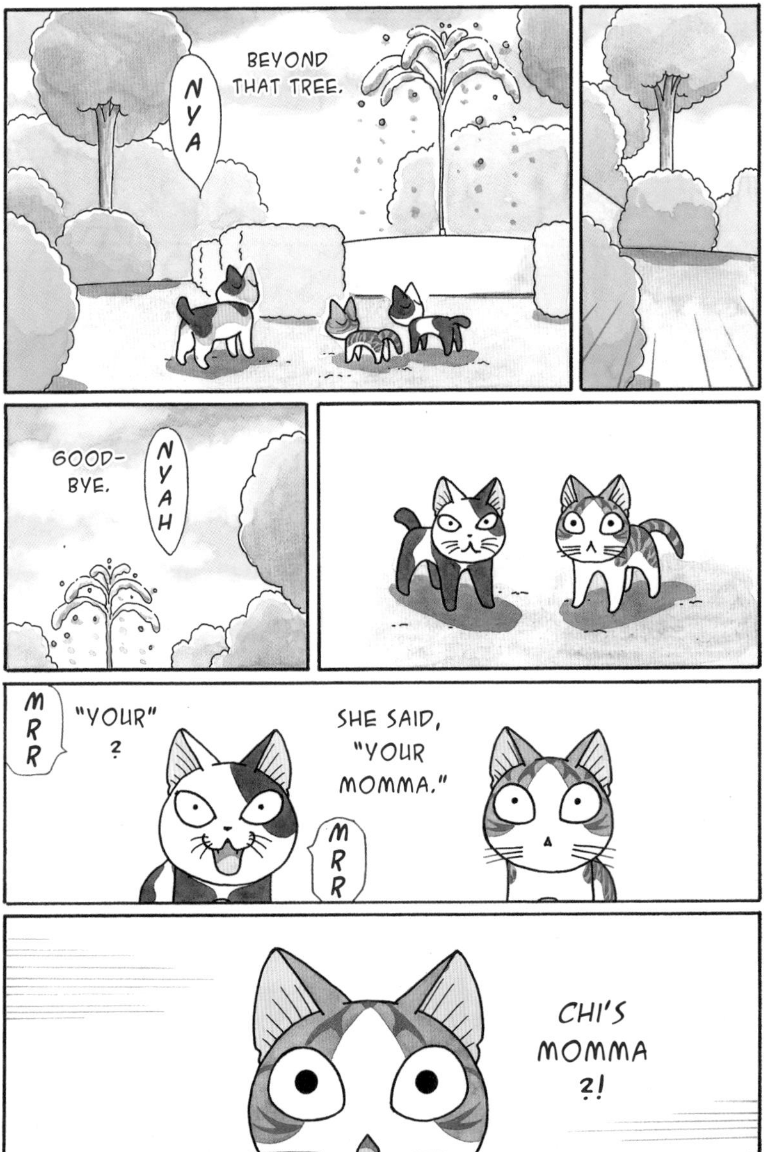
NYA
BEYOND THAT TREE.
GOOD-BYE.
NYAH
MRR
"YOUR"?
SHE SAID, "YOUR MOMMA."
MRR
CHI'S MOMMA ?!

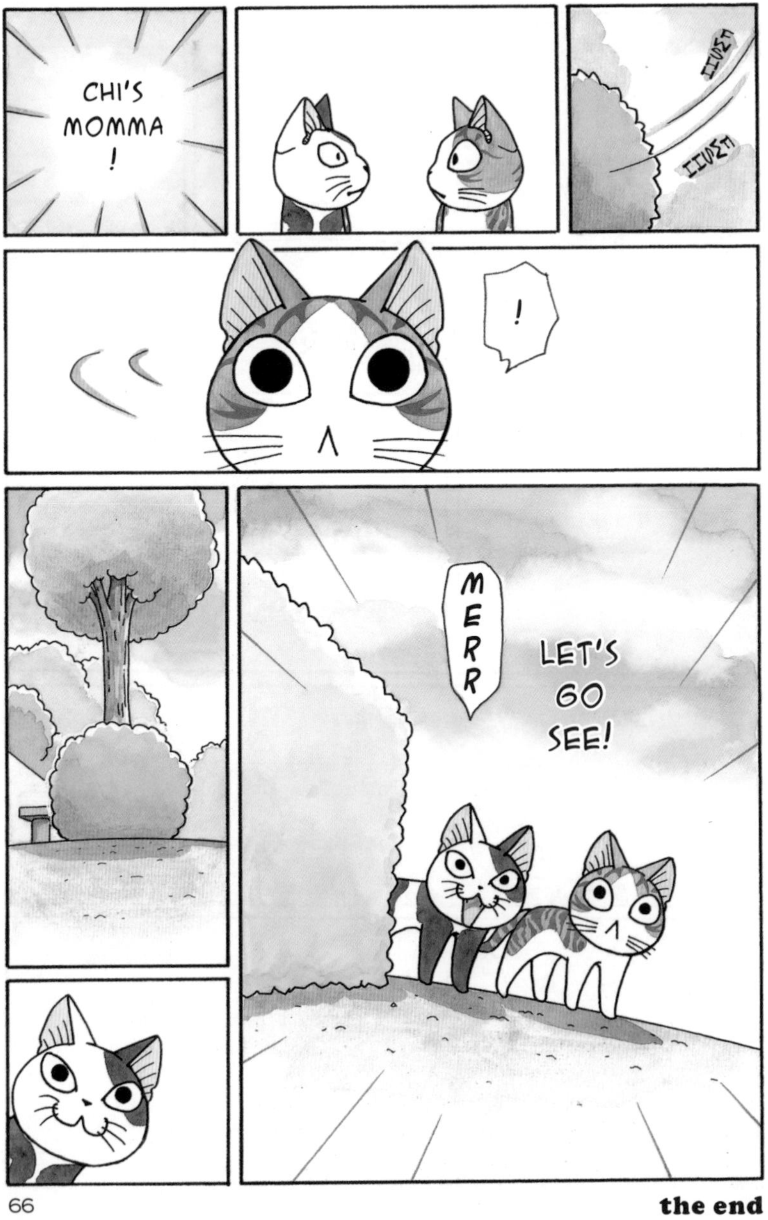
CHI'S MOMMA !
!
MERR
LET'S GO SEE!

the end

homemade 173: a cat goes to see

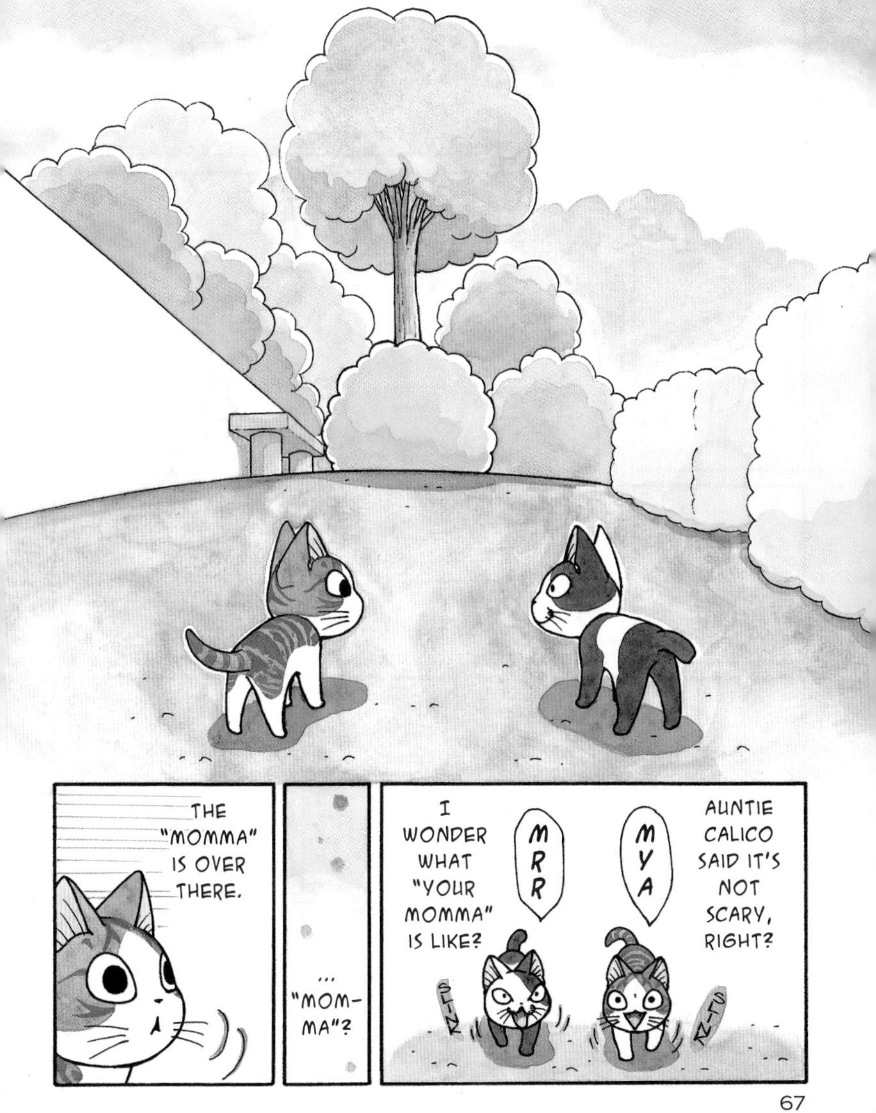
THE "MOMMA" IS OVER THERE.
... "MOM-MA"?
I WONDER WHAT "YOUR MOMMA" IS LIKE?
MRR
MYA
AUNTIE CALICO SAID IT'S NOT SCARY, RIGHT?
SLINK
SLINK

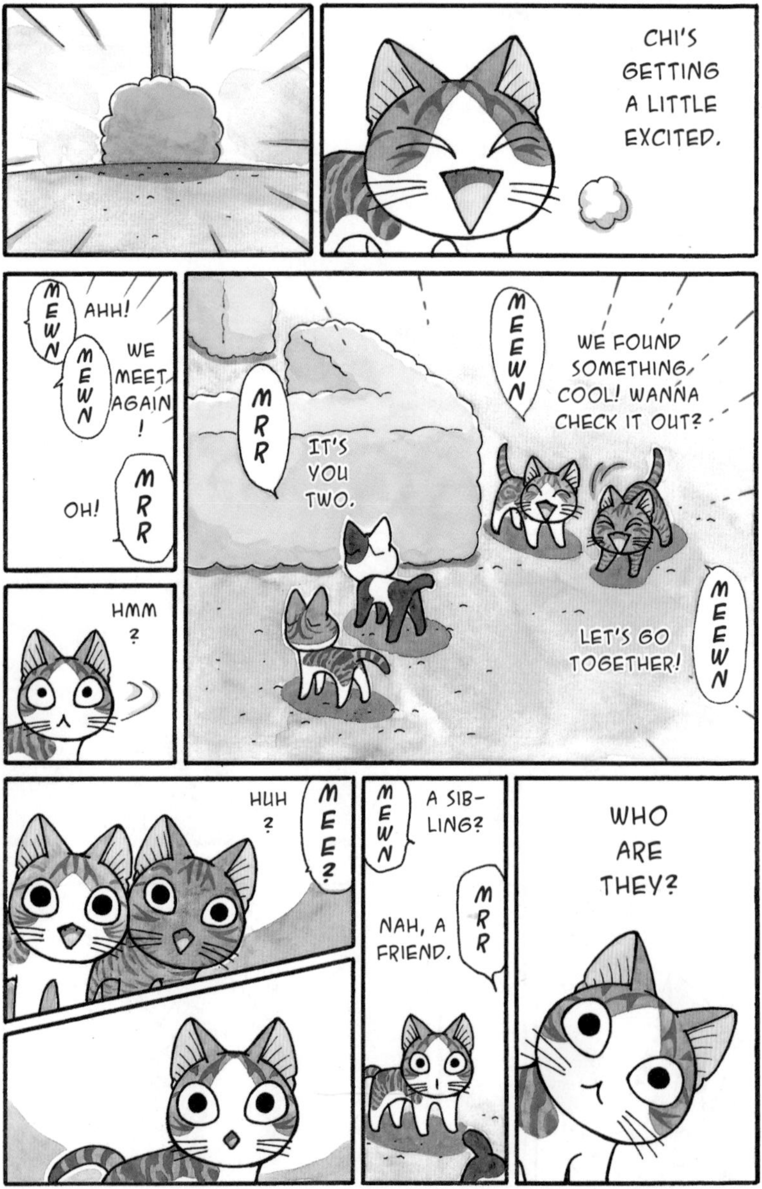
CHI'S GETTING A LITTLE EXCITED.
MEWN
AHH!
MEWN
WE MEET AGAIN!
MRR
OH!
HMM?
MRR
IT'S YOU TWO.
MEEWN
WE FOUND SOMETHING COOL! WANNA CHECK IT OUT?
MEEWN
LET'S GO TOGETHER!
HUH?
MEE?
MEWN
A SIB-LING?
MRR
NAH, A FRIEND.
WHO ARE THEY?

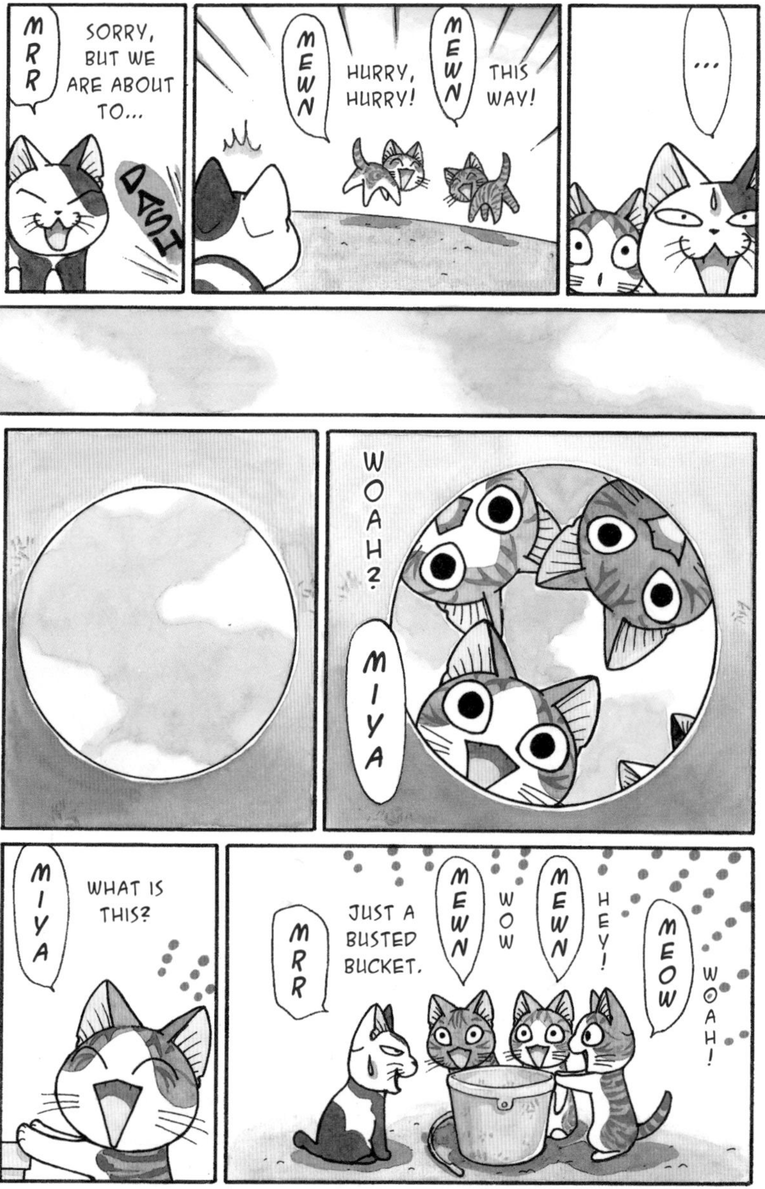
MRR
SORRY, BUT WE ARE ABOUT TO...
DASH
MEWN
HURRY, HURRY!
MEWN
THIS WAY!
...
WOAH?
MIYA
MIYA
WHAT IS THIS?
MRR
JUST A BUSTED BUCKET.
MEWN
WOW
MEWN
HEY!
MEOW
WOAH!

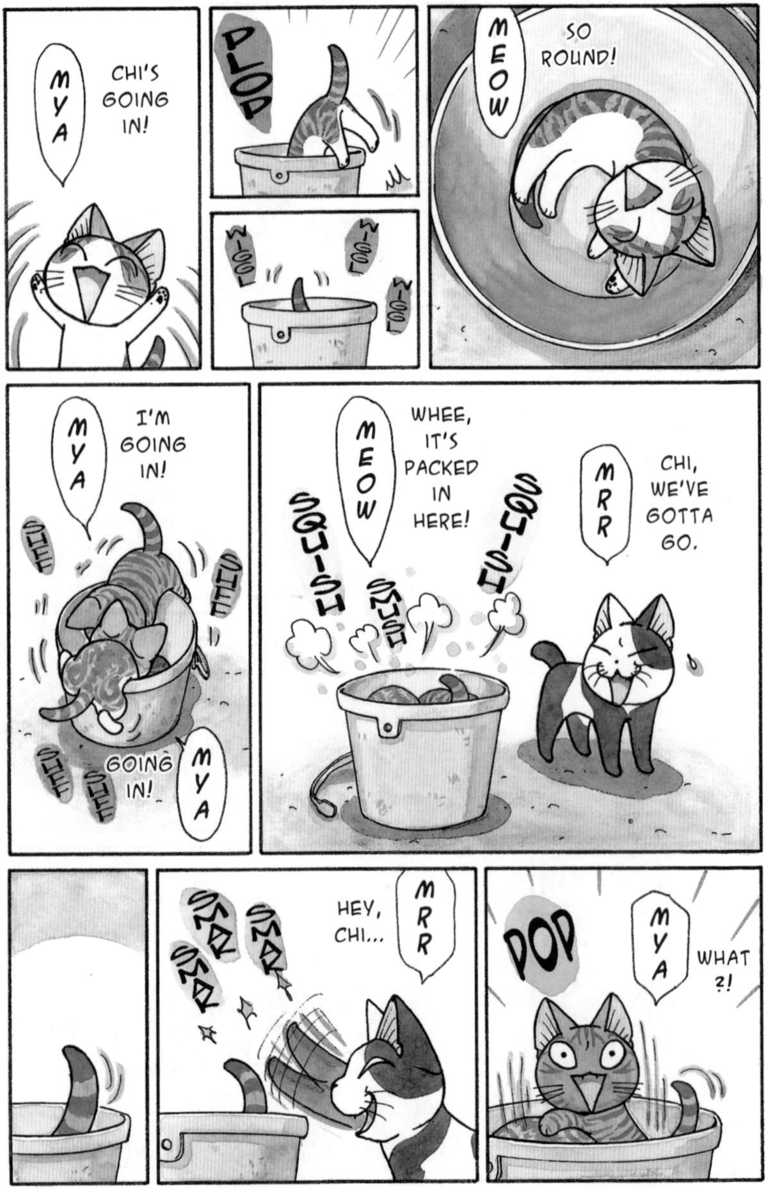
MYA
CHI'S GOING IN!
PLOP
WIGGL
WIGGL
WIGGL
MEOW
SO ROUND!
MYA
I'M GOING IN!
SHFF
SHFF
SHFF
SHFF
GOING IN!
MYA
MEOW
WHEE, IT'S PACKED IN HERE!
SQUISH
SMUSH
SQUISH
MRR
CHI, WE'VE GOTTA GO.
SMAK
SMAK
SMAK
HEY, CHI...
MRR
POP
MYA
WHAT?!

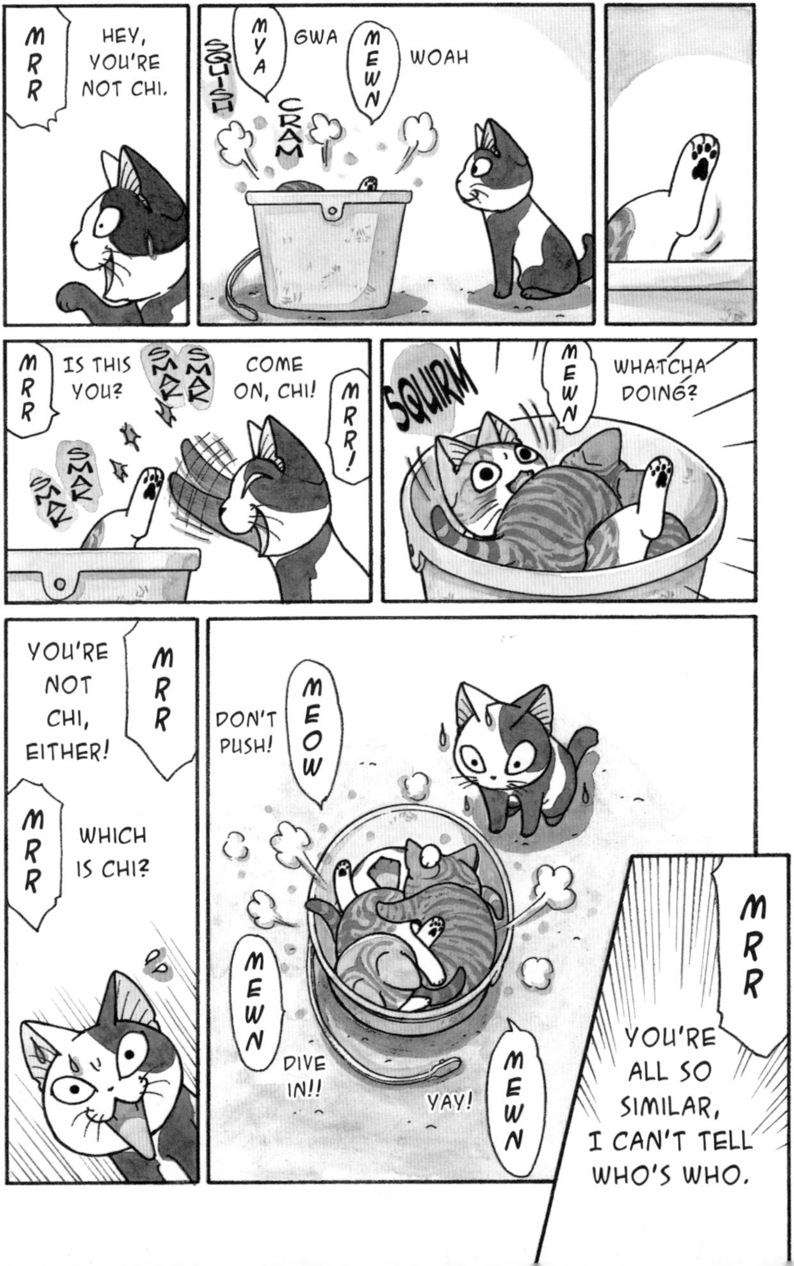

MRR
HEY, YOU'RE NOT CHI.
SQUISH
MYA
GWA
CRAM
MEWN
WOAH
MRR
IS THIS YOU?
SMAK SMAK
SMAK SMAK
COME ON, CHI!
MRR!
SQUIRM
MEWN
WHATCHA DOING?
YOU'RE NOT CHI, EITHER!
MRR
MRR
WHICH IS CHI?
DON'T PUSH!
MEOW
MEWN
DIVE IN!!
YAY!
MEWN
MRR
YOU'RE ALL SO SIMILAR, I CAN'T TELL WHO'S WHO.

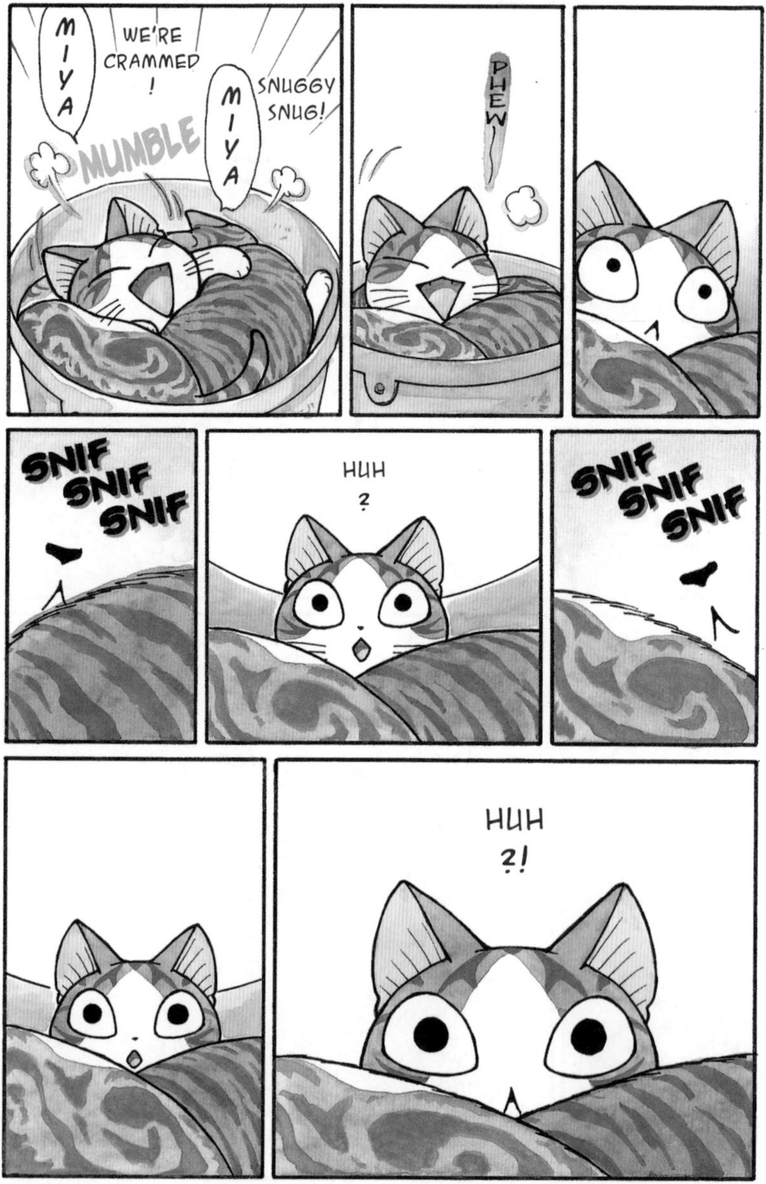
MIYA
WE'RE CRAMMED!
MIYA
SNUGGY SNUG!
MUMBLE
PHEW
SNIF SNIF SNIF
HUH?
SNIF SNIF SNIF
HUH?!

NUZZL
NUZZL

...

HAVE
I...

DONE
THIS
BEFORE?

RIGHT,

BACK
THEN.

REACH

STRETCH

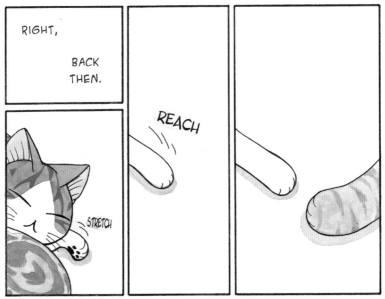

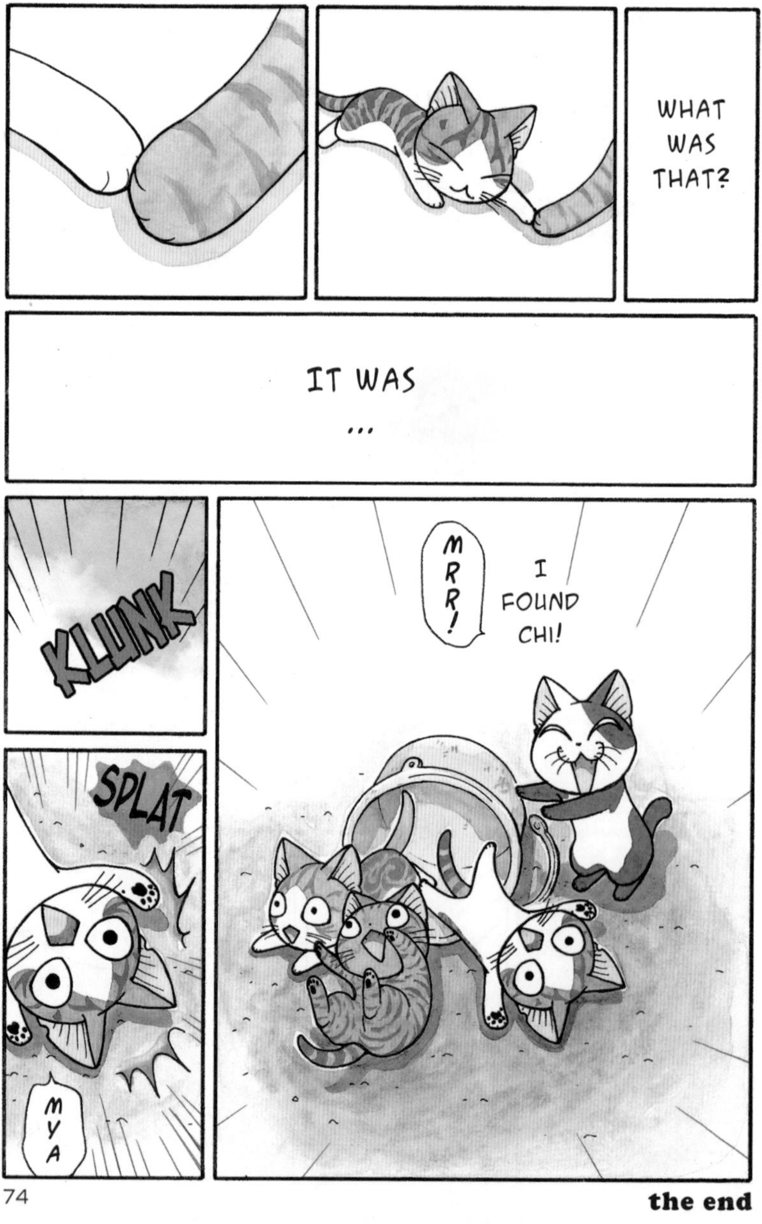
WHAT WAS THAT?
IT WAS ...
KLUNK
SPLAT
MYA
MRR!
I FOUND CHI!

the end

homemade 174: a cat ponders

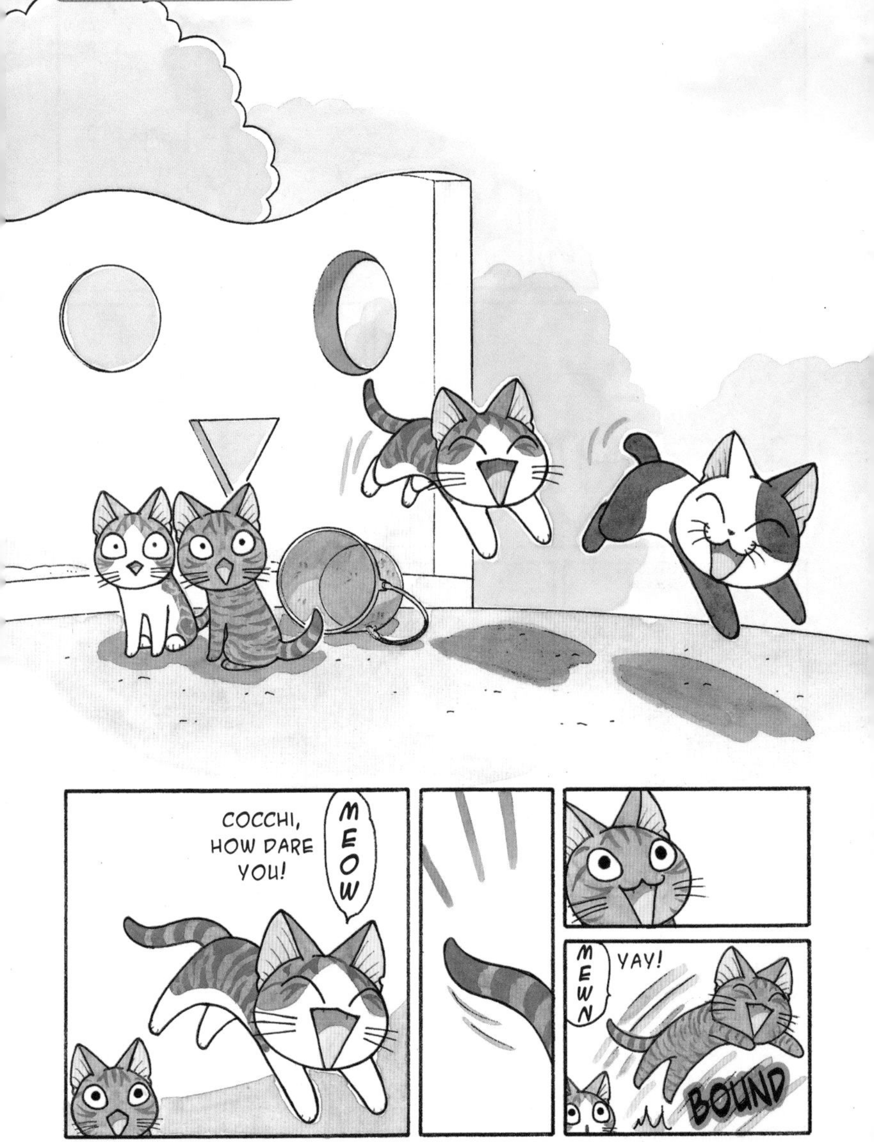
COCCHI, HOW DARE YOU!
MEOW
MEWN
YAY!
BOUND

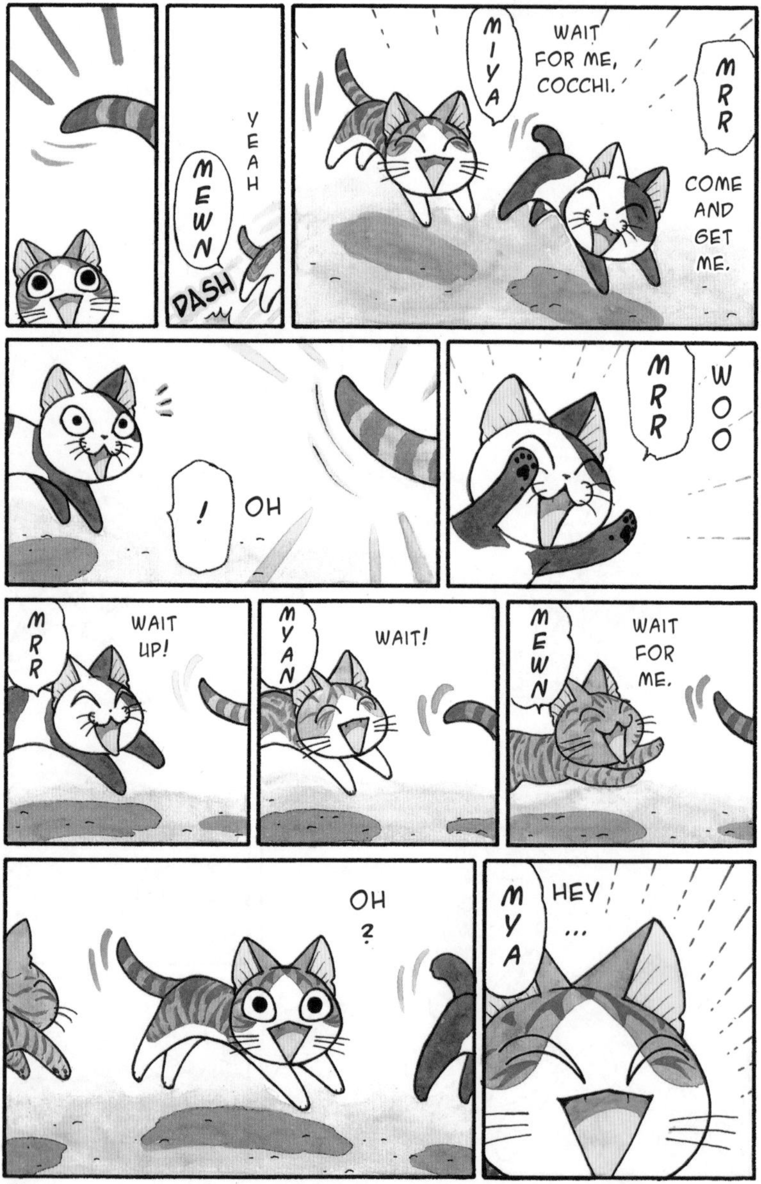
MEWN
YEAH
DASH
MIYA
WAIT FOR ME, COCCHI.
MRR
COME AND GET ME.
!
OH
MRR
WOO
MRR
WAIT UP!
MYAN
WAIT!
MEWN
WAIT FOR ME.
OH ?
MYA
HEY ...

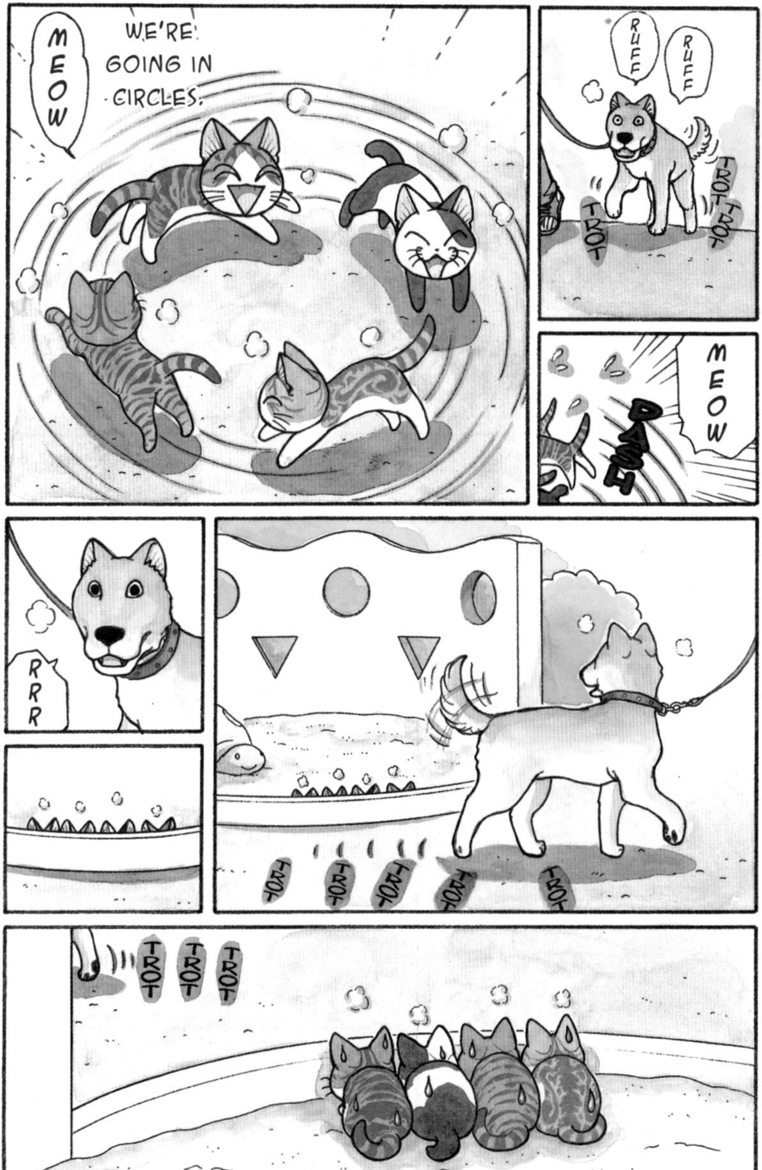
MEOW
WE'RE GOING IN CIRCLES.
RUFF
RUFF
TROT
TROT TROT
MEOW
DASH
RRR
TROT
TROT
TROT
TROT
TROT
TROT
TROT
TROT

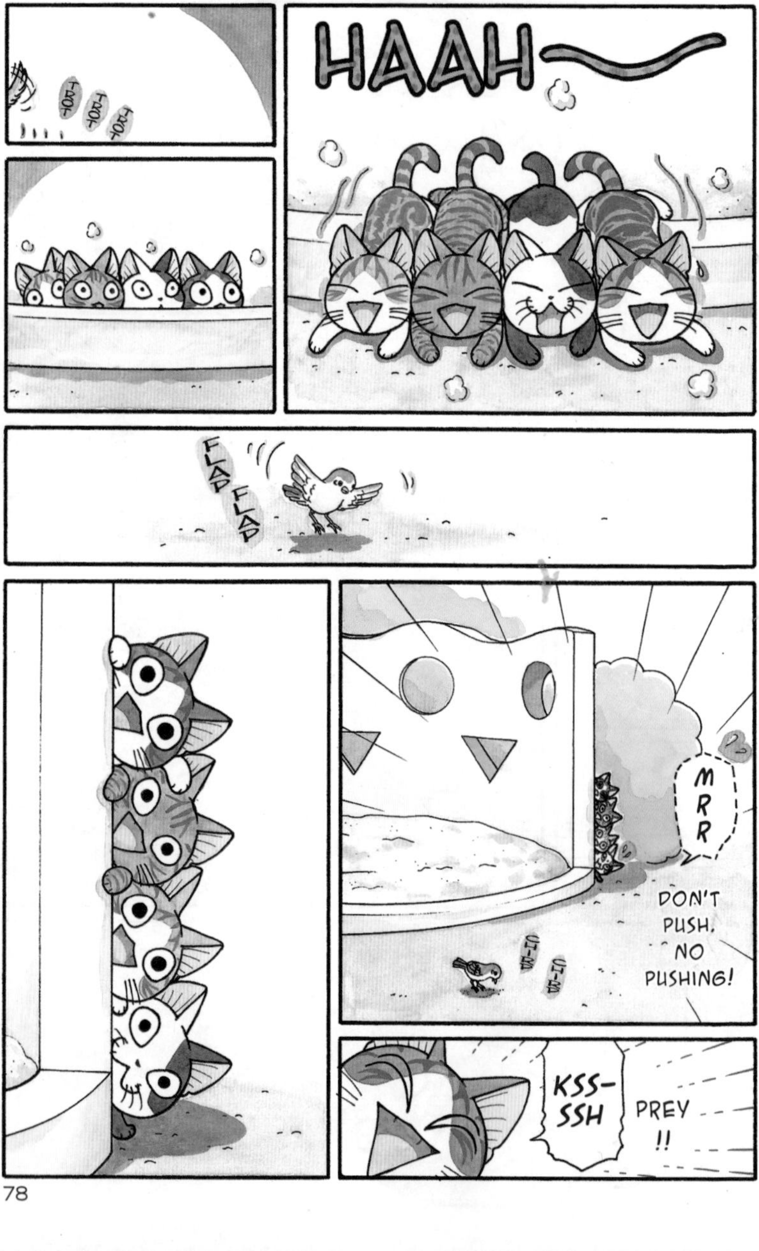
TROT
TROT
TROT
HAAH~
FLAP
FLAP
MRR
DON'T PUSH. NO PUSHING!
CHIB
CHIB
KSS-SSH
PREY !!

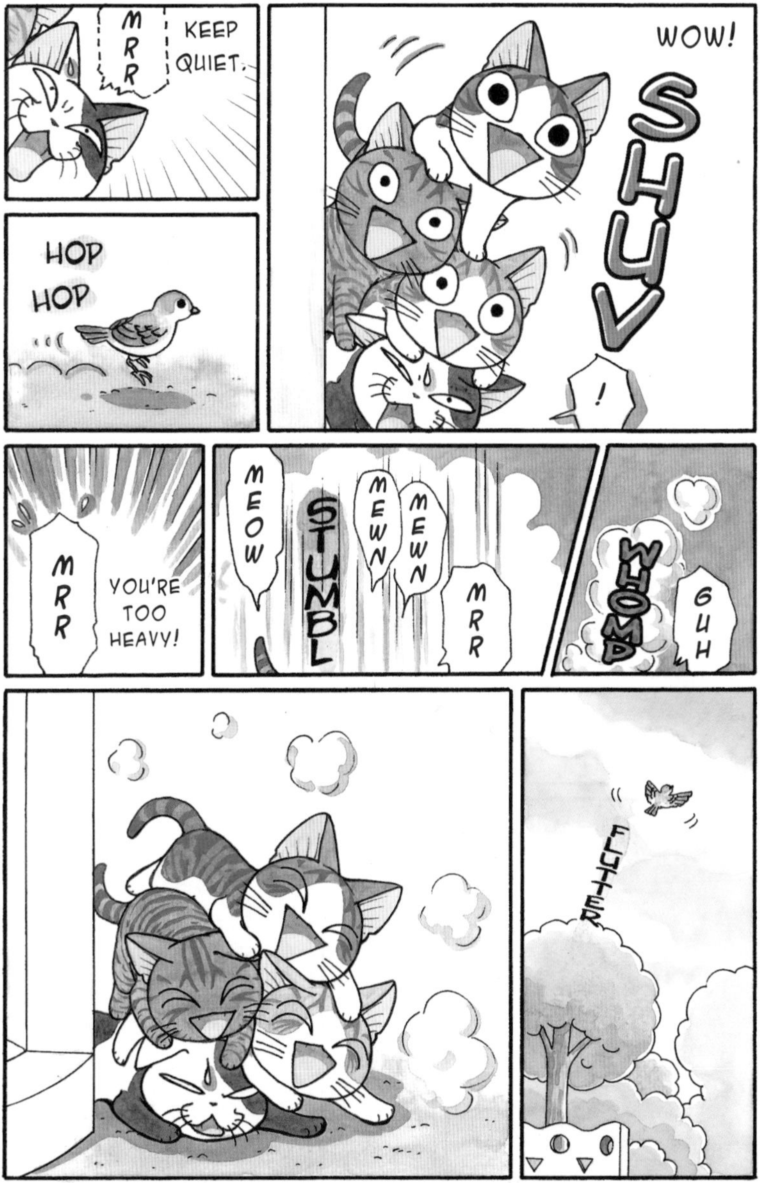

MRR
KEEP QUIET.
HOP
HOP
WOW!
SHUV
!
MRR
YOU'RE TOO HEAVY!
MEOW
STUMBL
MEWN
MEWN
MRR
WHOMP
GUH
FLUTTER

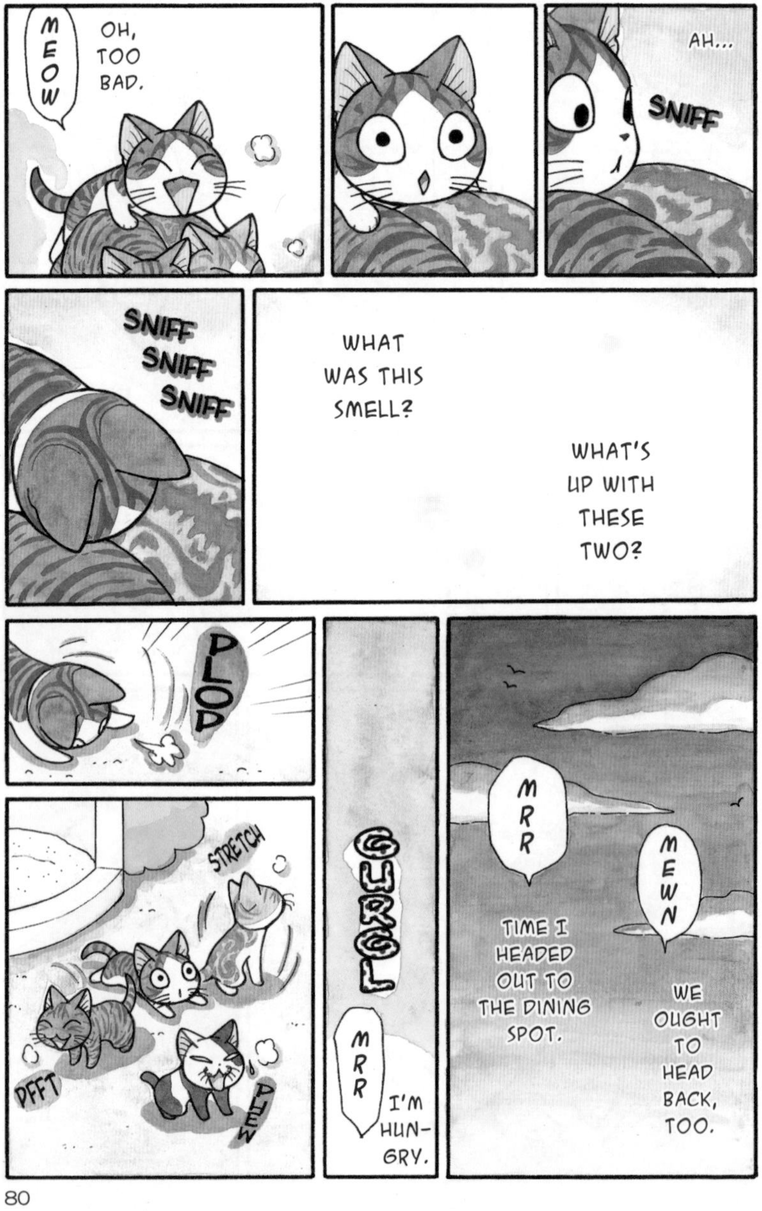

MEOW
OH, TOO BAD.
AH...
SNIFF
SNIFF
SNIFF
SNIFF
WHAT WAS THIS SMELL?
WHAT'S UP WITH THESE TWO?
PLOD
STRETCH
PFFT
PHEW
GURGL
MRR
I'M HUN-GRY.
MRR
MEWN
TIME I HEADED OUT TO THE DINING SPOT.
WE OUGHT TO HEAD BACK, TOO.

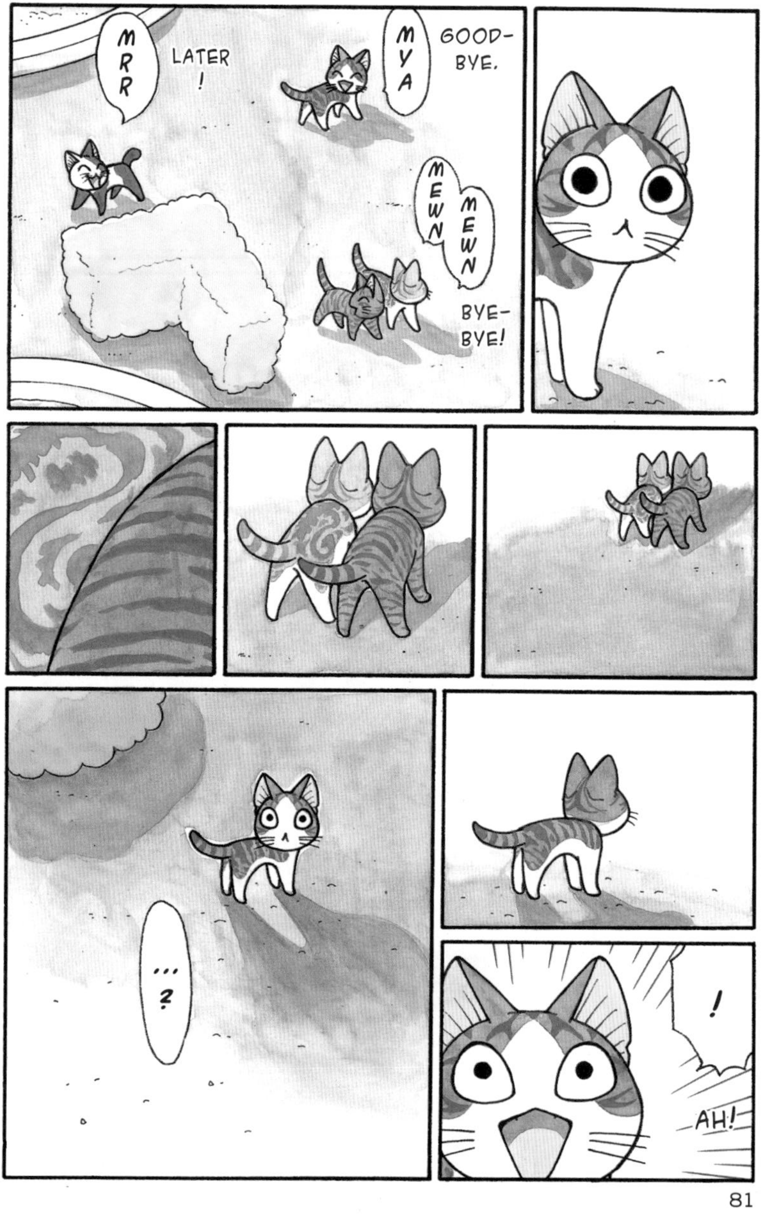
MRR
LATER!
MYA
GOOD-BYE.
MEWN
MEWN
BYE-BYE!
...?
!
AH!

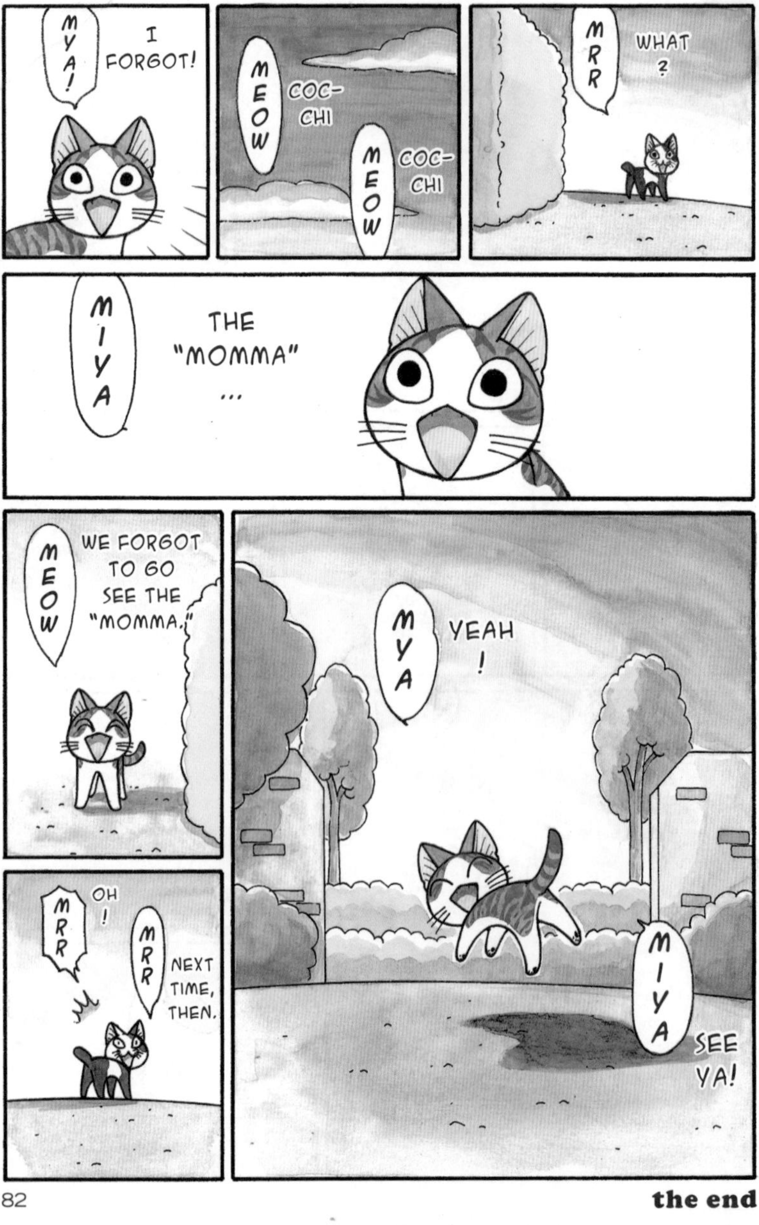
MYA!
I FORGOT!
MEOW
COC-CHI
MEOW
COC-CHI
MRR
WHAT?
MIYA
THE "MOMMA" ...
MEOW
WE FORGOT TO GO SEE THE "MOMMA."
MRR
OH!
MRR
NEXT TIME, THEN.
MYA
YEAH!
MIYA
SEE YA!

the end

homemade 175: a cat realizes

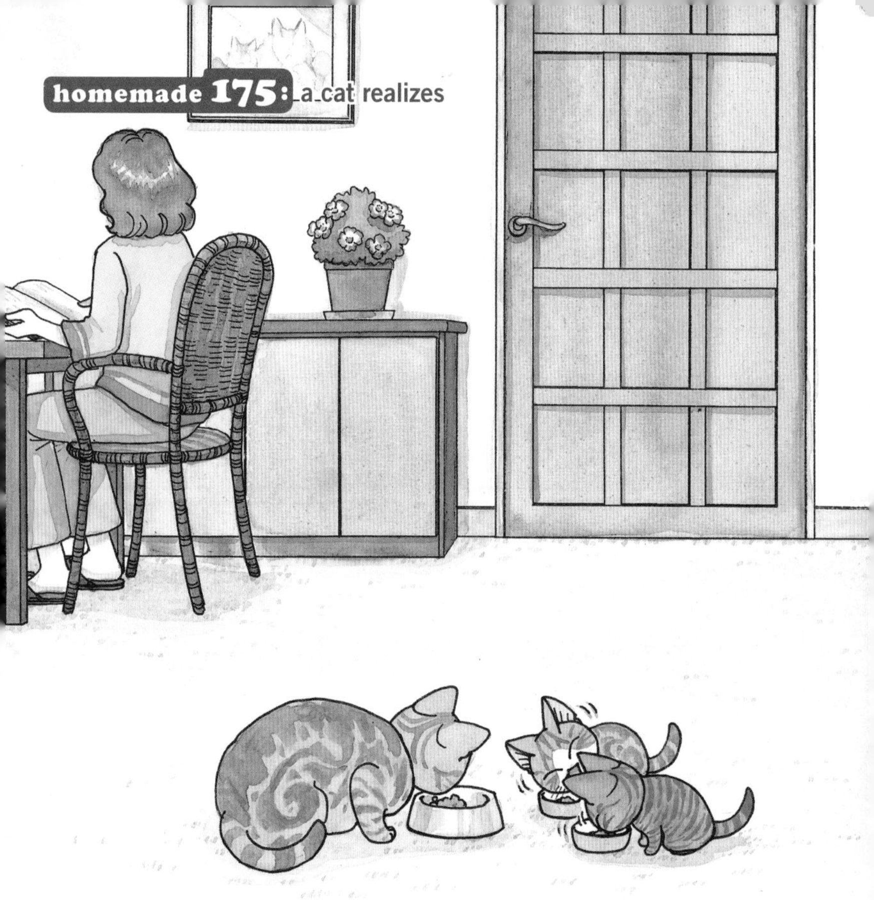

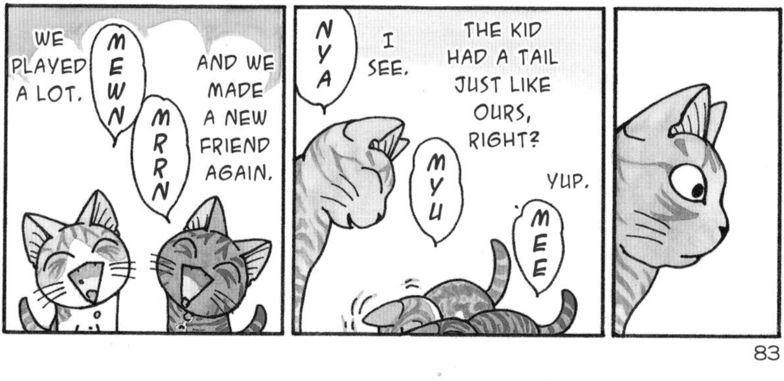

WE PLAYED A LOT.
MEWN
AND WE MADE A NEW FRIEND AGAIN.
MRRN
NYA
I SEE.
THE KID HAD A TAIL JUST LIKE OURS, RIGHT?
MYU
YUP.
MEE

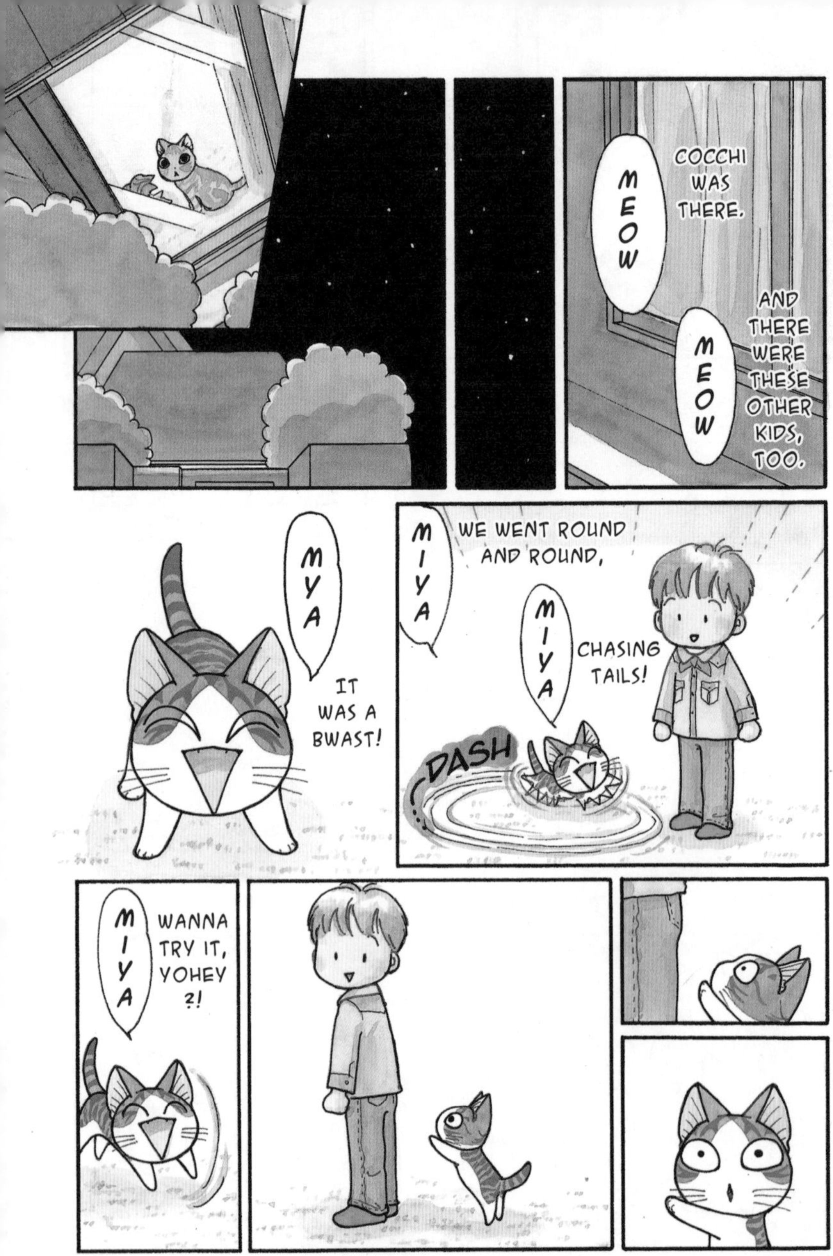
MEOW
COCCHI WAS THERE.
MEOW
AND THERE WERE THESE OTHER KIDS, TOO.
MYA
IT WAS A BWAST!
MIYA
WE WENT ROUND AND ROUND,
MIYA
CHASING TAILS!
DASH
MIYA
WANNA TRY IT, YOHEY ?!

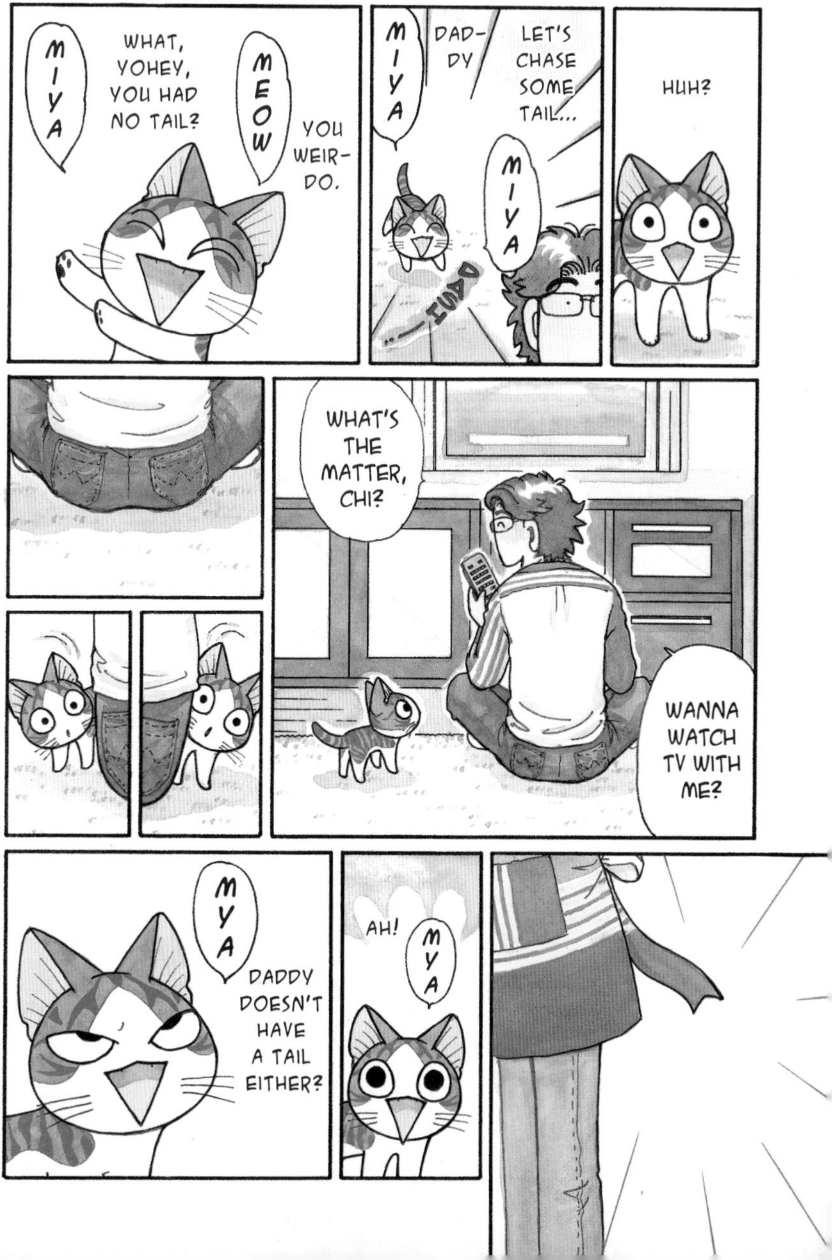
MIYA
WHAT, YOHEY, YOU HAD NO TAIL?
MEOW
YOU WEIRDO.
MIYA
DADDY
LET'S CHASE SOME TAIL...
MIYA
DASH
HUH?
WHAT'S THE MATTER, CHI?
WANNA WATCH TV WITH ME?
MYA
DADDY DOESN'T HAVE A TAIL EITHER?
AH!
MYA

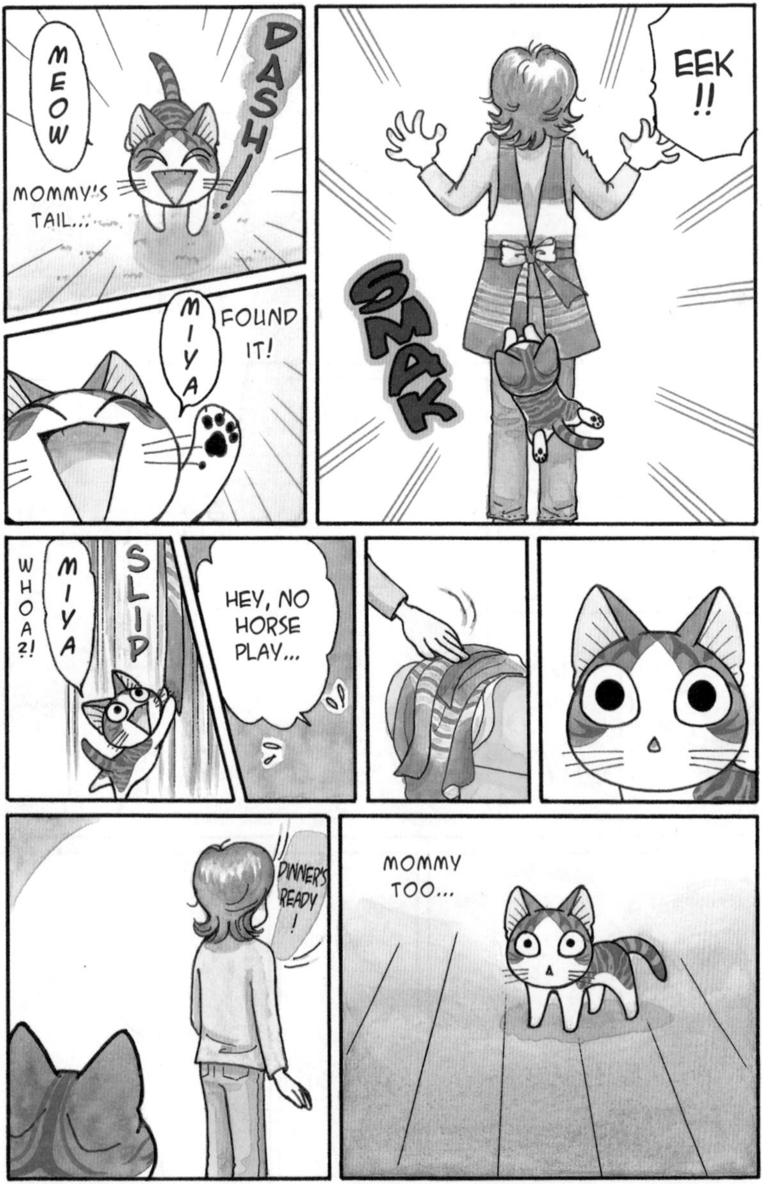
MEOW
DASH!
MOMMY'S TAIL...
EEK!!
SMAK
MIYA
FOUND IT!
WHOA?!
MIYA
SLIP
HEY, NO HORSE PLAY...
DINNER'S READY!
MOMMY TOO...

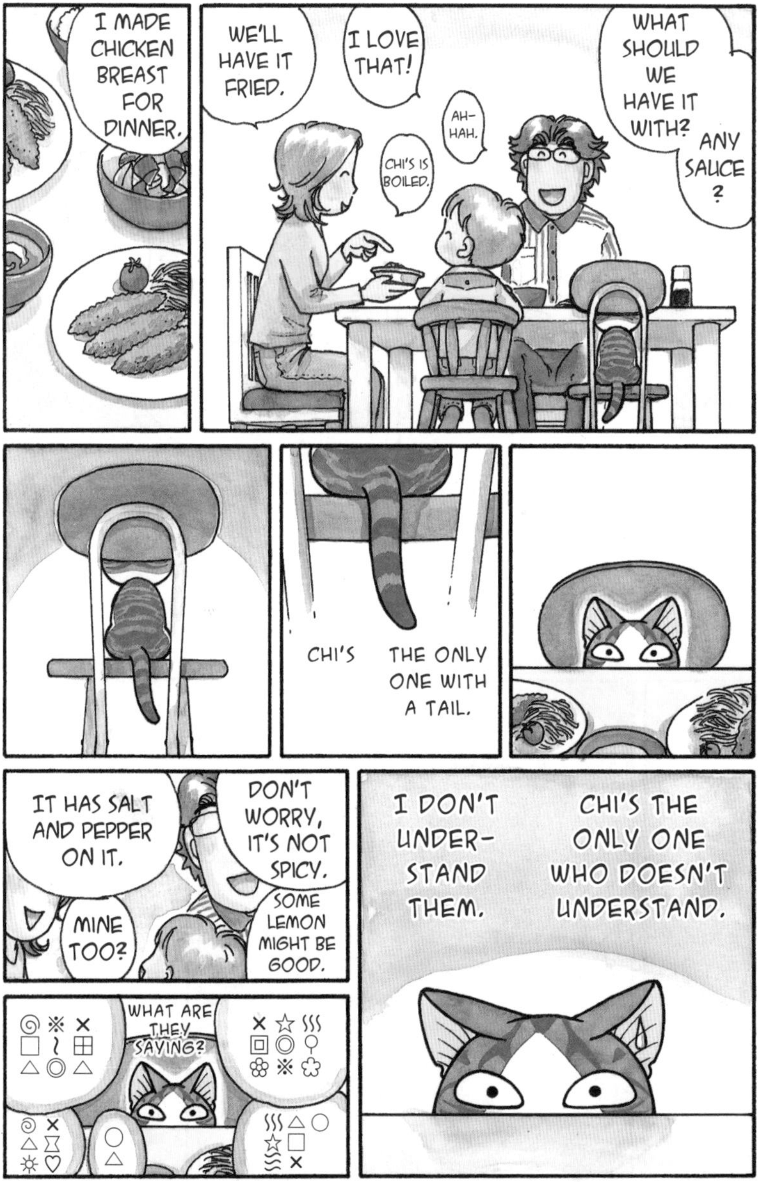

I MADE CHICKEN BREAST FOR DINNER.
WE'LL HAVE IT FRIED.
I LOVE THAT!
CHI'S IS BOILED.
AH-HAH.
WHAT SHOULD WE HAVE IT WITH?
ANY SAUCE?
CHI'S
THE ONLY ONE WITH A TAIL.
IT HAS SALT AND PEPPER ON IT.
DON'T WORRY, IT'S NOT SPICY.
MINE TOO?
SOME LEMON MIGHT BE GOOD.
WHAT ARE THEY SAYING?
I DON'T UNDER-STAND THEM.
CHI'S THE ONLY ONE WHO DOESN'T UNDERSTAND.

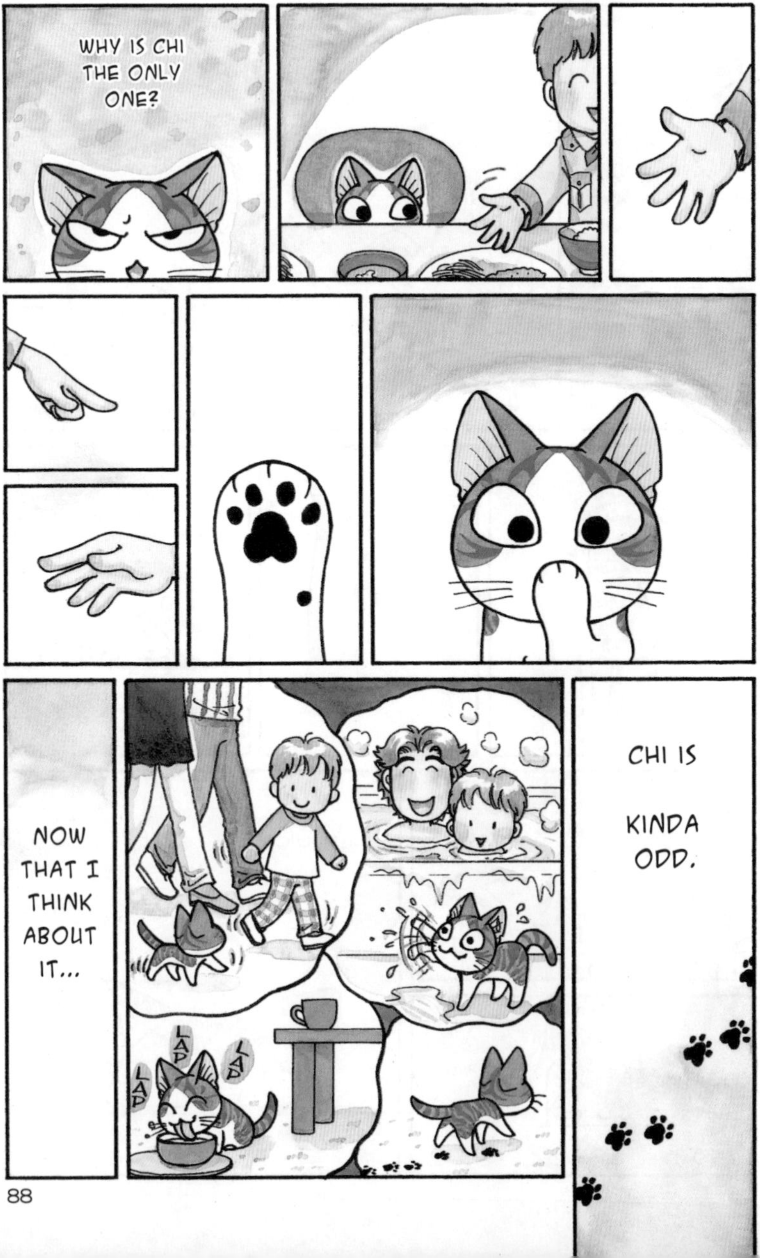
WHY IS CHI THE ONLY ONE?
NOW THAT I THINK ABOUT IT...
LAP
LAP
LAP
CHI IS
KINDA ODD.

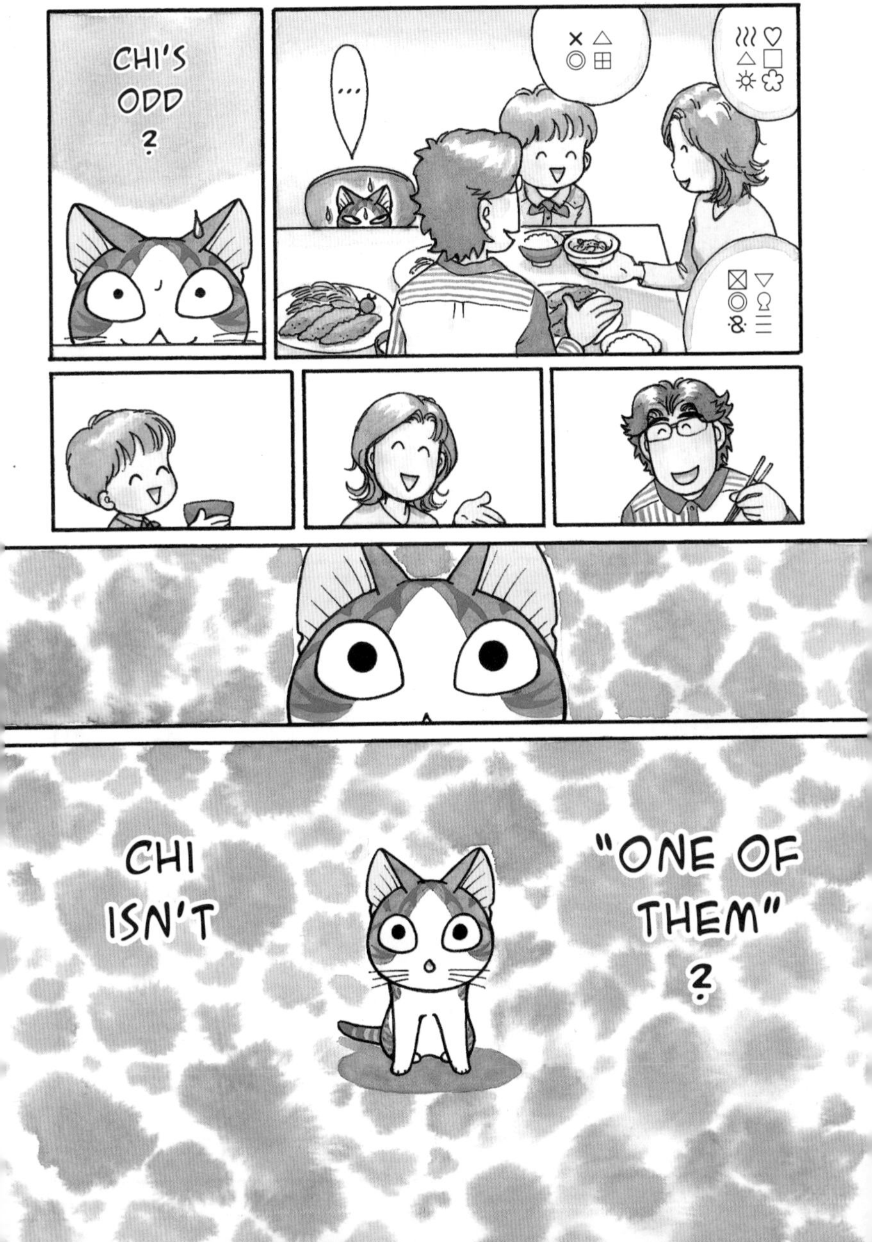
CHI'S ODD ?
...
CHI ISN'T
"ONE OF THEM" ?

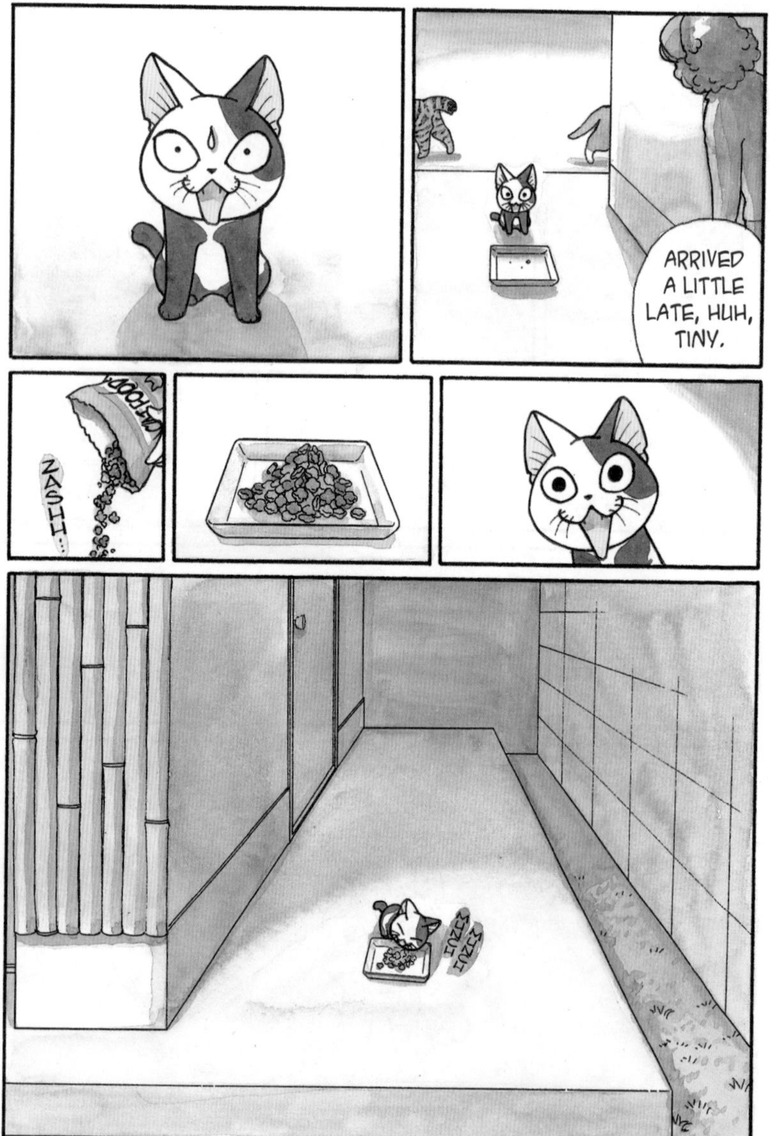
ARRIVED A LITTLE LATE, HUH, TINY.
ZASHH...

the end

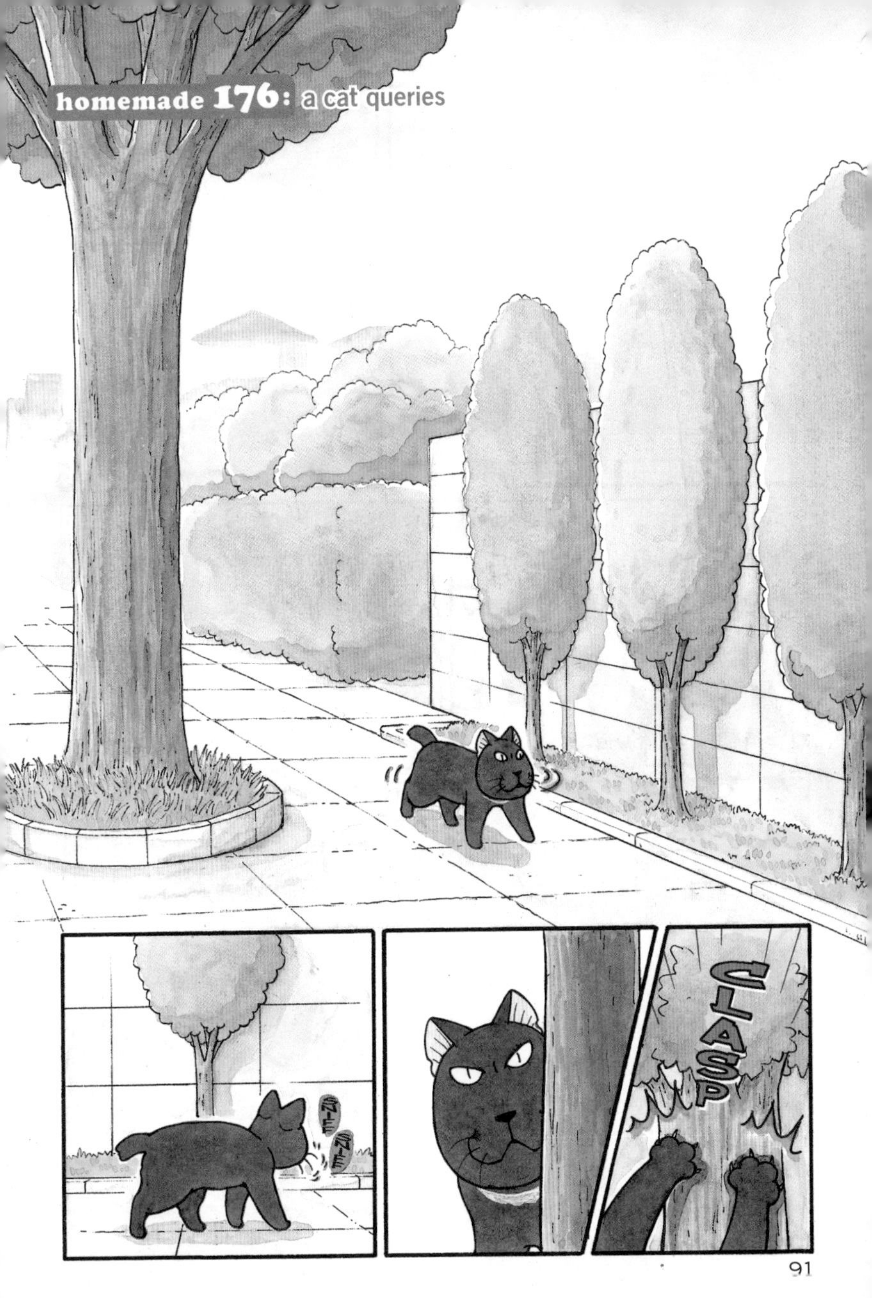
homemade 176: a cat queries
SNIFF
SNIFF
CLASP

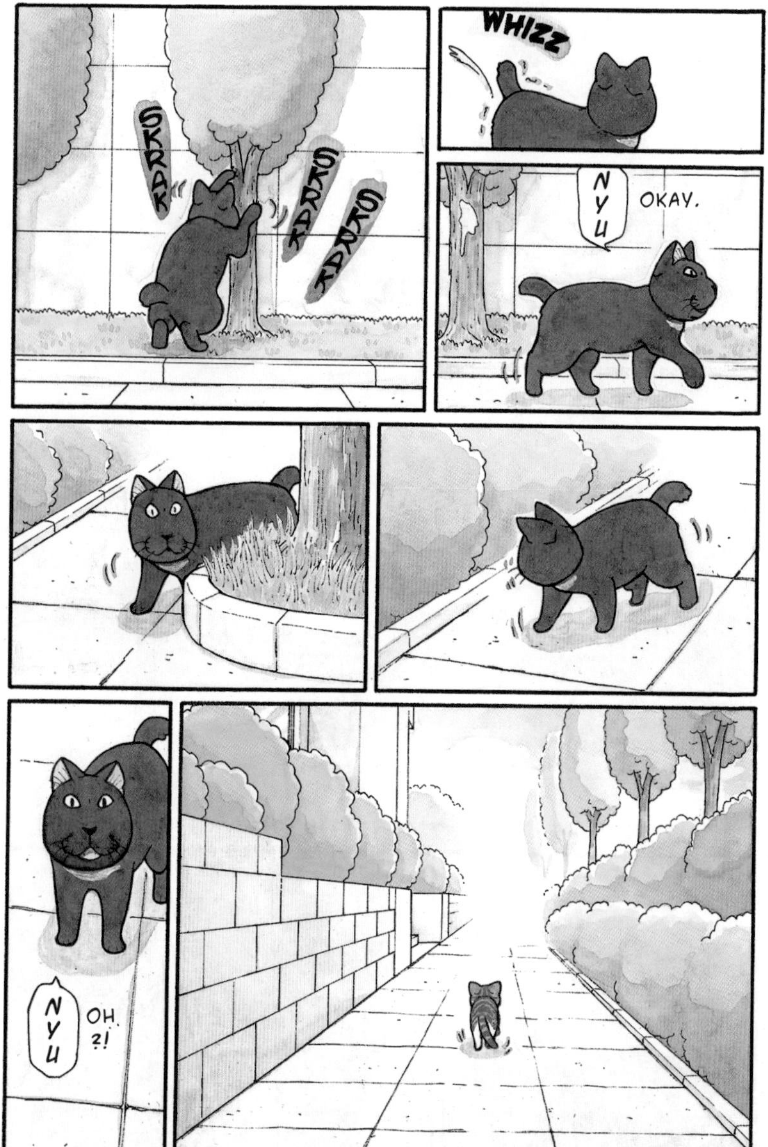
SKRAK
SKRAK
SKRAK
WHIZZ
NYU
OKAY.
NYU
OH?!

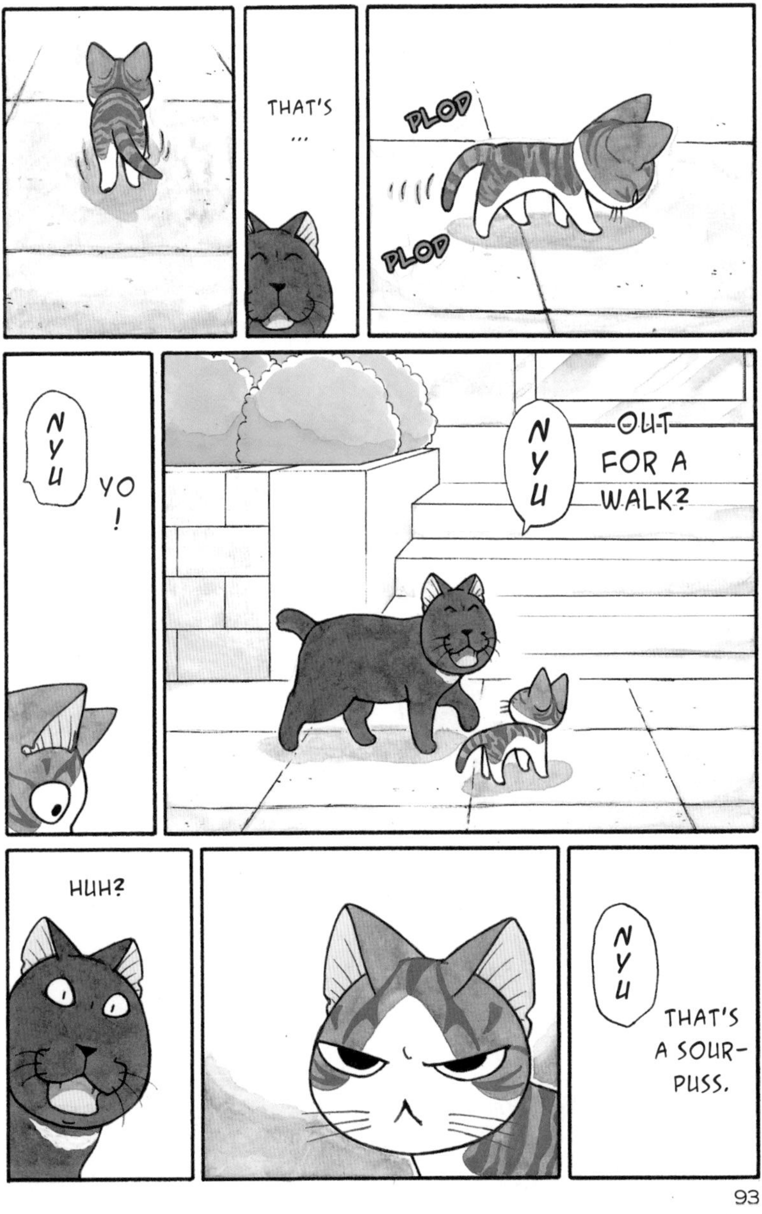
THAT'S ...
PLOD
PLOD
NYU
YO!
NYU
OUT FOR A WALK?
HUH?
NYU
THAT'S A SOUR-PUSS.

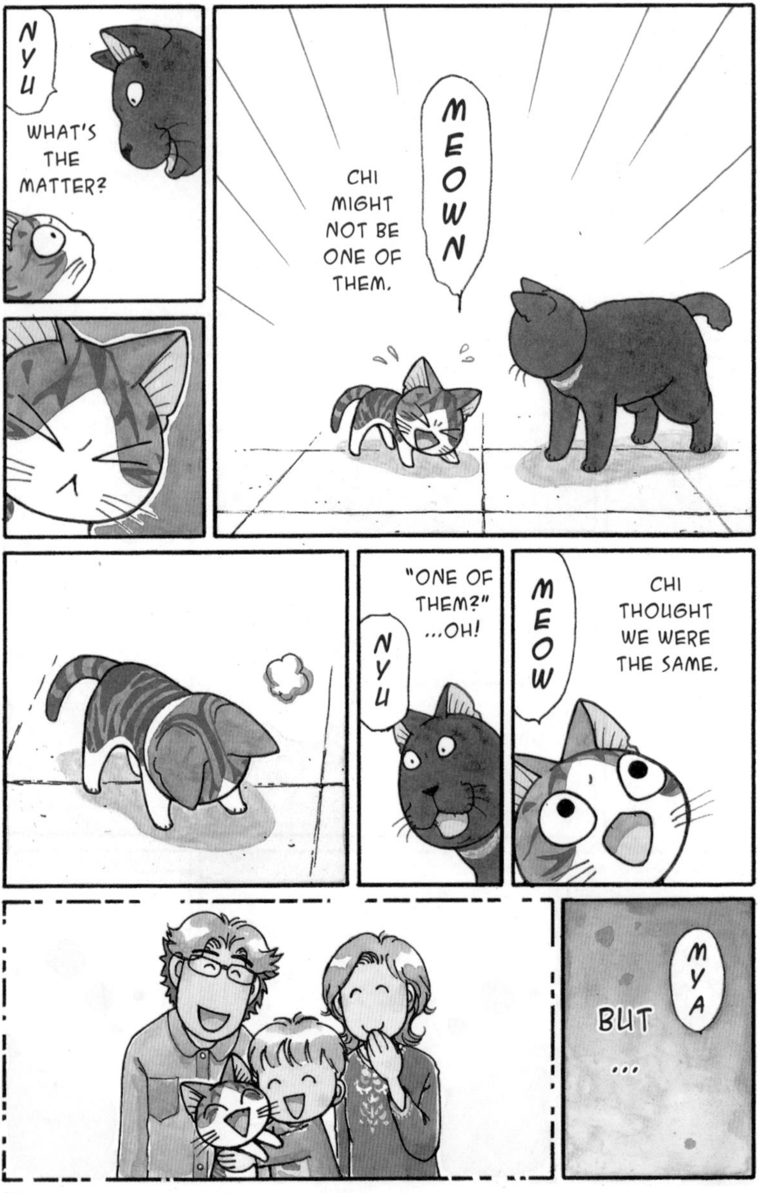
NYU
WHAT'S THE MATTER?
MEOWN
CHI MIGHT NOT BE ONE OF THEM.
"ONE OF THEM?" ...OH!
NYU
MEOW
CHI THOUGHT WE WERE THE SAME.
MYA
BUT ...

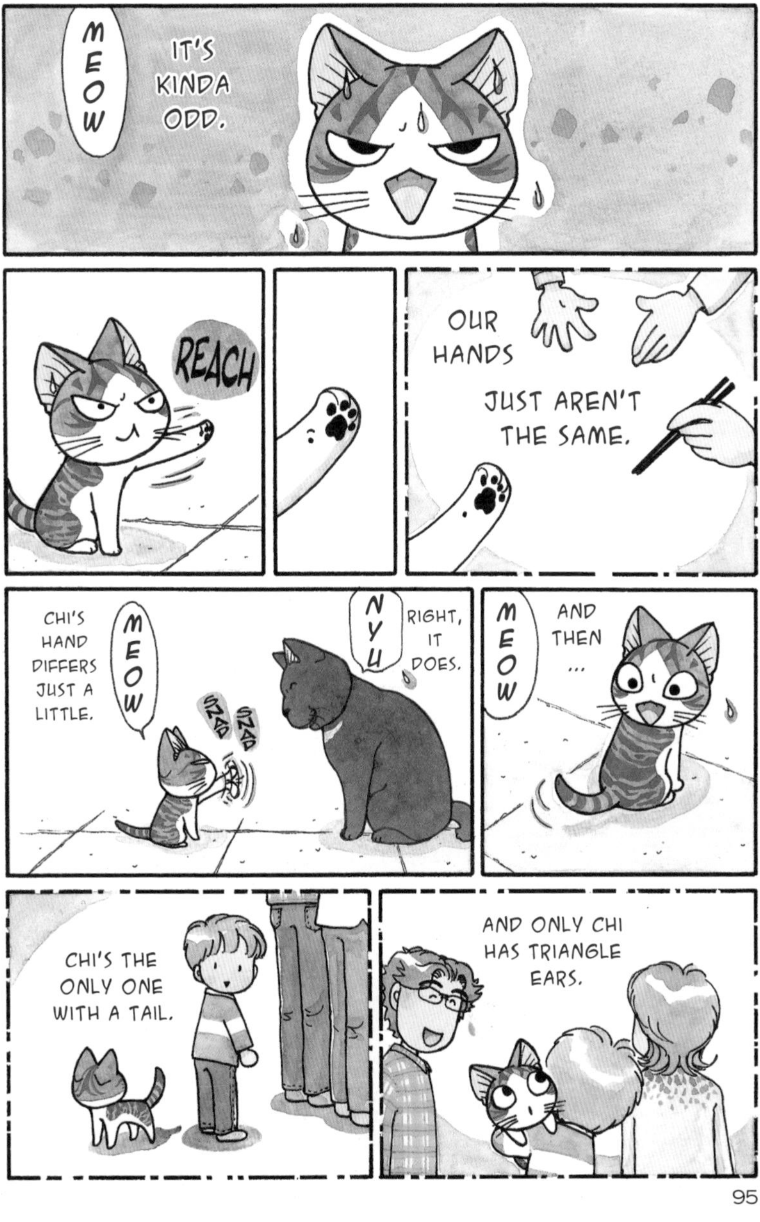
MEOW
IT'S KINDA ODD.
REACH
OUR HANDS
JUST AREN'T THE SAME.
CHI'S HAND DIFFERS JUST A LITTLE.
MEOW
SNAP
SNAP
NYU
RIGHT, IT DOES.
MEOW
AND THEN ...
CHI'S THE ONLY ONE WITH A TAIL.
AND ONLY CHI HAS TRIANGLE EARS.

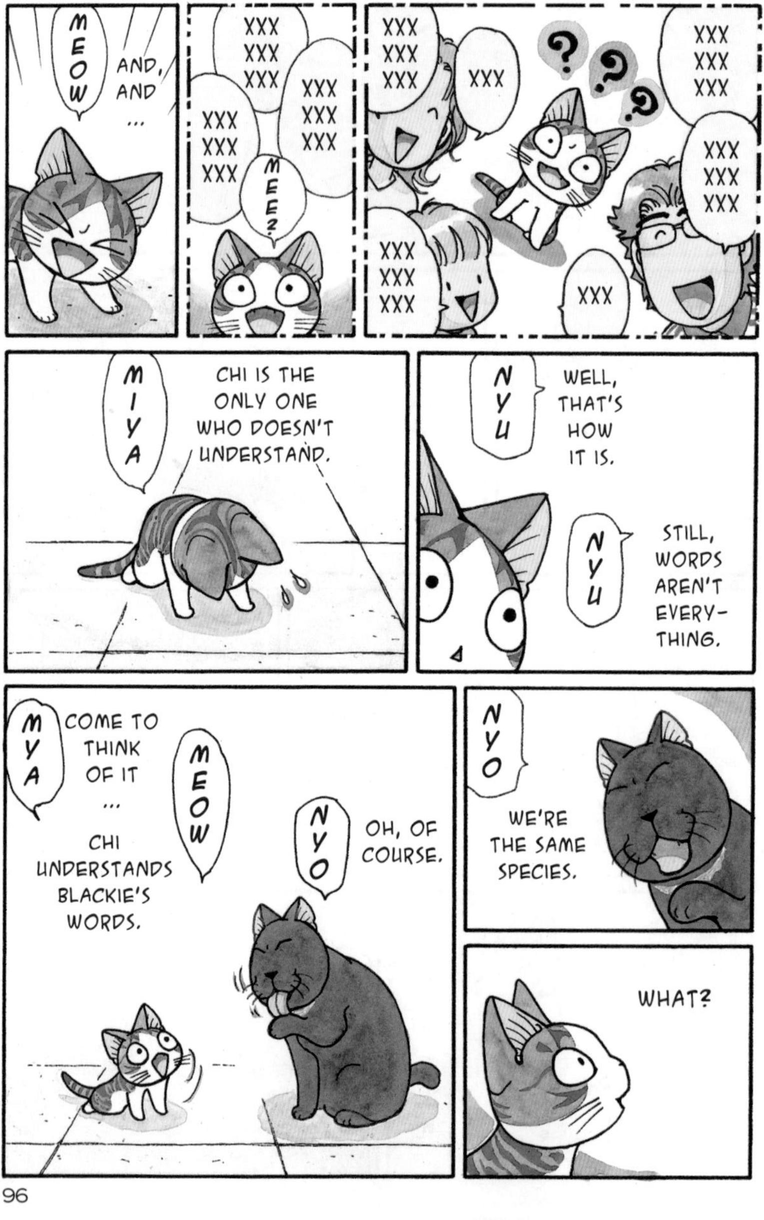
MEOW
AND, AND ...
XXX XXX XXX
XXX XXX XXX
XXX XXX XXX
MEE?
XXX XXX XXX
XXX
? ? ?
XXX XXX XXX
XXX XXX XXX
XXX XXX XXX
XXX
MIYA
CHI IS THE ONLY ONE WHO DOESN'T UNDERSTAND.
NYU
WELL, THAT'S HOW IT IS.
NYU
STILL, WORDS AREN'T EVERY-THING.
MYA
COME TO THINK OF IT ...
CHI UNDERSTANDS BLACKIE'S WORDS.
MEOW
NYO
OH, OF COURSE.
NYO
WE'RE THE SAME SPECIES.
WHAT?

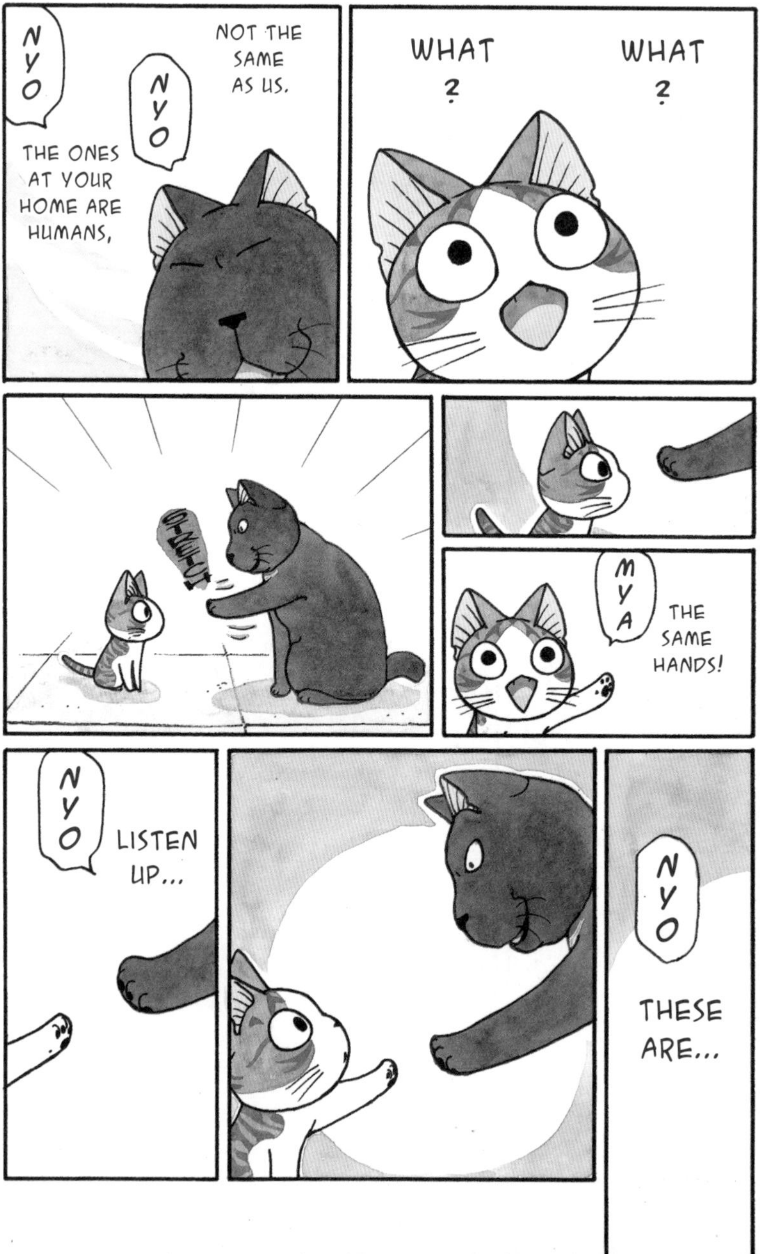

NYO
THE ONES AT YOUR HOME ARE HUMANS,
NYO
NOT THE SAME AS US.
WHAT ?
WHAT ?
STRETCH
MYA
THE SAME HANDS!
NYO
LISTEN UP...
NYO
THESE ARE...

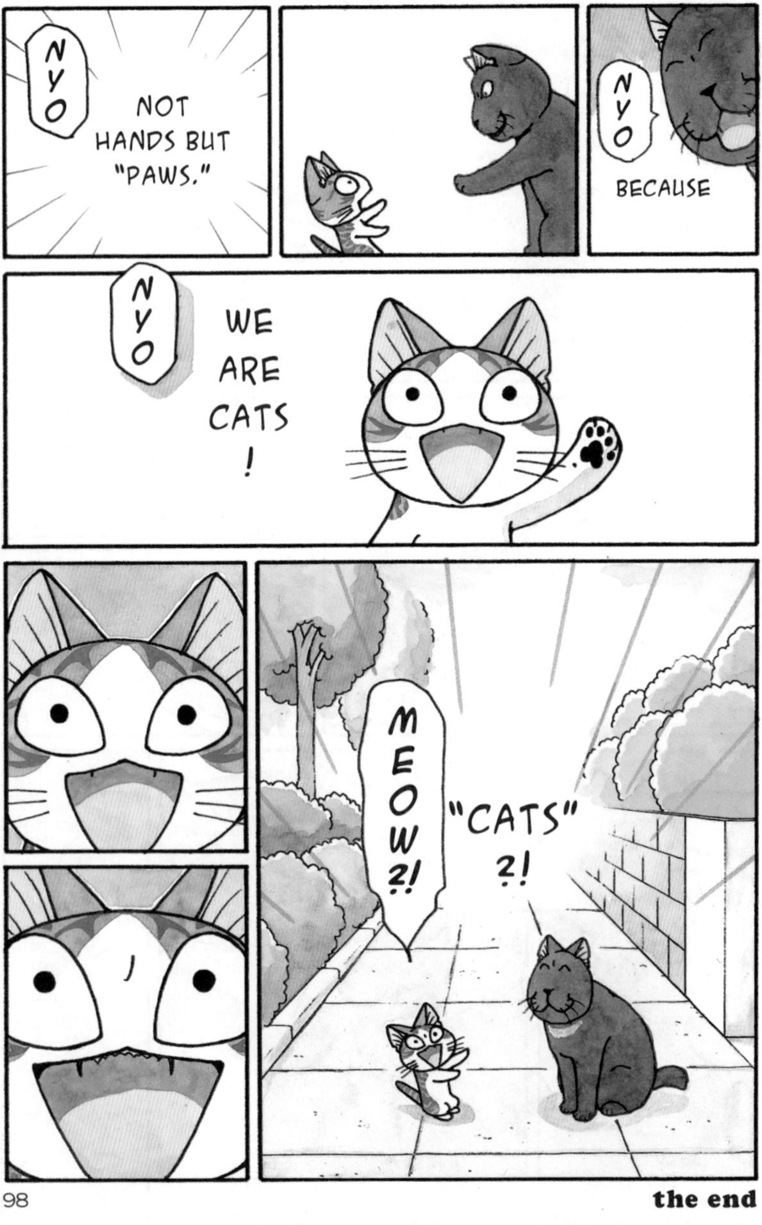
NYO
NOT HANDS BUT "PAWS."
NYO
BECAUSE
NYO
WE ARE CATS !
MEOW ?!
"CATS" ?!

the end

homemade 177: a cat is briefed

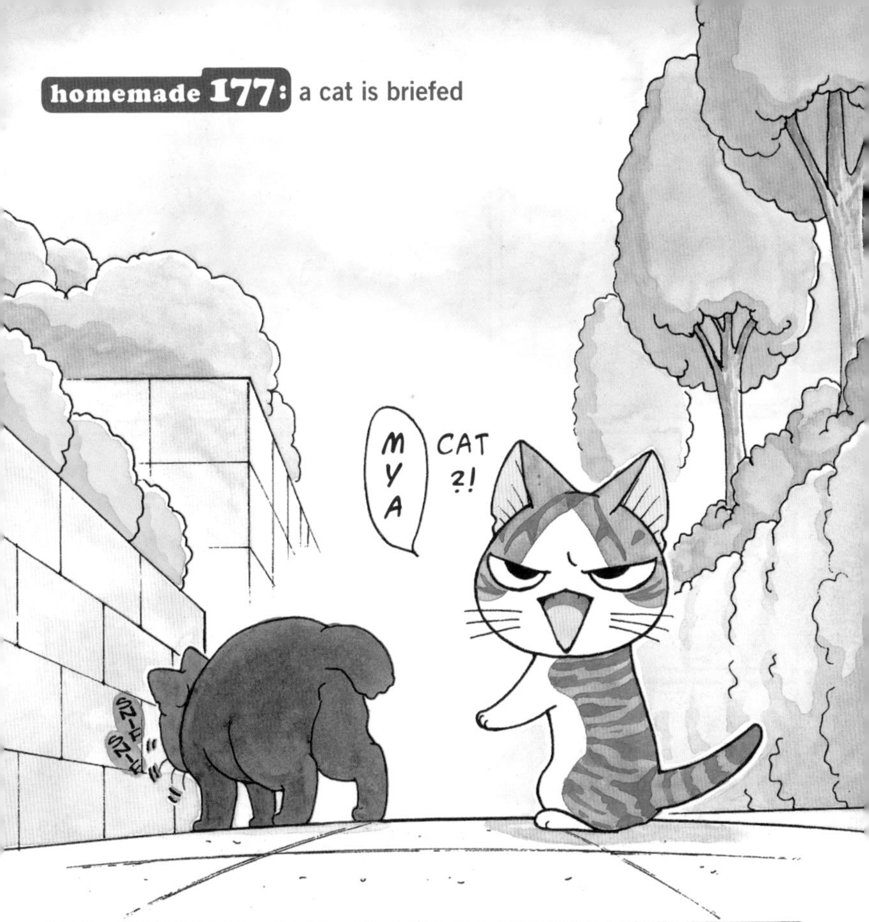
MYA
CAT?!
SNIFF
SNIFF

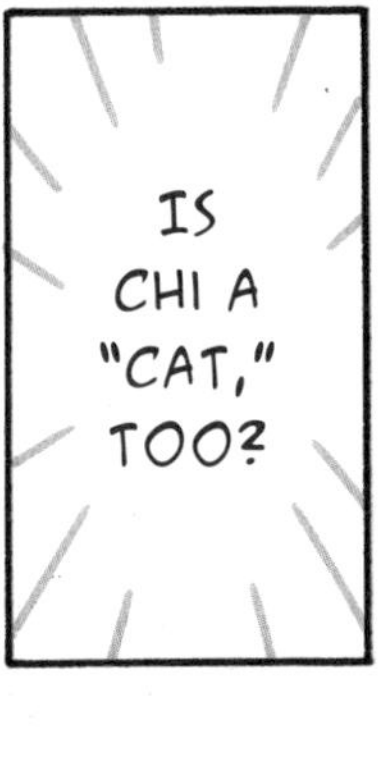
IS CHI A "CAT," TOO?

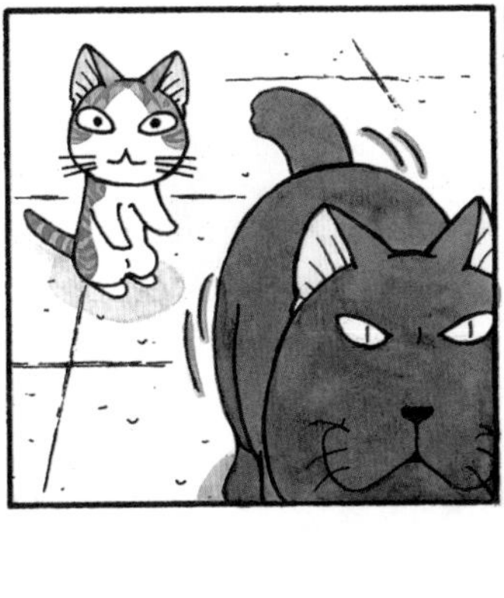

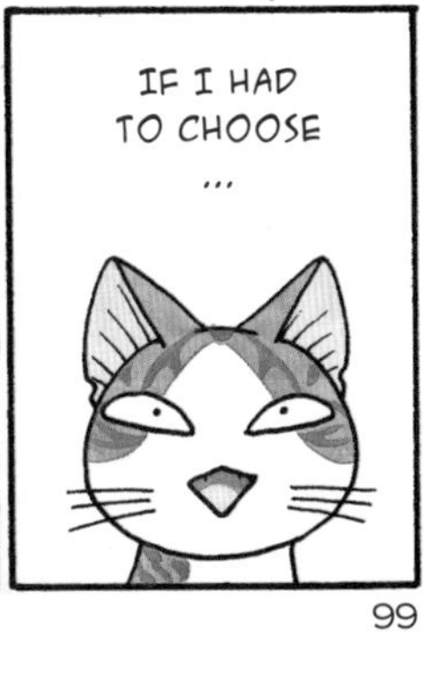
IF I HAD TO CHOOSE ...

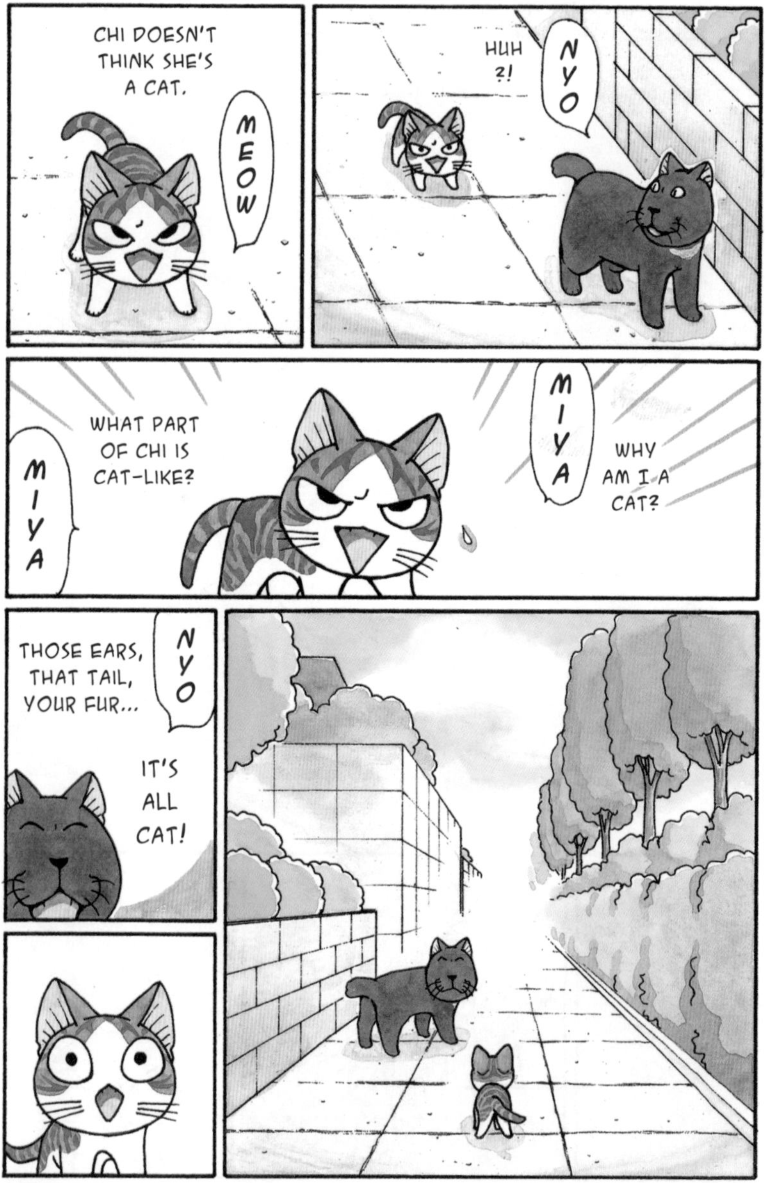
CHI DOESN'T THINK SHE'S A CAT.
MEOW
HUH ?!
NYO
MIYA
WHAT PART OF CHI IS CAT-LIKE?
MIYA
WHY AM I A CAT?
THOSE EARS, THAT TAIL, YOUR FUR...
NYO
IT'S ALL CAT!

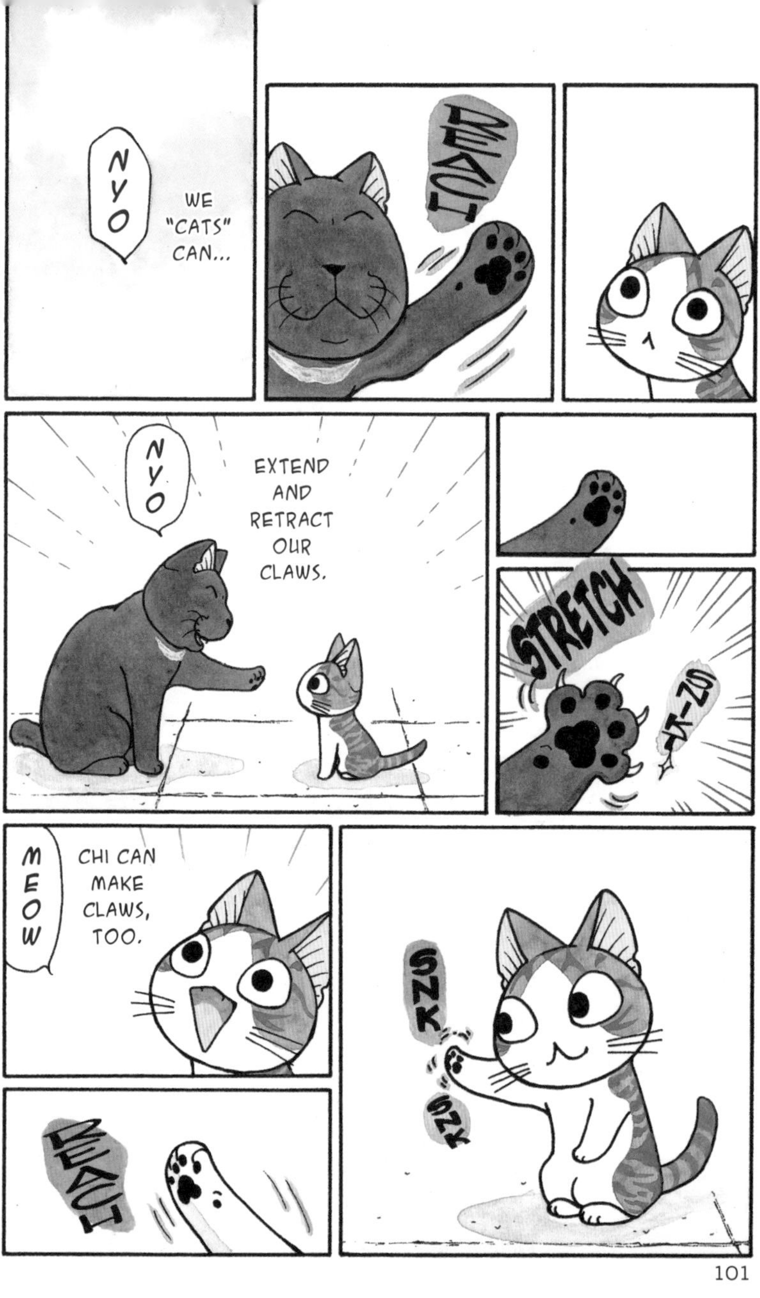
NYO
WE "CATS" CAN...
REACH
NYO
EXTEND AND RETRACT OUR CLAWS.
STRETCH
MEOW
CHI CAN MAKE CLAWS, TOO.
REACH
SNK
SNK

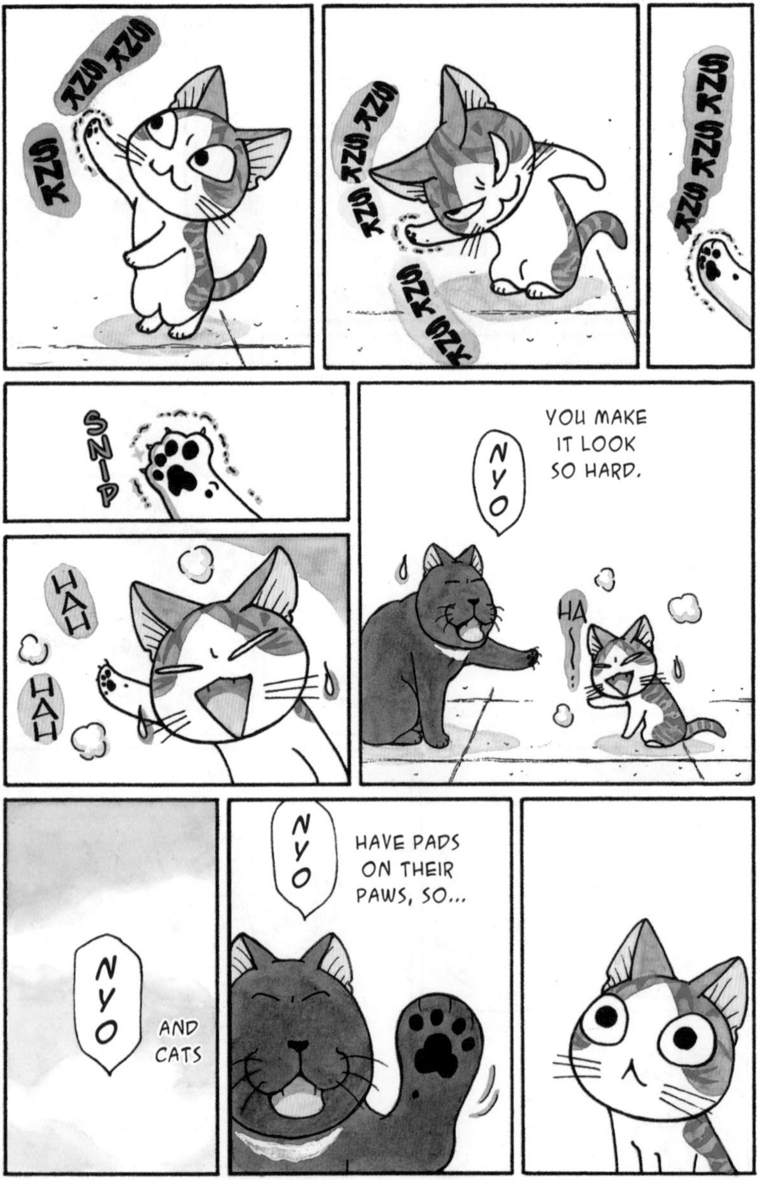
SNK
SNK SNK
SNK SNK SNK
SNK SNK
SNK SNK SNK SNK
SNIP
NYO
YOU MAKE IT LOOK SO HARD.
HAH HAH
HA
NYO
AND CATS
NYO
HAVE PADS ON THEIR PAWS, SO...

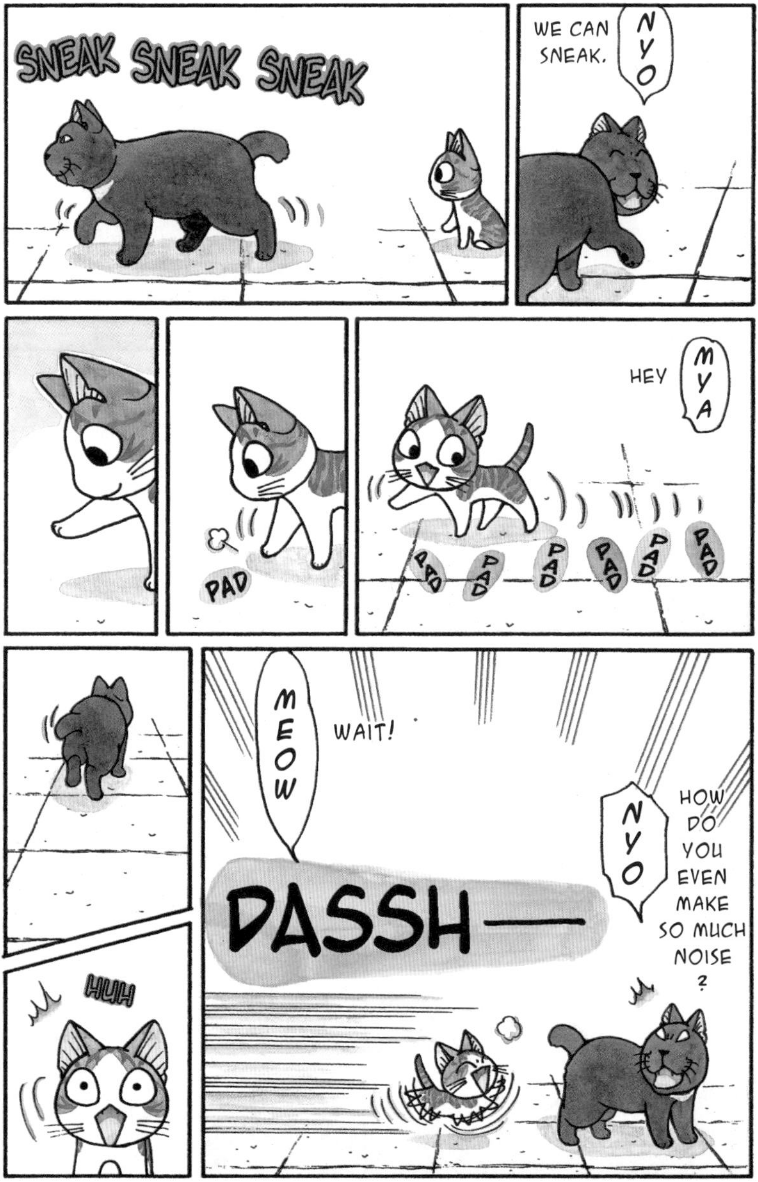
SNEAK SNEAK SNEAK
WE CAN SNEAK.
NYO
PAD
HEY
MYA
PAD PAD PAD PAD PAD PAD
HUH
MEOW
WAIT!
DASSH—
NYO
HOW DO YOU EVEN MAKE SO MUCH NOISE?

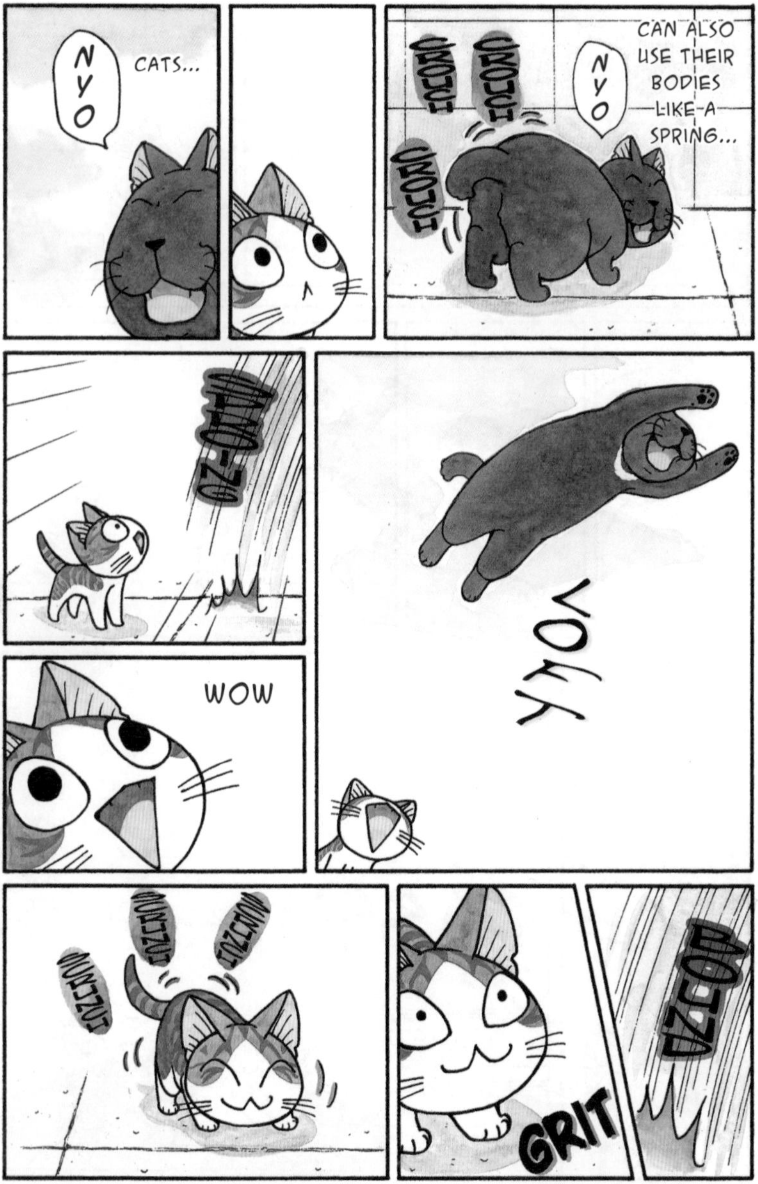
NYO
CATS...
CROUCH
CROUCH
CROUCH
NYO
CAN ALSO USE THEIR BODIES LIKE A SPRING...
WOW
GRIT

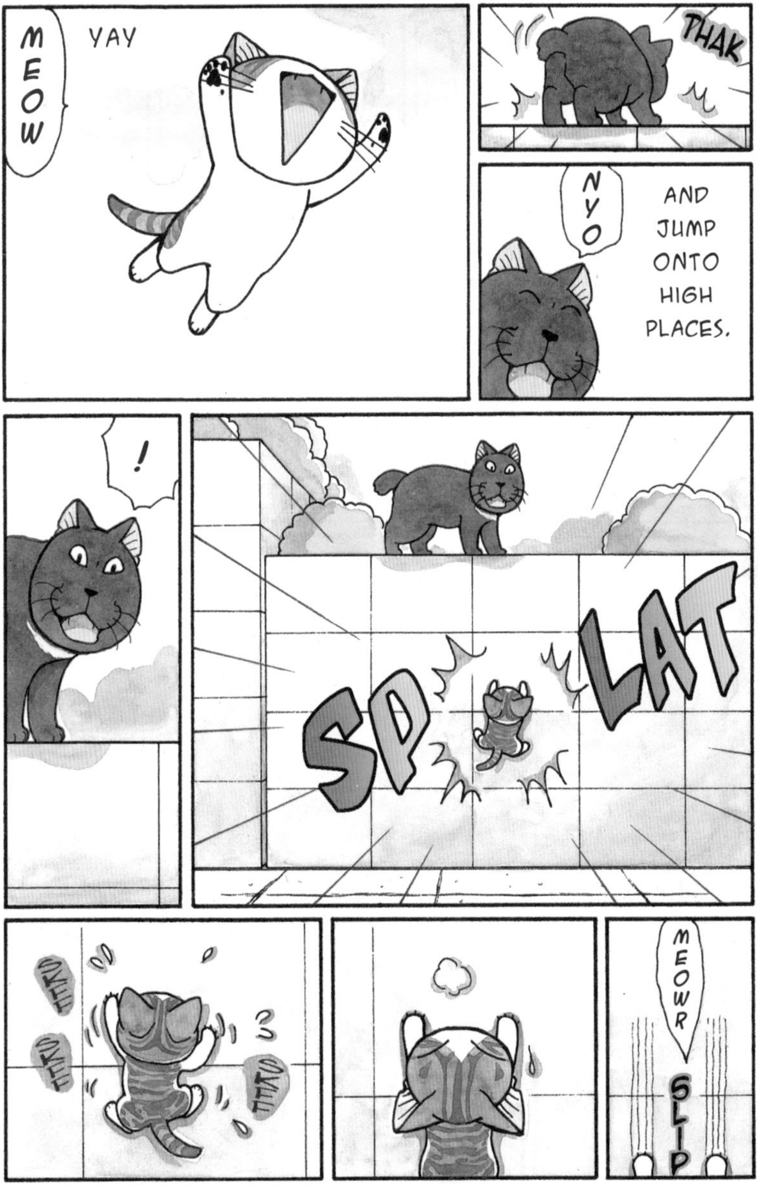
MEOW
YAY
THAK
NYO
AND JUMP ONTO HIGH PLACES.
!
SPLAT
SKFF
SKFF
SKFF
MEOWR
SLIP

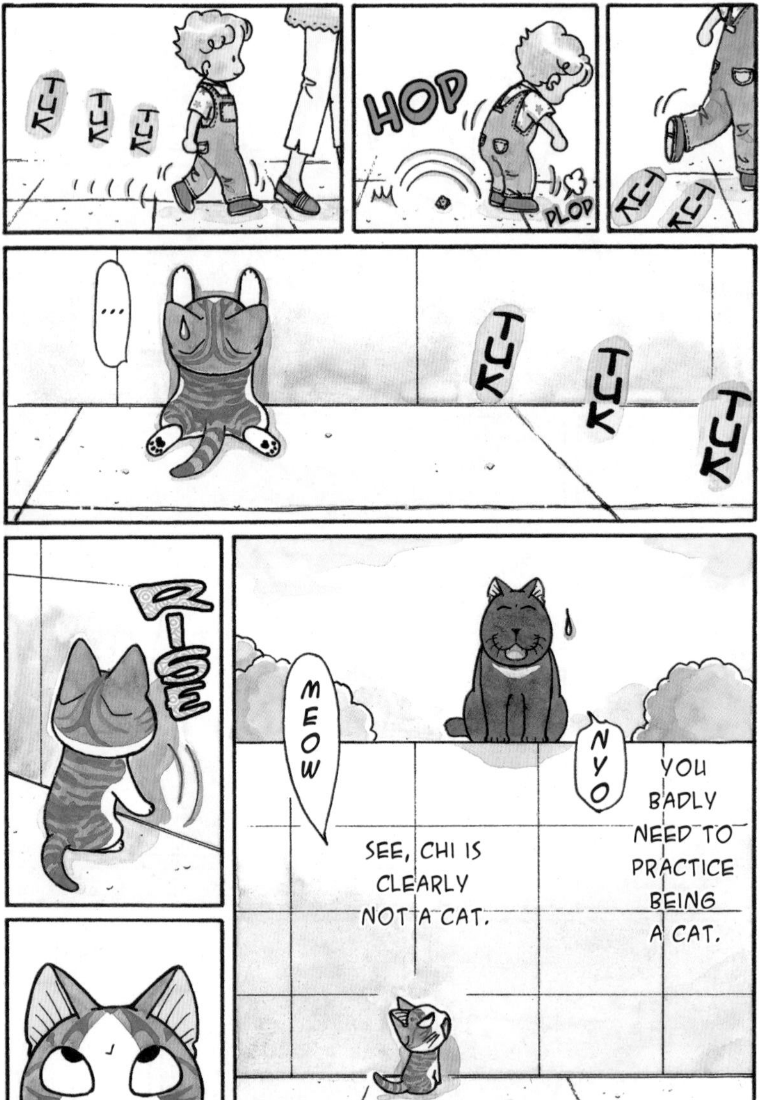
TUK
TUK
TUK
HOP
PLOP
TUK
TUK
...
TUK
TUK
TUK
RISE
MEOW
NYO
SEE, CHI IS CLEARLY NOT A CAT.
YOU BADLY NEED TO PRACTICE BEING A CAT.

the end

homemade 178: a cat trains

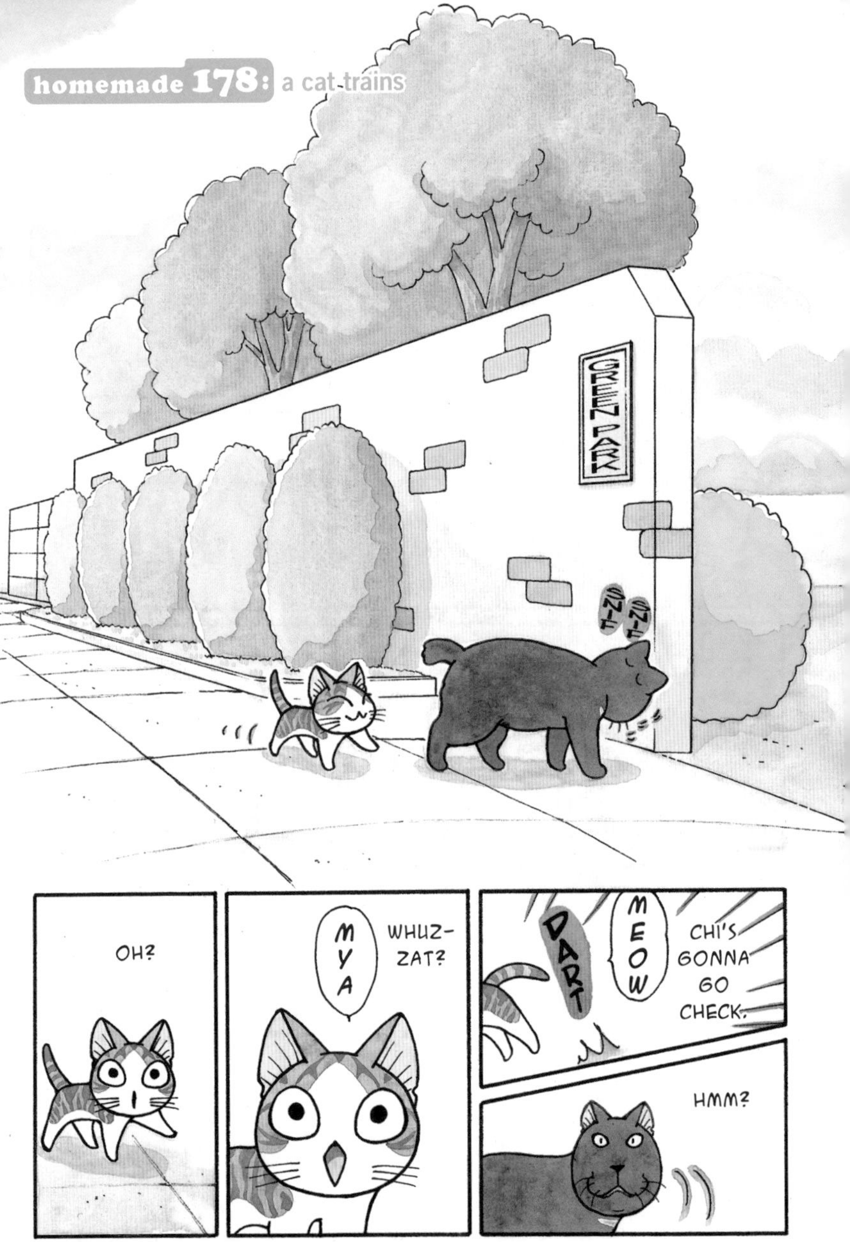
GREEN PARK
SNIF
SNIF
OH?
MYA
WHUZ-ZAT?
DART
MEOW
CHI'S GONNA GO CHECK.
HMM?

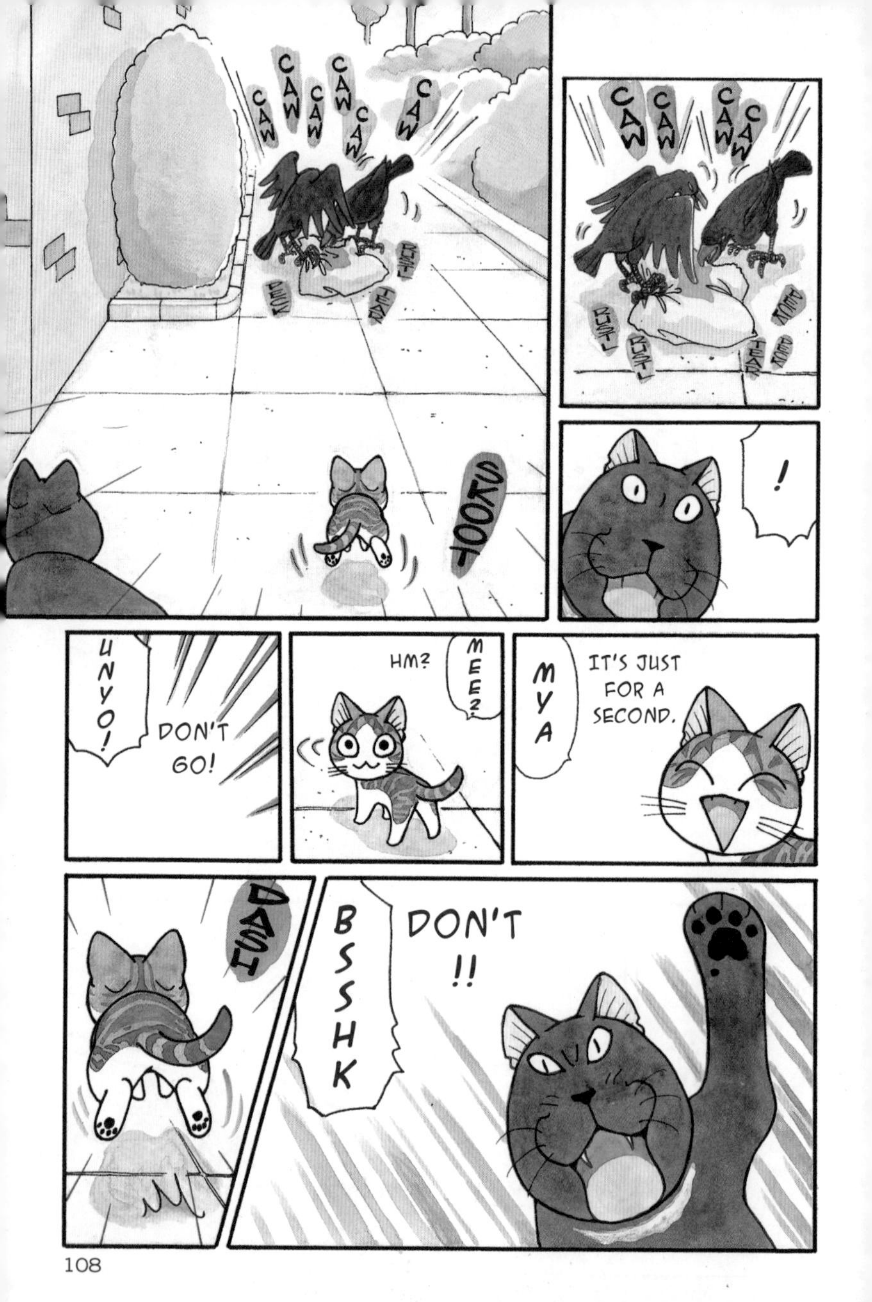
CAW
CAW
CAW
CAW
CAW
RUSTL
PECK
TEAR
SKOOT
CAW
CAW
CAW
CAW
RUSTL
RUSTL
TEAR
PECK
PECK
!
UNYO!
DON'T GO!
HM?
MEE?
MYA
IT'S JUST FOR A SECOND.
DASH
BSSHK
DON'T !!

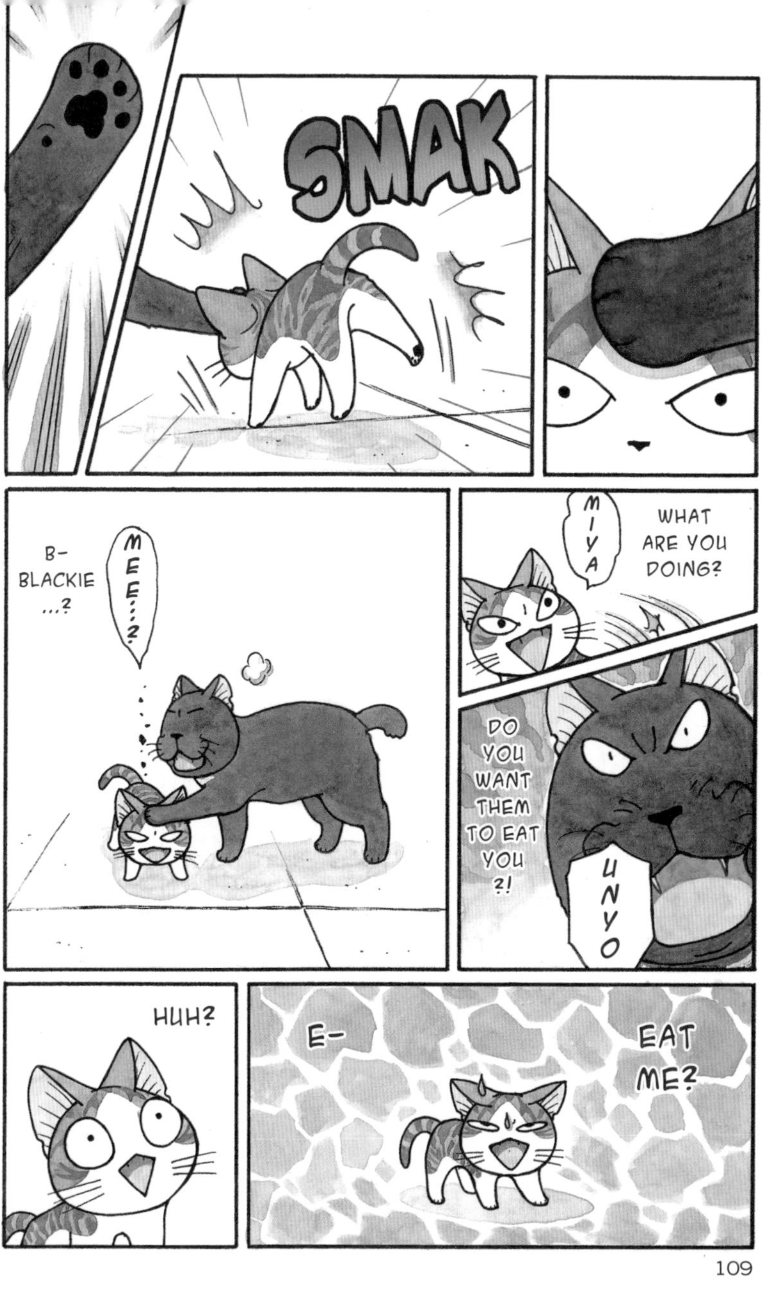
SMAK
B- BLACKIE ...?
MEE...?
MIYA
WHAT ARE YOU DOING?
DO YOU WANT THEM TO EAT YOU ?!
UNYO
HUH?
E-
EAT ME?

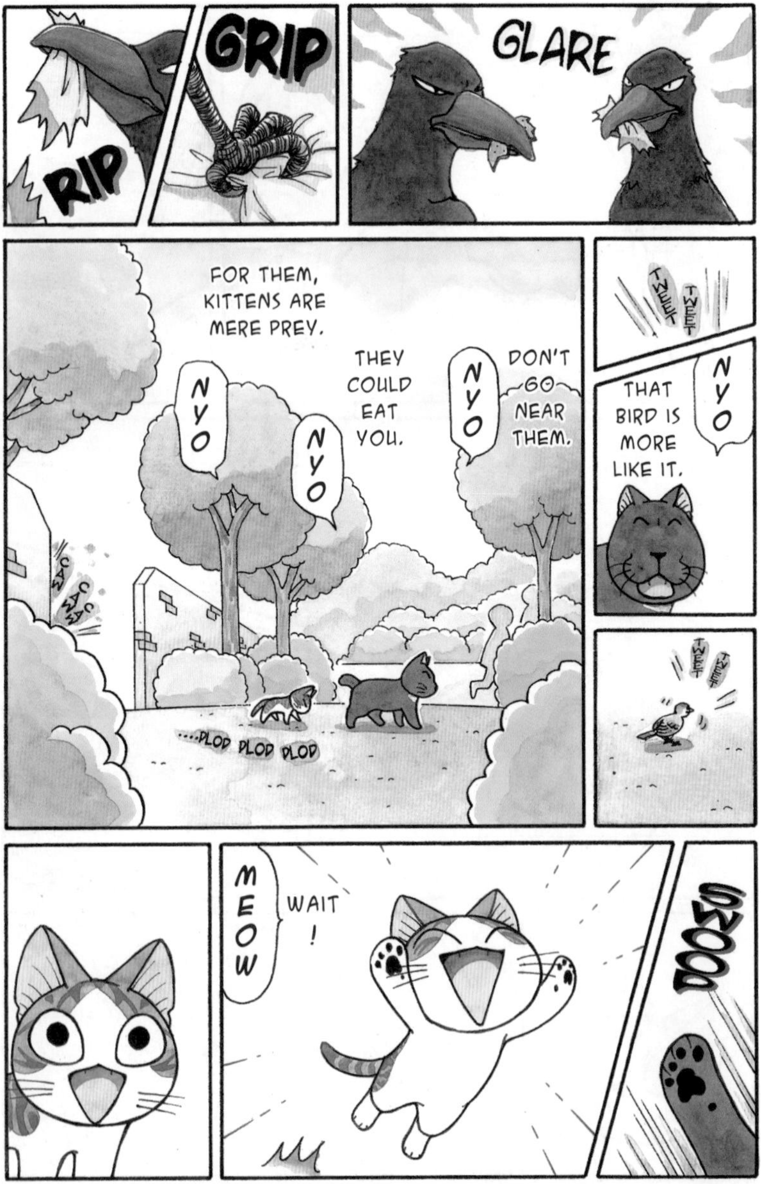
RIP
GRIP
GLARE
FOR THEM, KITTENS ARE MERE PREY.
NYO
NYO
THEY COULD EAT YOU.
NYO
DON'T GO NEAR THEM.
CAW CAW
....PLOD PLOD PLOD
TWEET TWEET
THAT BIRD IS MORE LIKE IT.
NYO
TWEET TWEET
MEOW
WAIT!
SWOOP

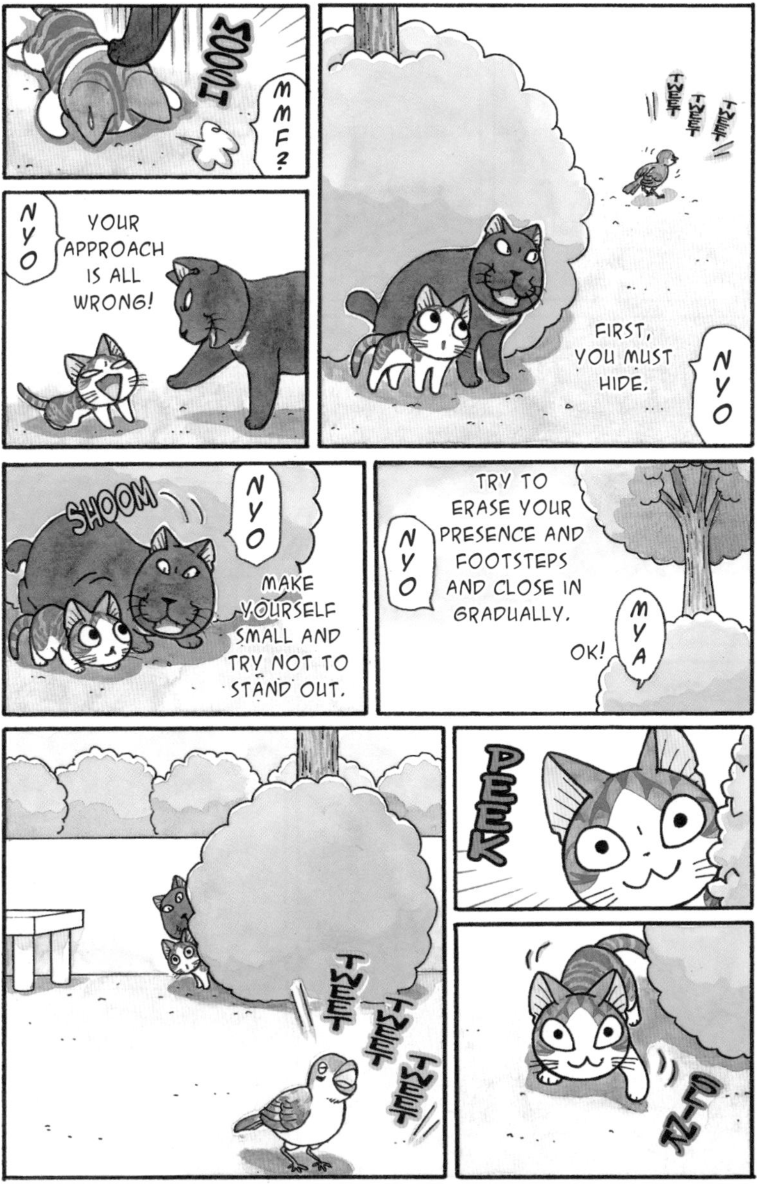

WOOSH
MMF?
TWEET TWEET TWEET
NYO
YOUR APPROACH IS ALL WRONG!
FIRST, YOU MUST HIDE.
NYO
SHOOM
NYO
MAKE YOURSELF SMALL AND TRY NOT TO STAND OUT.
NYO
TRY TO ERASE YOUR PRESENCE AND FOOTSTEPS AND CLOSE IN GRADUALLY.
MYA
OK!
TWEET TWEET TWEET
PEEK
SPIN

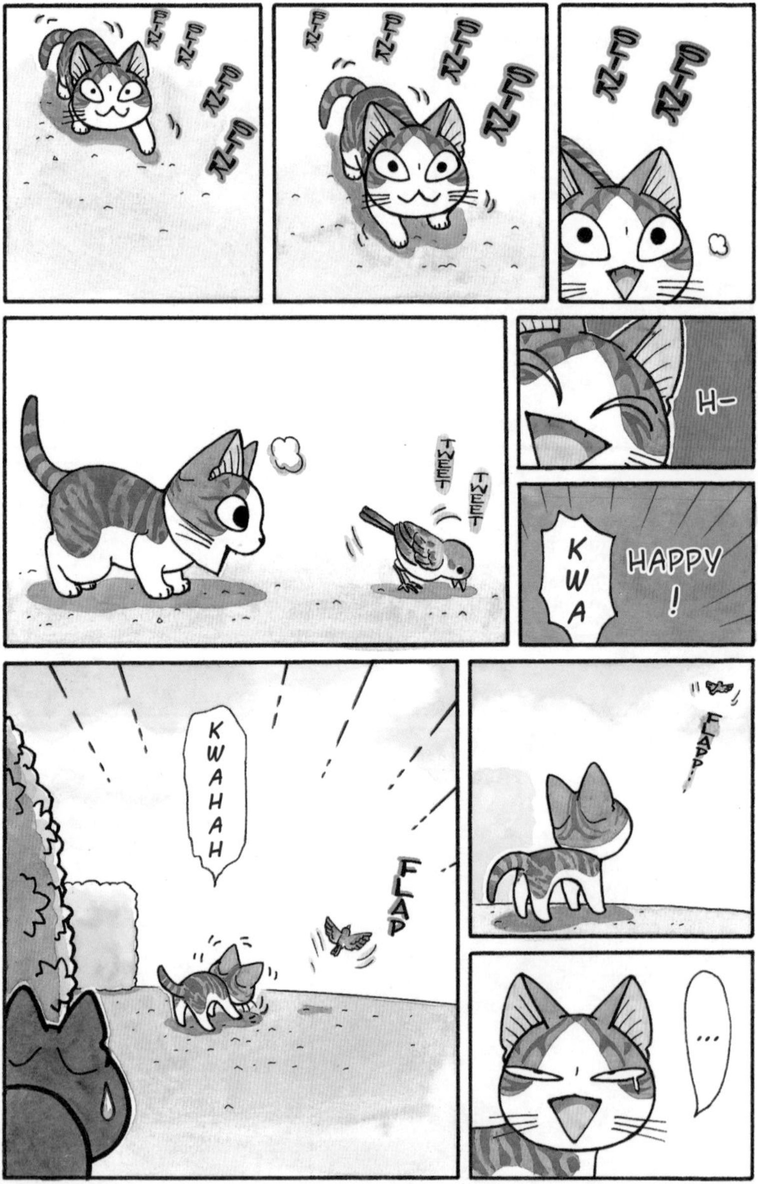
PINK
PINK
PINK
PINK
PINK
PINK
PINK
PINK
PINK
PINK
TWEET
TWEET
H-
KWA
HAPPY!
KWAHAHAH
FLAP
FLAPP...
...

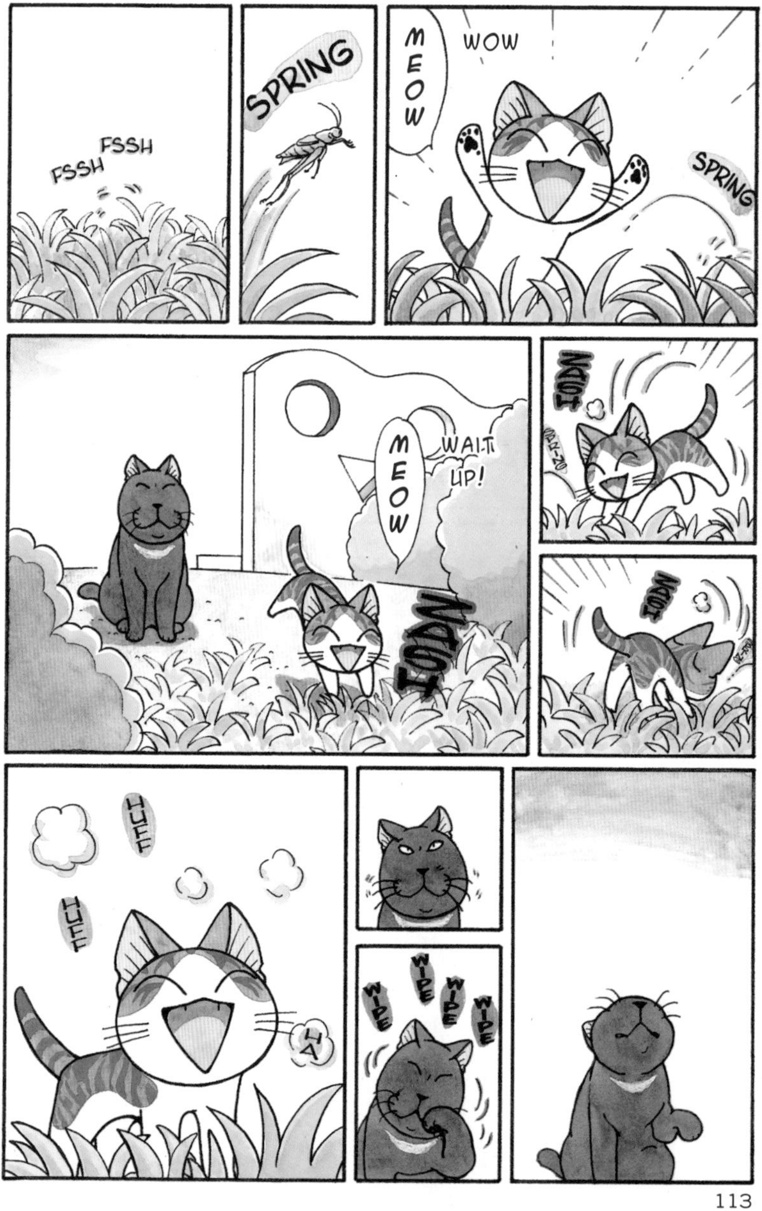
FSSH
FSSH
SPRING
MEOW
WOW
SPRING
MEOW
WAIT UP!
ZOOM!
ZOOM!
ZOOM!
HUFF
HUFF
HA
WIPE
WIPE
WIPE
WIPE

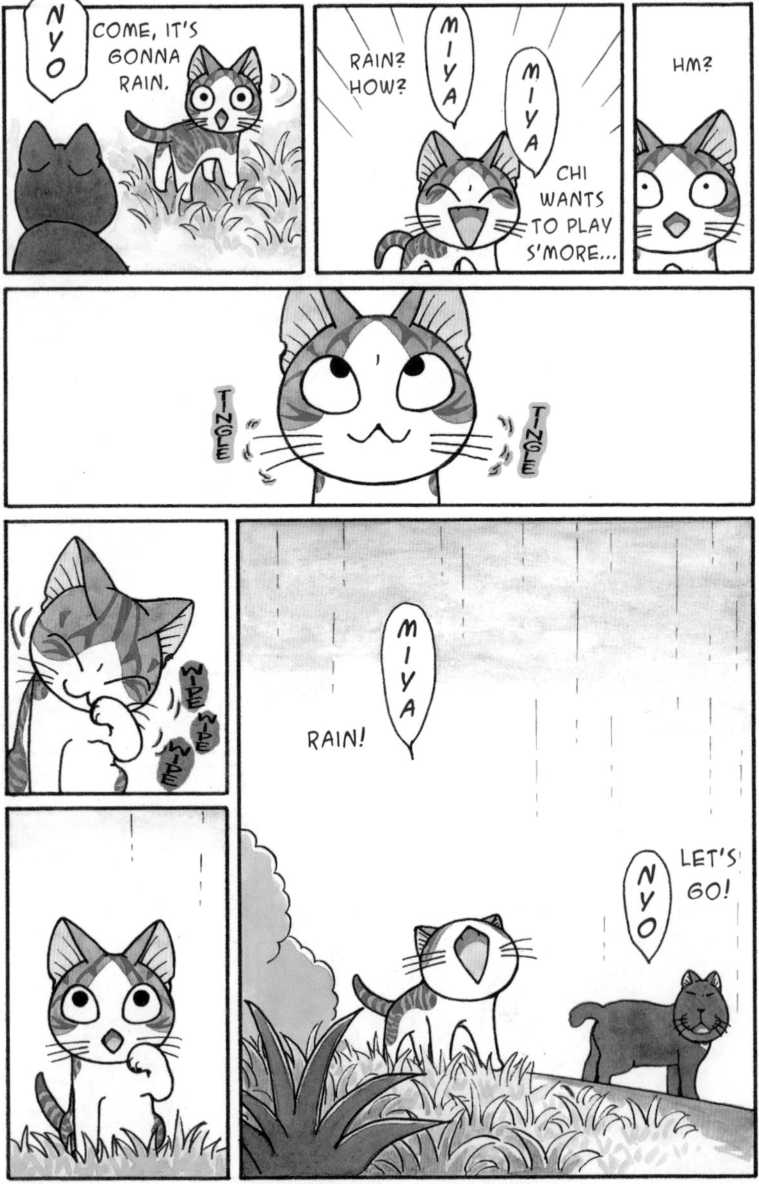
NYO
COME, IT'S GONNA RAIN.
RAIN? HOW?
MIYA
MIYA
CHI WANTS TO PLAY S'MORE...
HM?
TINGLE
TINGLE
WIPE
WIPE
WIPE
MIYA
RAIN!
NYO
LET'S GO!

the end

homemade 179: a cat holds

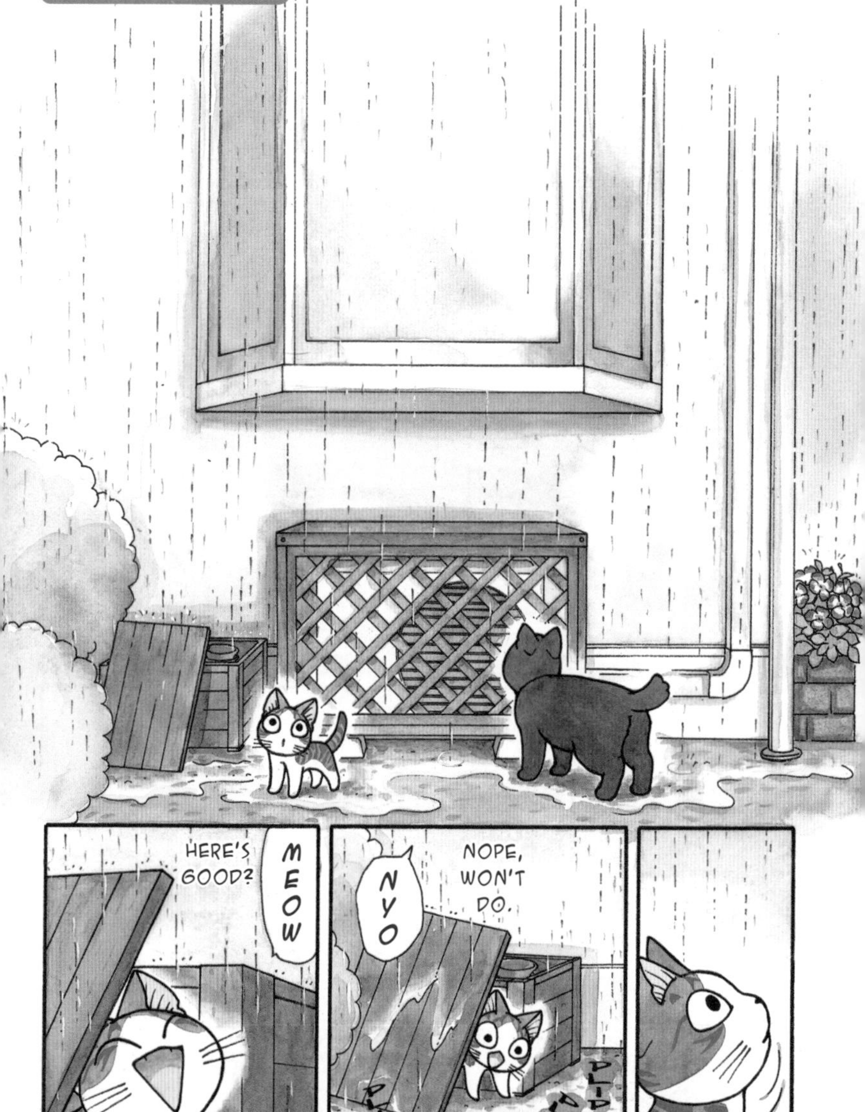
HERE'S GOOD?
MEOW
NYO
NOPE, WON'T DO.

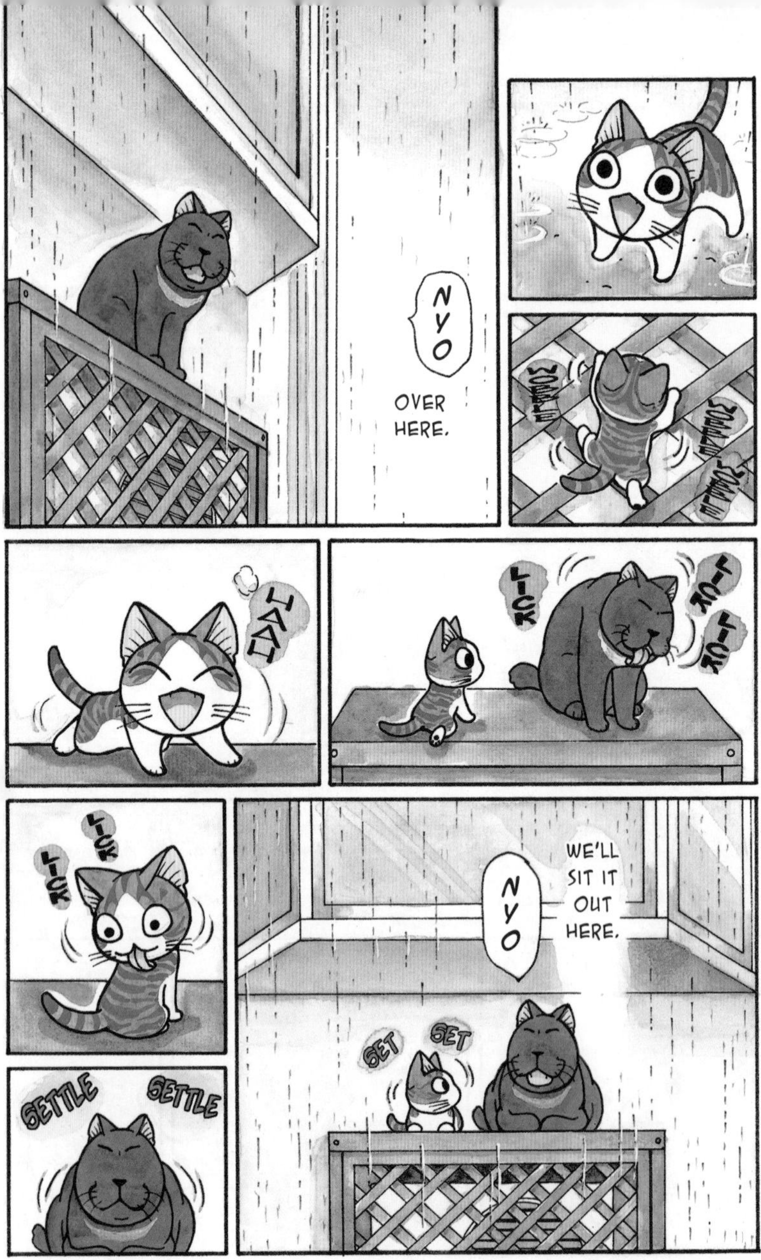
WOBBLE
WOBBLE
WOBBLE
NYO
OVER HERE.
LICK
LICK
LICK
HAAH
NYO
WE'LL SIT IT OUT HERE.
SET
SET
LICK
LICK
SETTLE
SETTLE

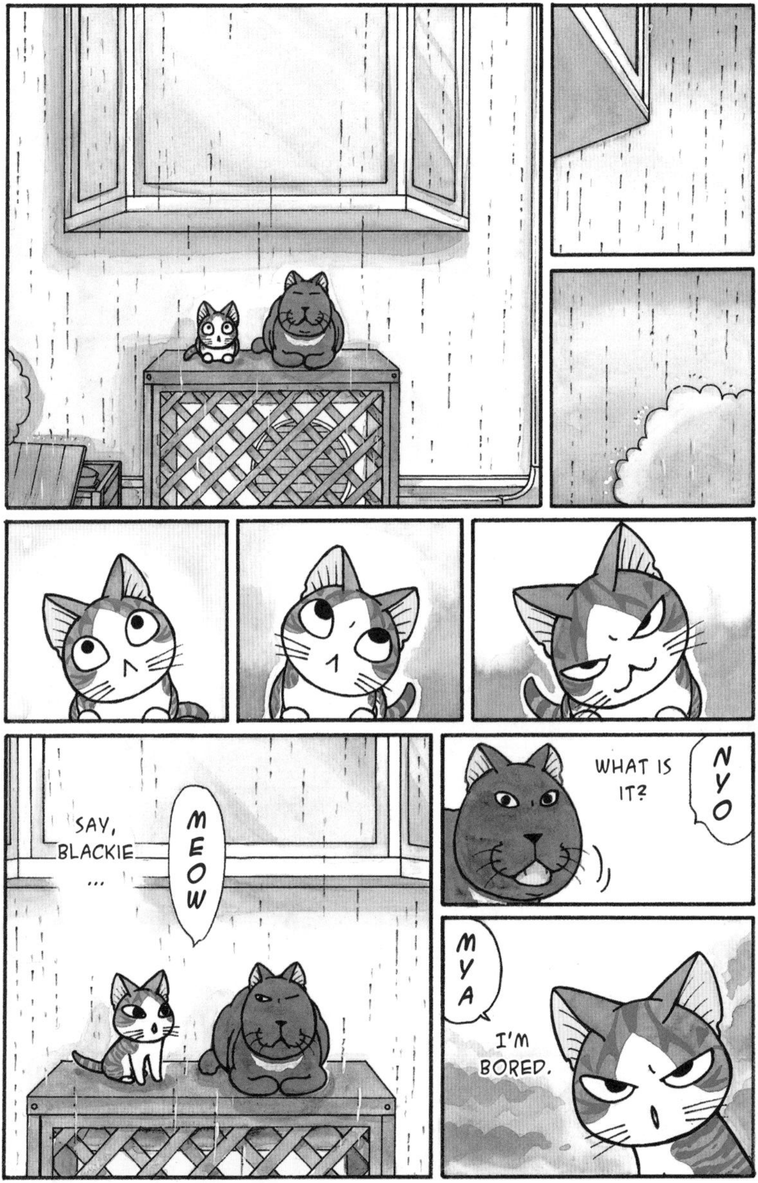
SAY, BLACKIE ...
MEOW
WHAT IS IT?
NYO
MYA
I'M BORED.

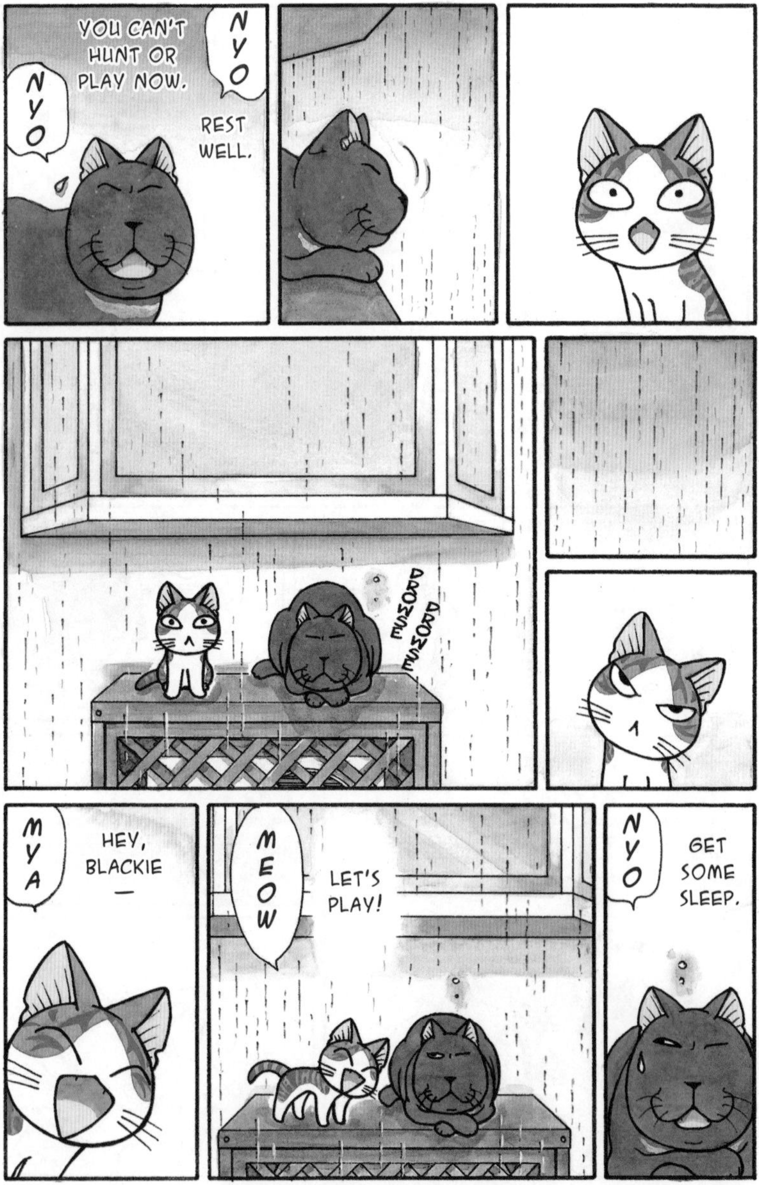
NYO
YOU CAN'T HUNT OR PLAY NOW.
NYO
REST WELL.
DROWSE DROWSE
MYA
HEY, BLACKIE —
MEOW
LET'S PLAY!
NYO
GET SOME SLEEP.

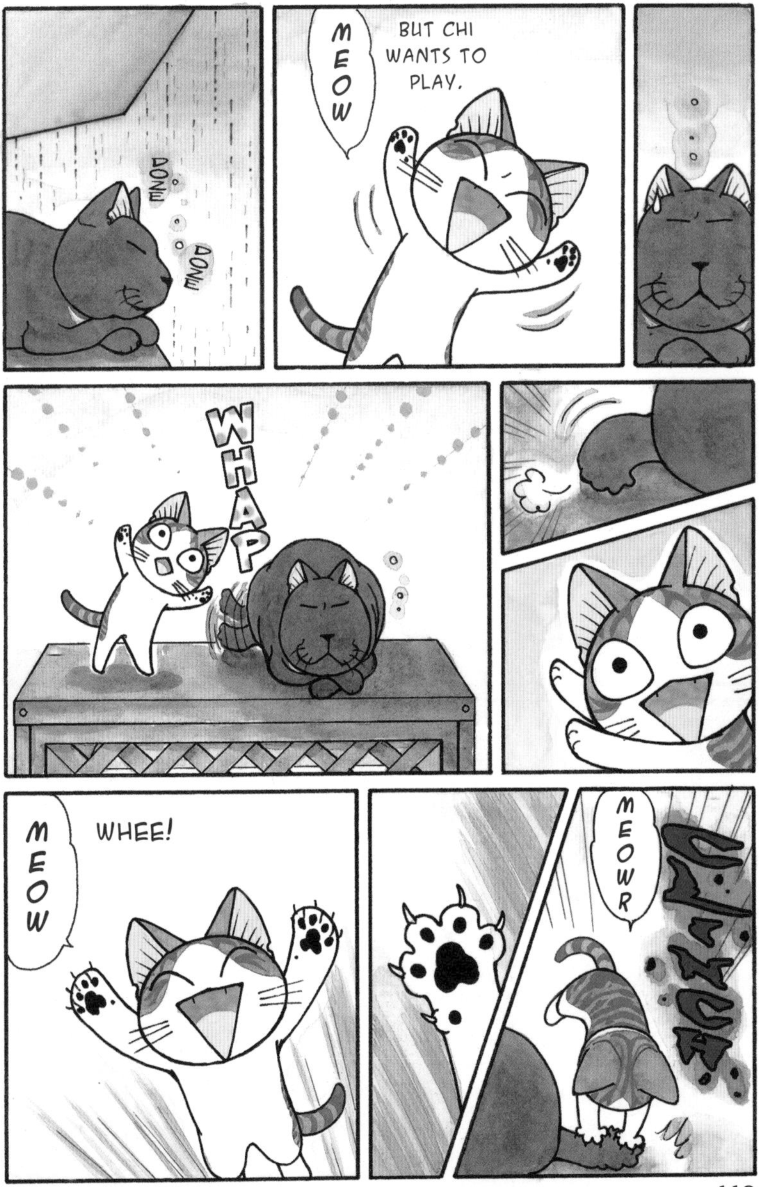
DONE
DONE
MEOW
BUT CHI WANTS TO PLAY.
WHAP
MEOW
WHEE!
MEOWR
CRUNCH

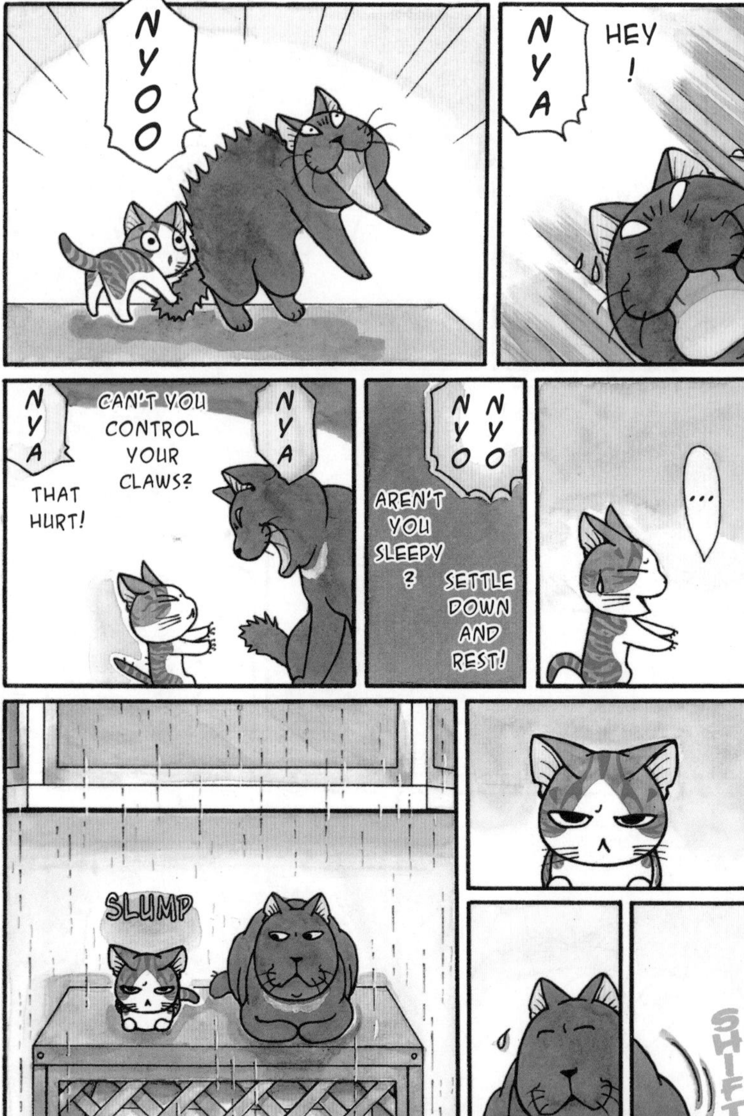
NYOO
NYA
HEY!
NYA
CAN'T YOU CONTROL YOUR CLAWS?
NYA
THAT HURT!
NYO NYO
AREN'T YOU SLEEPY?
SETTLE DOWN AND REST!
...
SLUMP
SHIFT

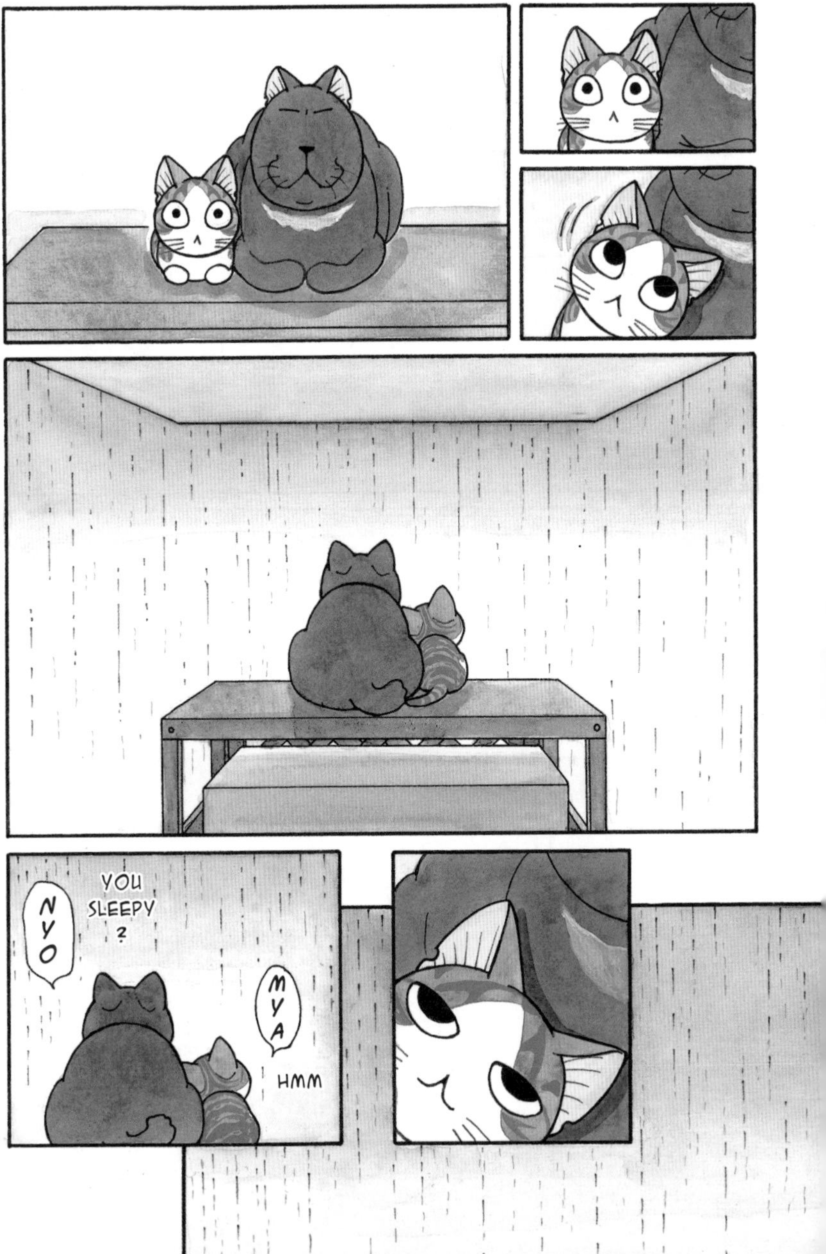
YOU SLEEPY ?
NYO
MYA
HMM

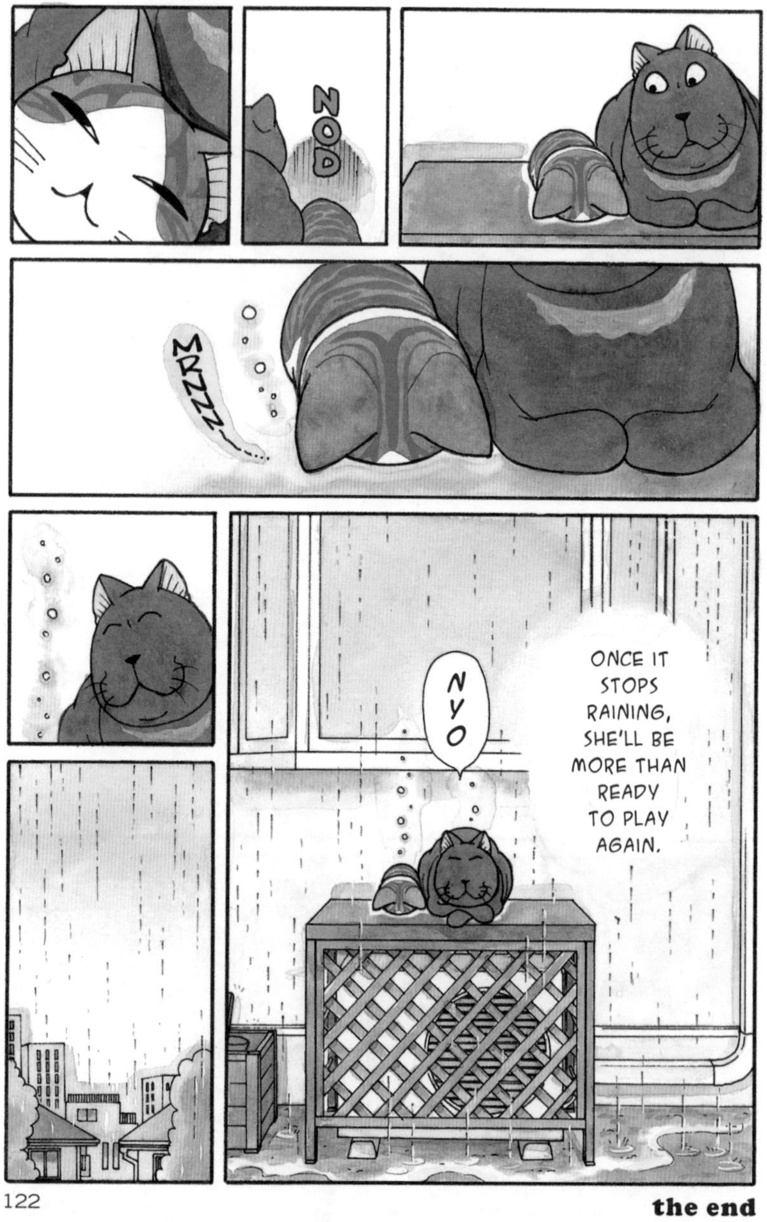
NOD
MRNZZZ
NYO
ONCE IT STOPS RAINING, SHE'LL BE MORE THAN READY TO PLAY AGAIN.

the end

homemade 180: a cat masters

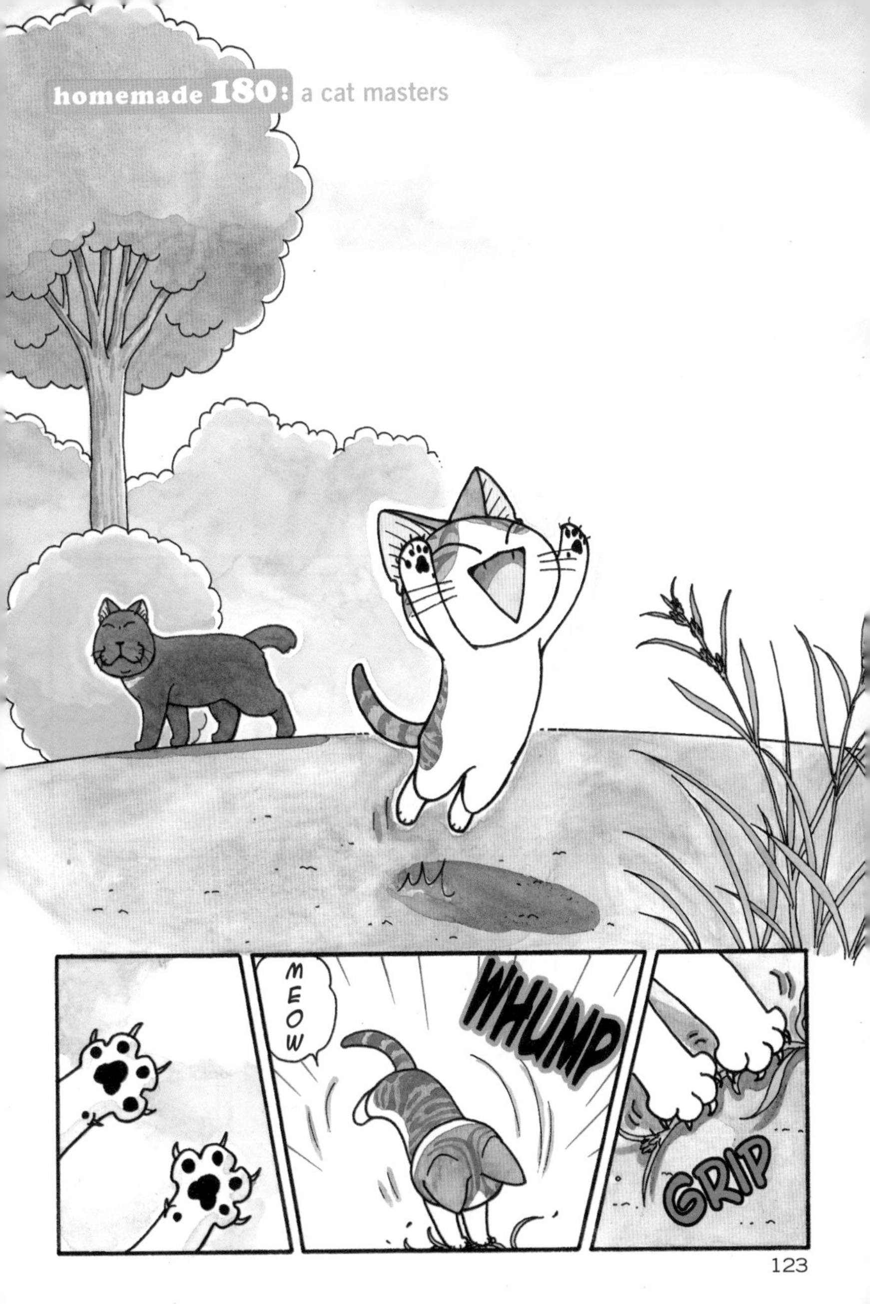
MEOW
WHUMP
GRIP

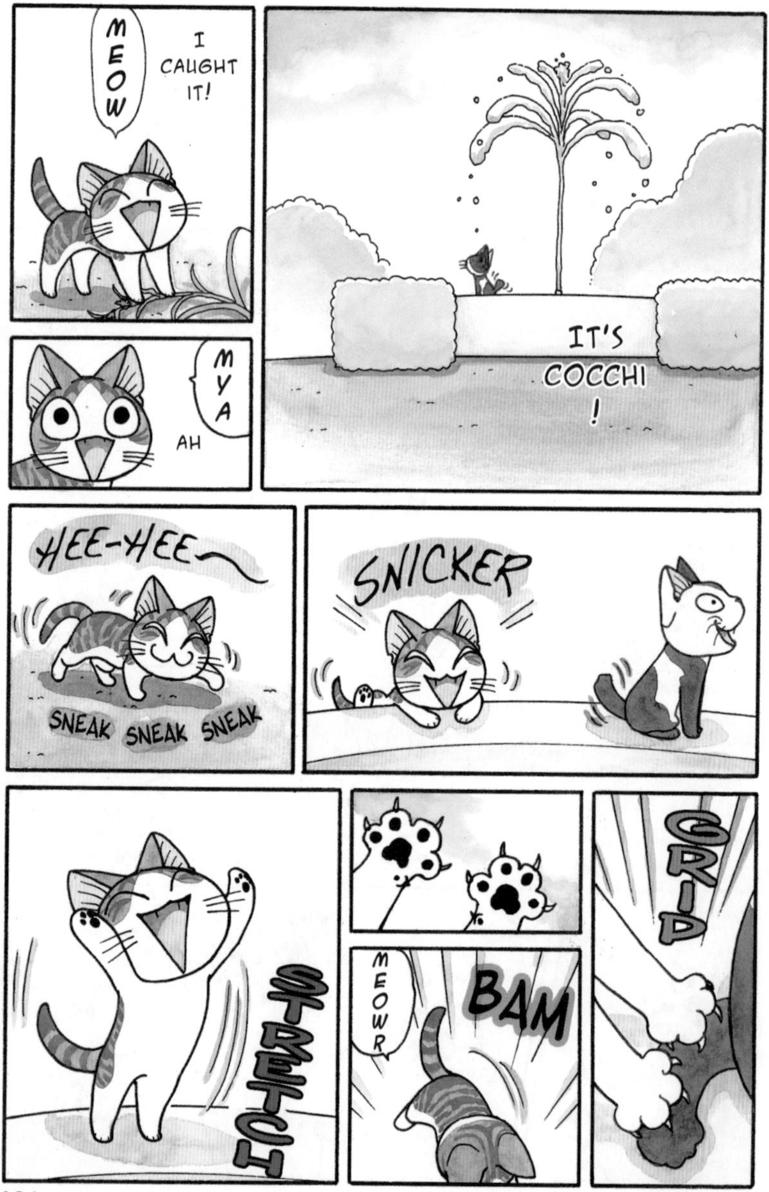
MEOW
I CAUGHT IT!
MYA
AH
IT'S COCCHI!
HEE-HEE~
SNEAK SNEAK SNEAK
SNICKER
STRETCH
MEOWR
BAM
GRIP

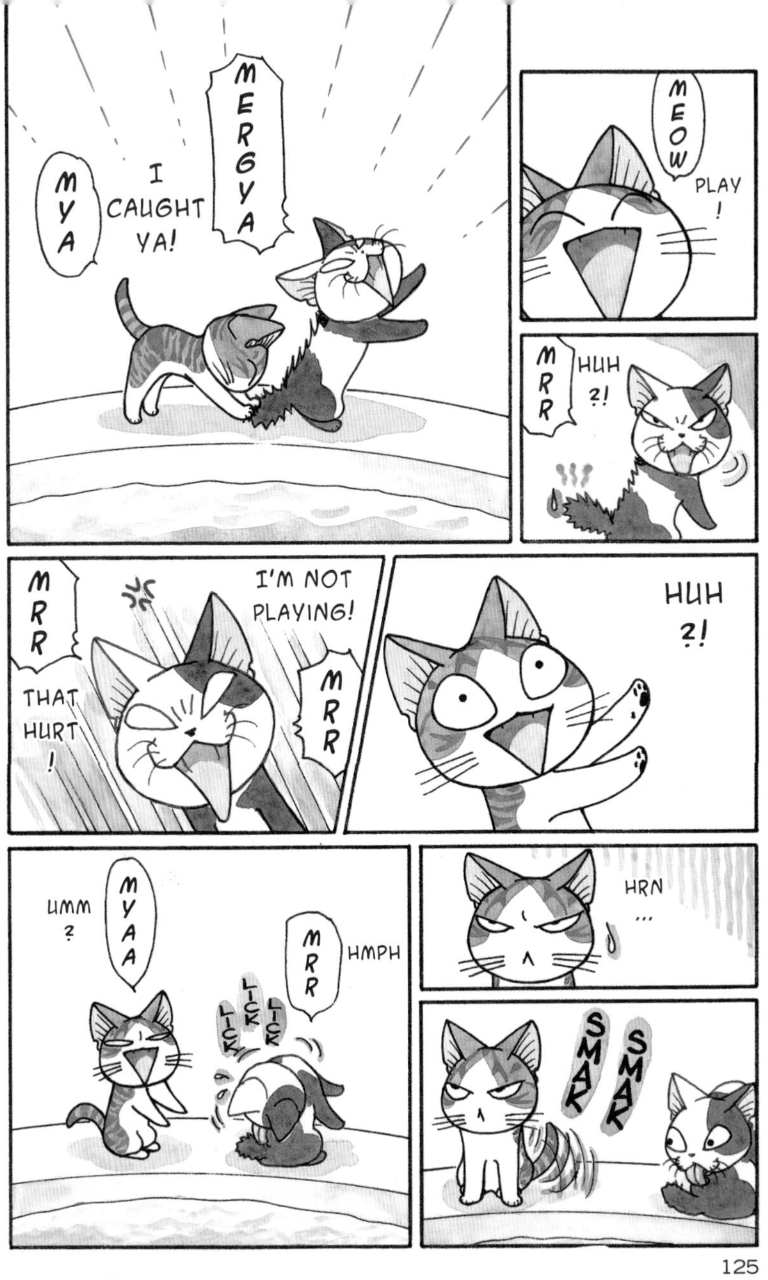
MYA
I CAUGHT YA!
MERGYA
MEOW
PLAY!
MRR
HUH ?!
MRR
THAT HURT!
I'M NOT PLAYING!
MRR
HUH ?!
UMM ?
MYAA
LICK LICK LICK
MRR
HMPH
HRN ...
SMAK SMAK

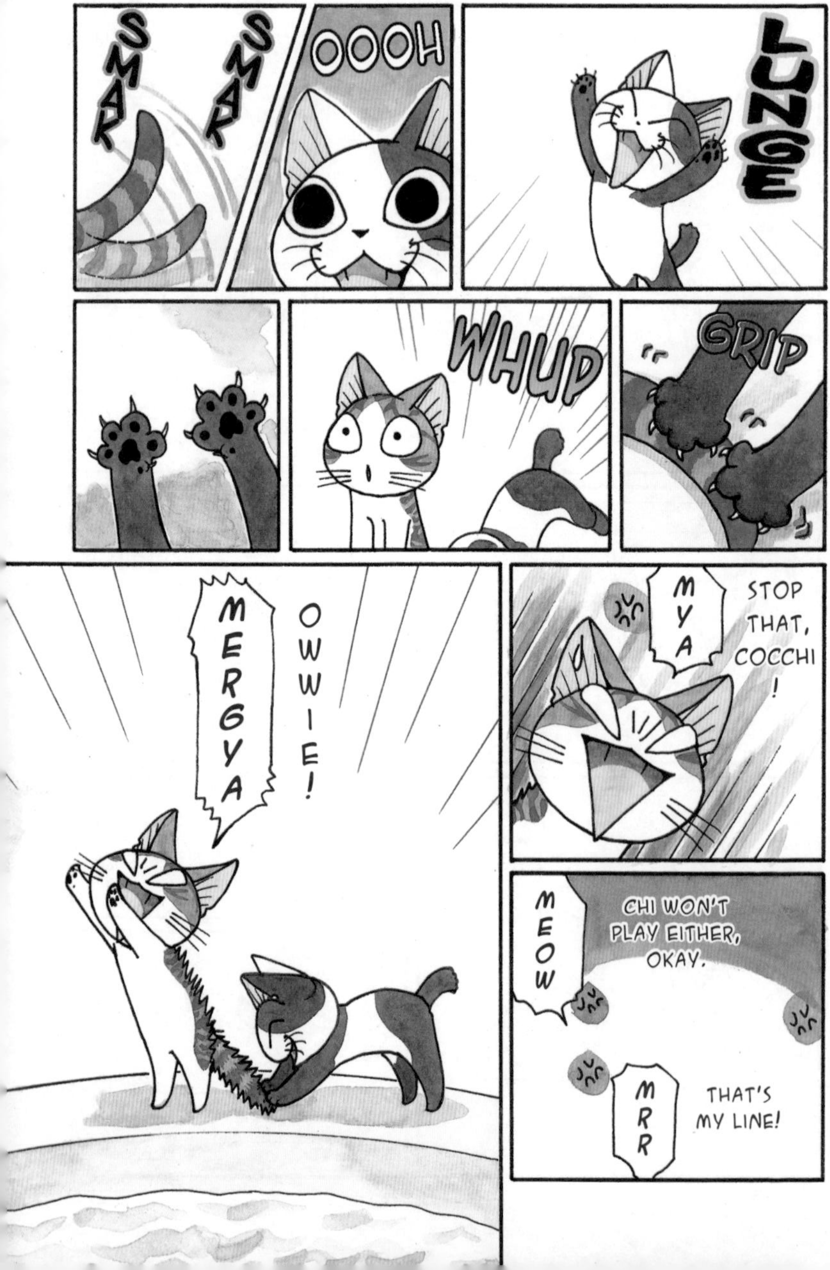
SMAR
SMAR
OOOH
LUNGE
WHUD
GRIP
MERGYA
OWWIE!
MYA
STOP THAT, COCCHI!
MEOW
CHI WON'T PLAY EITHER, OKAY.
MRR
THAT'S MY LINE!

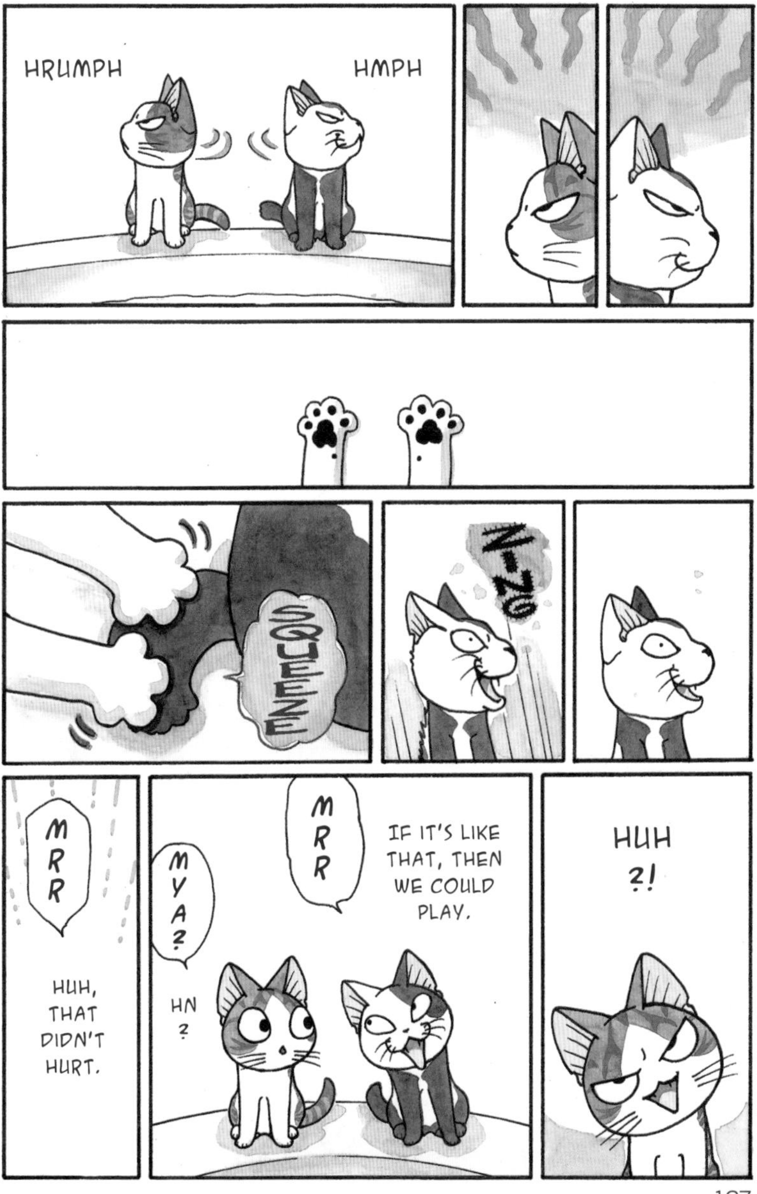
HRUMPH
HMPH
SQUEEZE
N-NG
MRR
HUH, THAT DIDN'T HURT.
MYA?
HN?
MRR
IF IT'S LIKE THAT, THEN WE COULD PLAY.
HUH?!

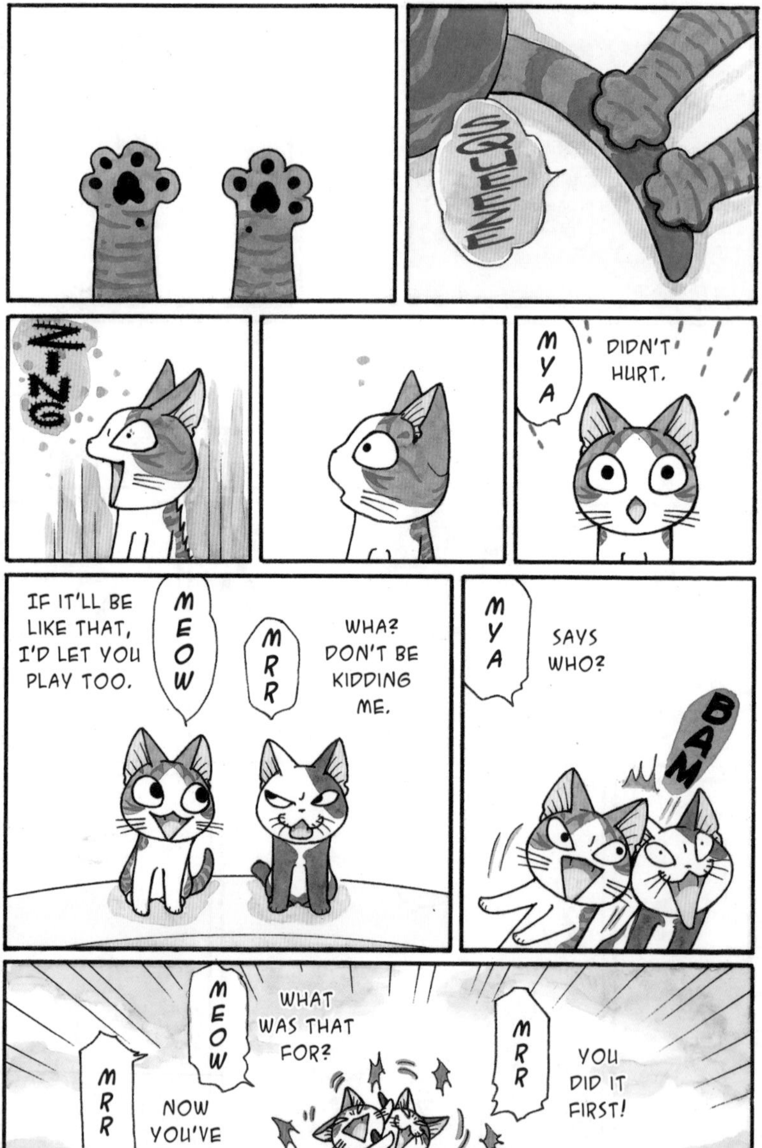
SQUEEZE
ZING
MYA
DIDN'T HURT.
IF IT'LL BE LIKE THAT, I'D LET YOU PLAY TOO.
MEOW
MRR
WHA? DON'T BE KIDDING ME.
MYA
SAYS WHO?
BAM
MRR
NOW YOU'VE DONE IT!
MEOW
WHAT WAS THAT FOR?
MRR
YOU DID IT FIRST!

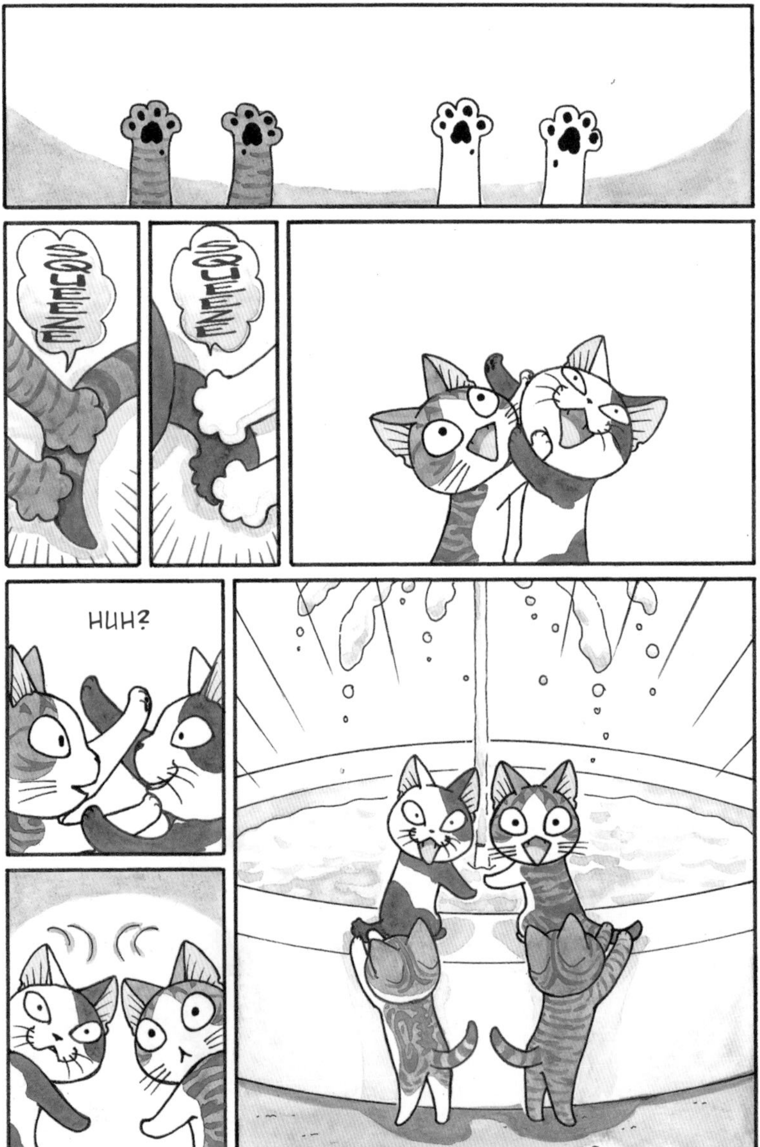
SQUEEZE
SQUEEZE
HUH?

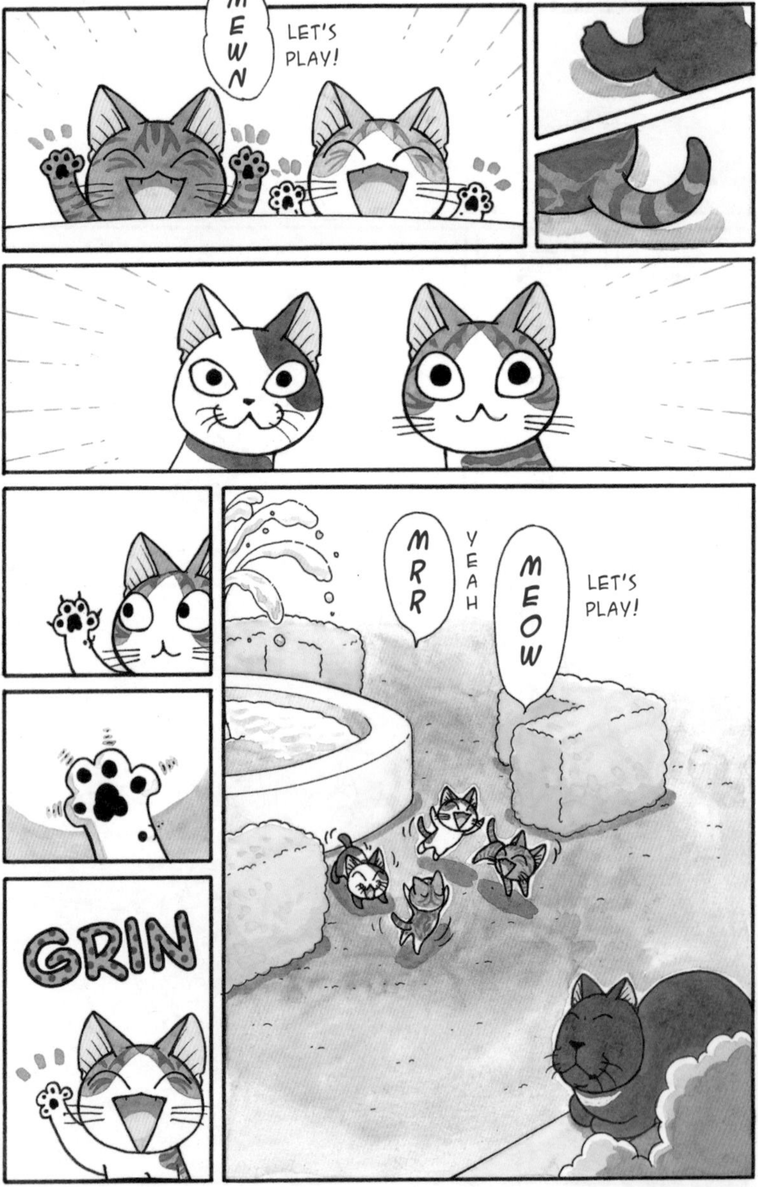
MEWN
LET'S PLAY!
GRIN
MRR
YEAH
MEOW
LET'S PLAY!

the end

homemade 181: a cat joins up

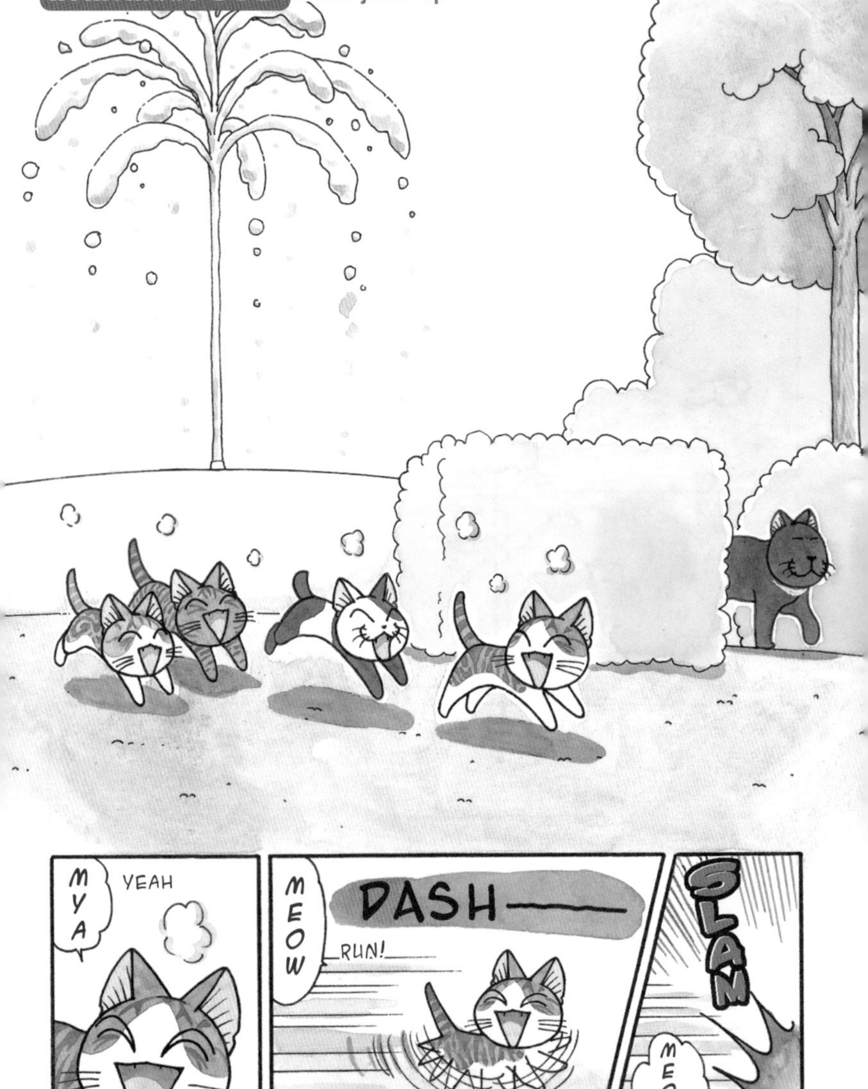
MYA
YEAH
MEOW
DASH——
RUN!
SLAM
MEOWN

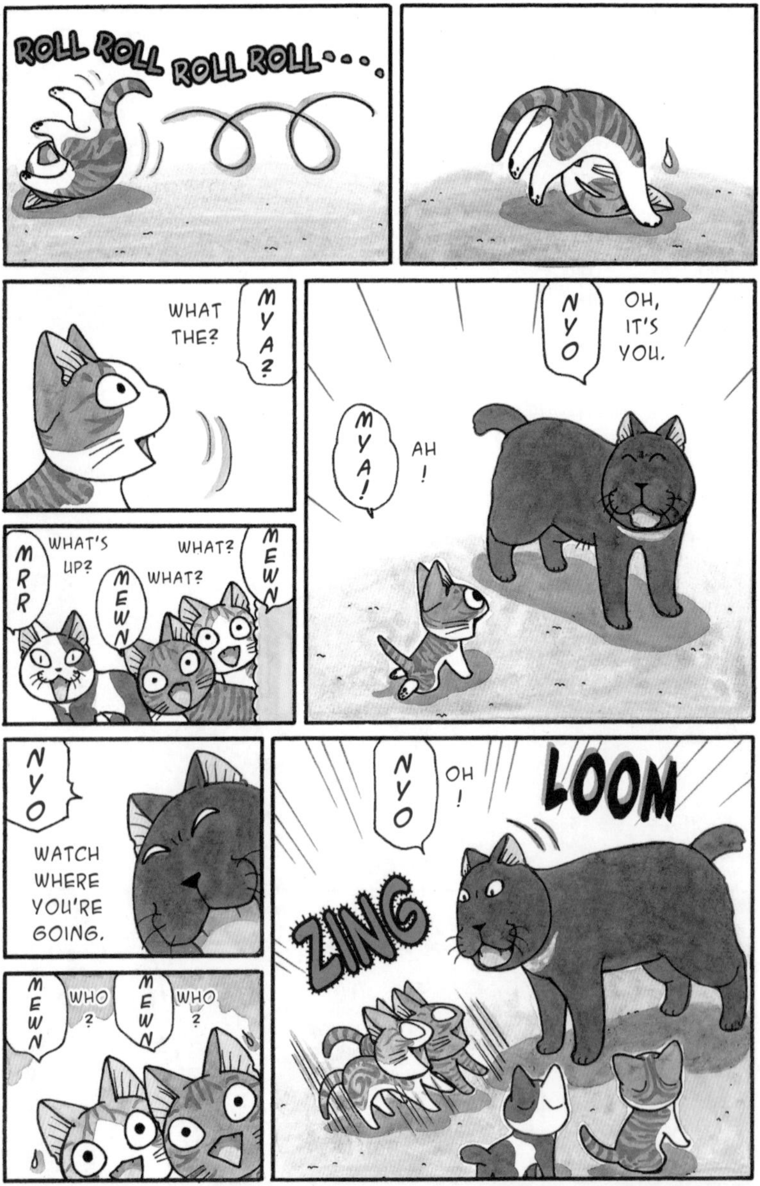
ROLL ROLL ROLL ROLL....
MYA?
WHAT THE?
MRR
WHAT'S UP?
MEWN
WHAT?
WHAT?
MEWN
NYO
OH, IT'S YOU.
MYA!
AH!
NYO
WATCH WHERE YOU'RE GOING.
MEWN
WHO?
MEWN
WHO?
NYO
OH!
LOOM
ZING

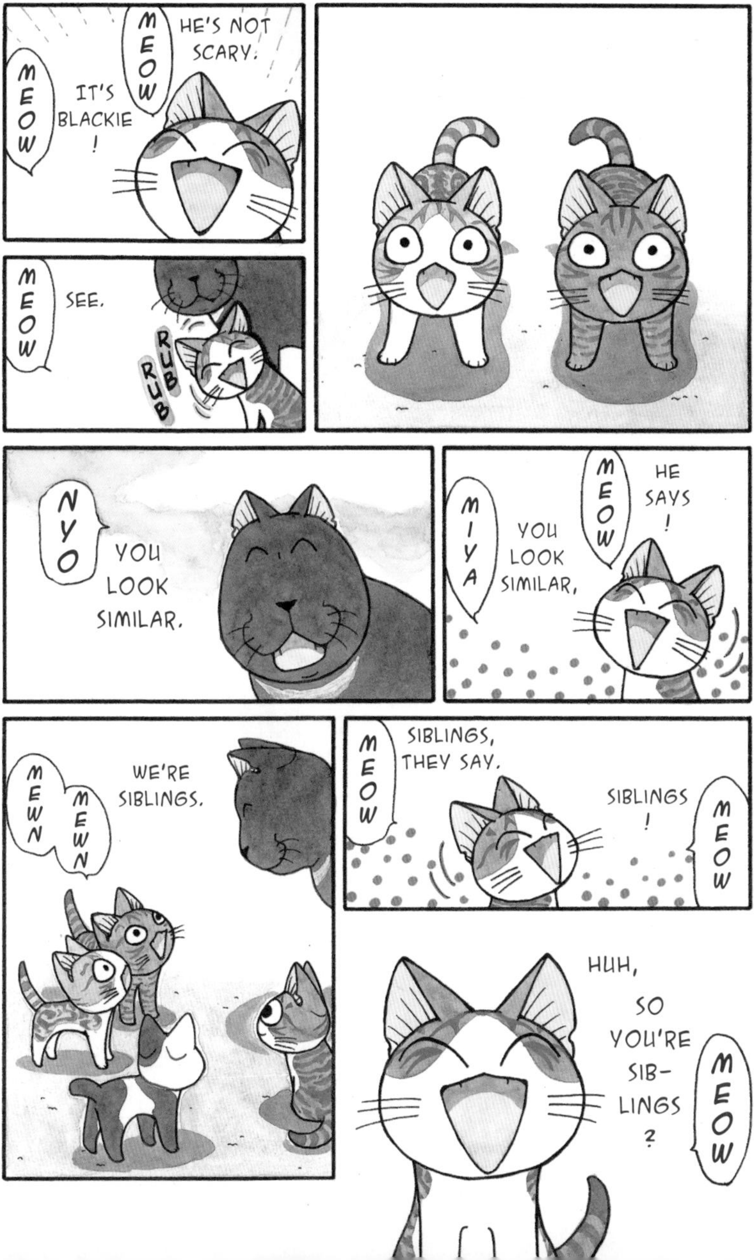
MEOW
IT'S BLACKIE!
MEOW
HE'S NOT SCARY.
MEOW
SEE.
RUB
RUB
NYO
YOU LOOK SIMILAR.
MIYA
YOU LOOK SIMILAR,
MEOW
HE SAYS!
MEWN
MEWN
WE'RE SIBLINGS.
MEOW
SIBLINGS, THEY SAY.
SIBLINGS!
MEOW
HUH, SO YOU'RE SIB-LINGS?
MEOW

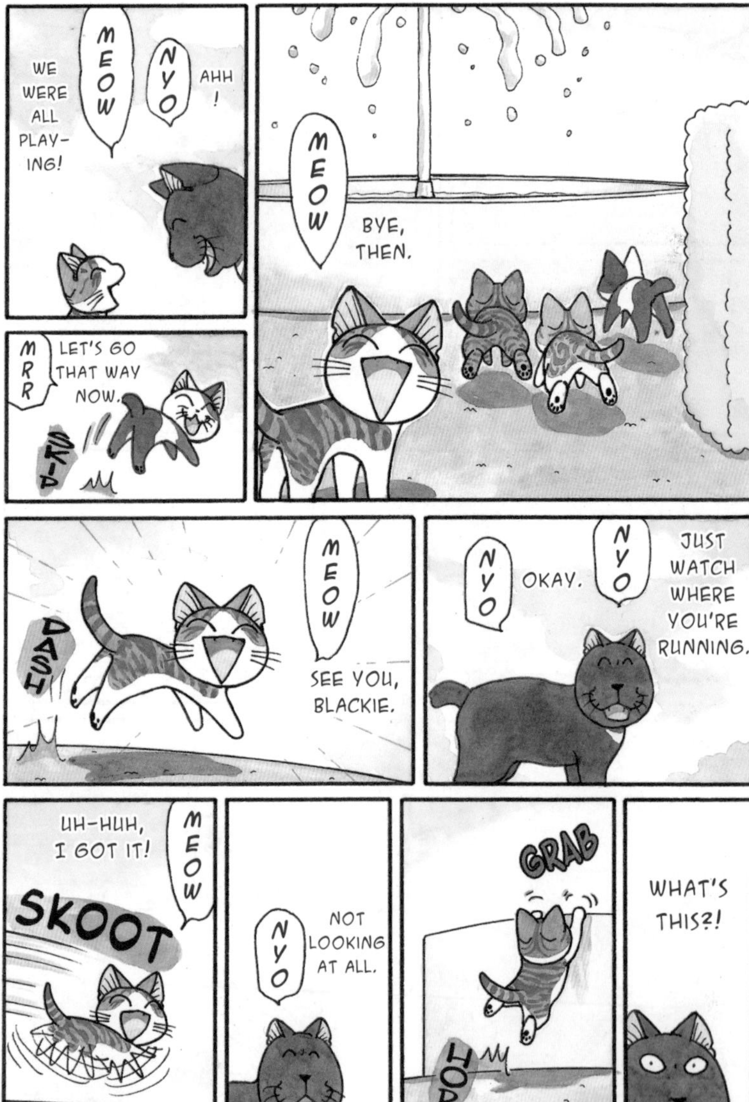

WE WERE ALL PLAYING!
MEOW
NYO
AHH!
MRR
LET'S GO THAT WAY NOW.
SKID
MEOW
BYE, THEN.
DASH
MEOW
SEE YOU, BLACKIE.
NYO
OKAY.
NYO
JUST WATCH WHERE YOU'RE RUNNING.
UH-HUH, I GOT IT!
MEOW
SKOOT
NYO
NOT LOOKING AT ALL.
GRAB
HOP
WHAT'S THIS?!

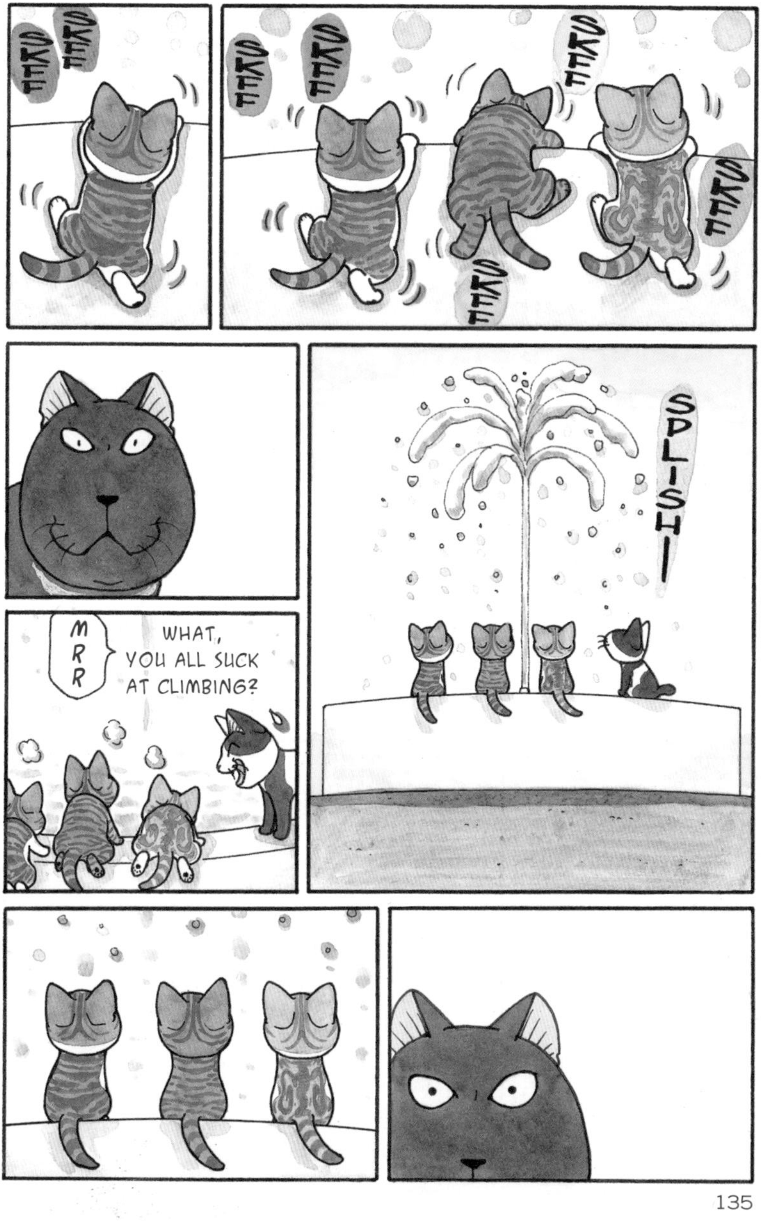
SKEE
SKEE
SKEE
SKEE
SKEE
SKEE
SKEE
MRR
WHAT, YOU ALL SUCK AT CLIMBING?
SPLISH!

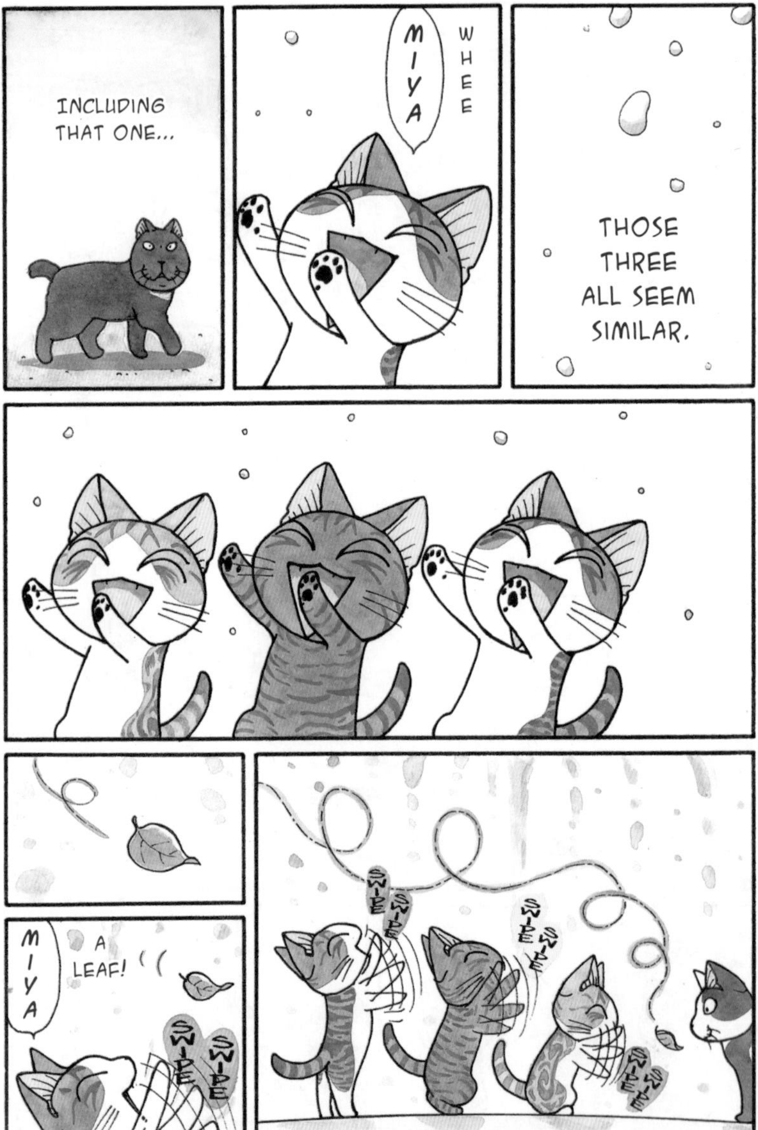
INCLUDING THAT ONE...
MIYA
WHEE
THOSE THREE ALL SEEM SIMILAR.
MIYA
A LEAF!
SWIPE
SWIPE
SWIPE
SWIPE
SWIPE
SWIPE
SWIPE
SWIPE

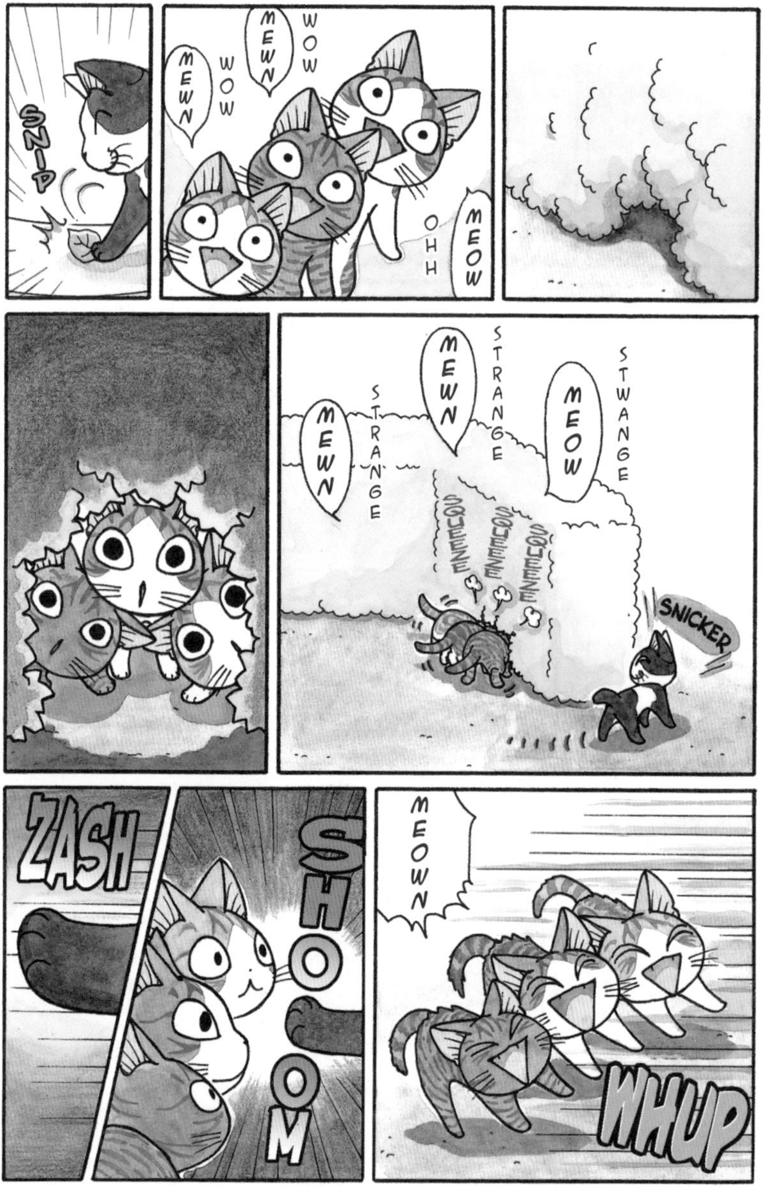
SNIP
MEWN
WOW
MEWN
WOW
OHH
MEOW
MEWN
STRANGE
MEWN
STRANGE
MEOW
STWANGE
SQUEEZE
SQUEEZE
SQUEEZE
SNICKER
ZASH
SHOOM
MEOWN
WHUP

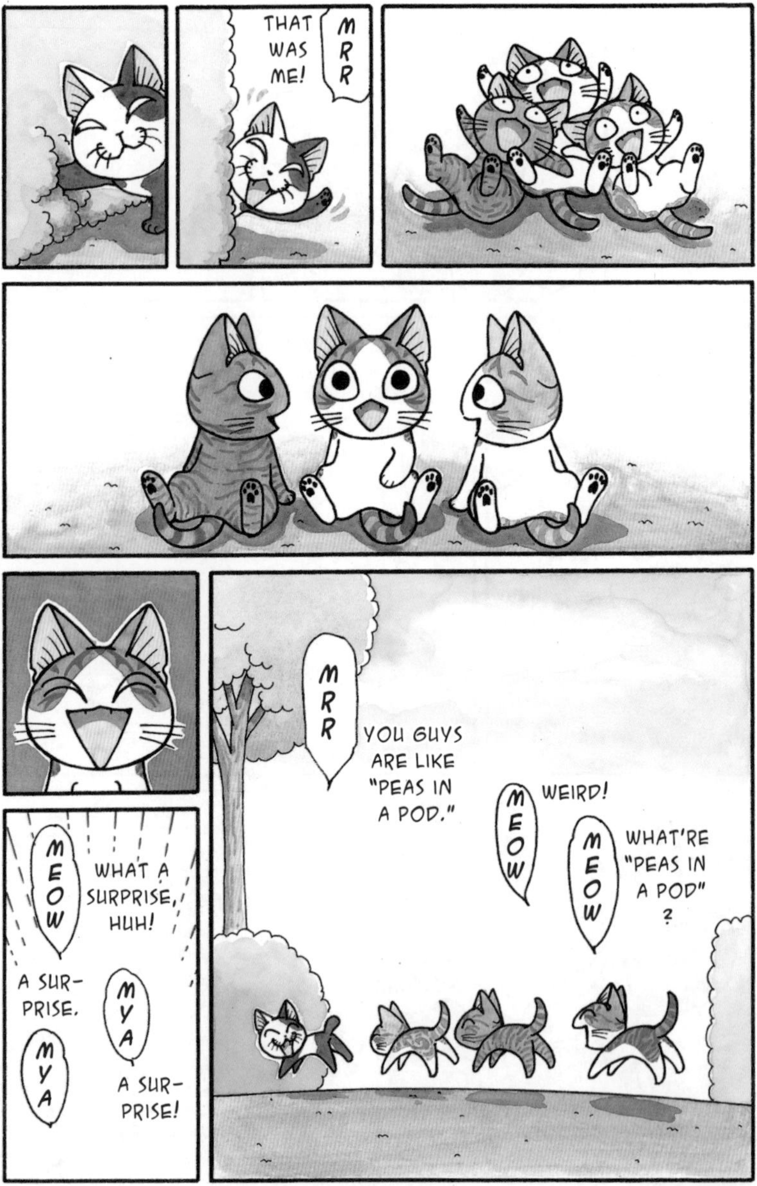
THAT WAS ME!
MRR
MEOW
WHAT A SURPRISE, HUH!
A SUR-PRISE.
MYA
MYA
A SUR-PRISE!
MRR
YOU GUYS ARE LIKE "PEAS IN A POD."
MEOW
WEIRD!
MEOW
WHAT'RE "PEAS IN A POD"?

the end

homemade 182: a cat begins to change

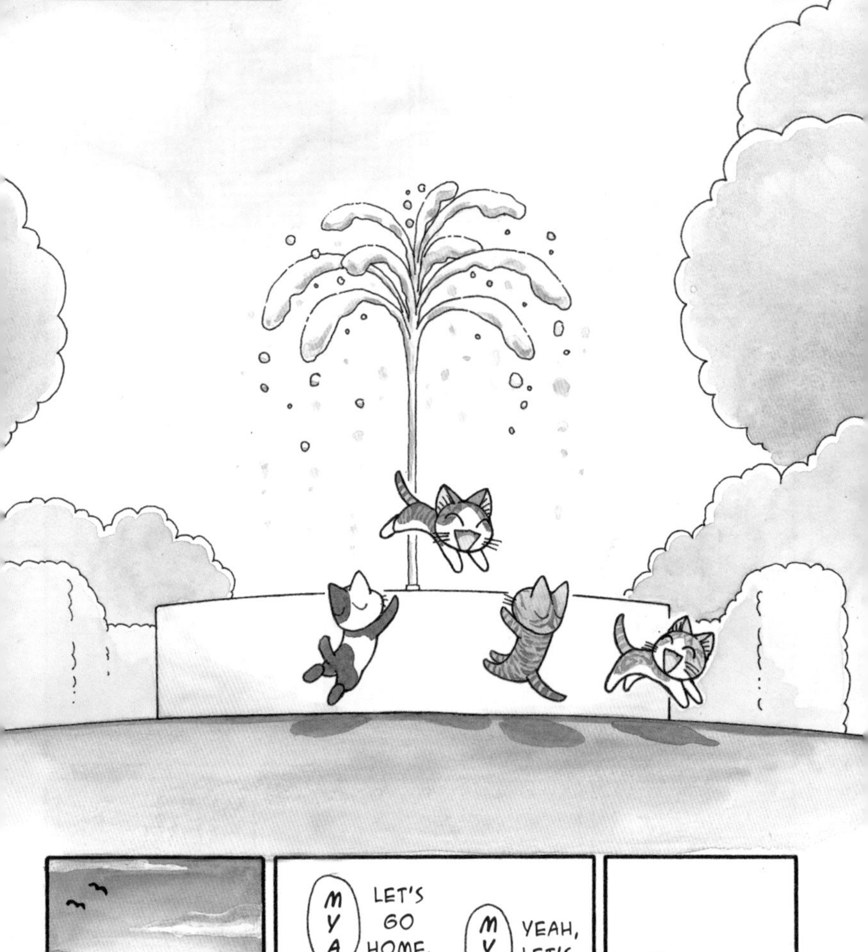
MYA
LET'S GO HOME.
MYA
YEAH, LET'S.

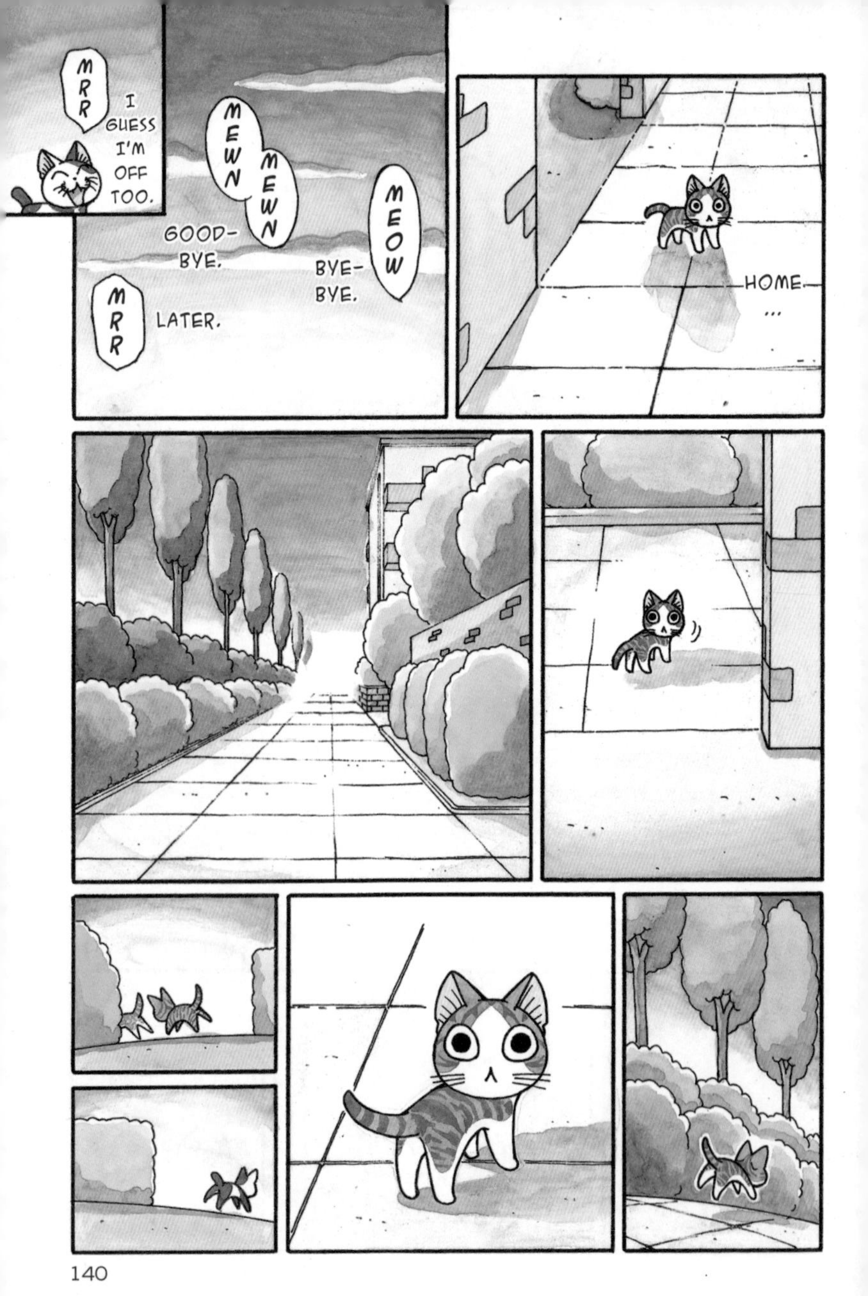
MRR
I GUESS I'M OFF TOO.
MEWN
MEWN
GOOD-BYE.
MEOW
BYE-BYE.
MRR
LATER.
HOME...

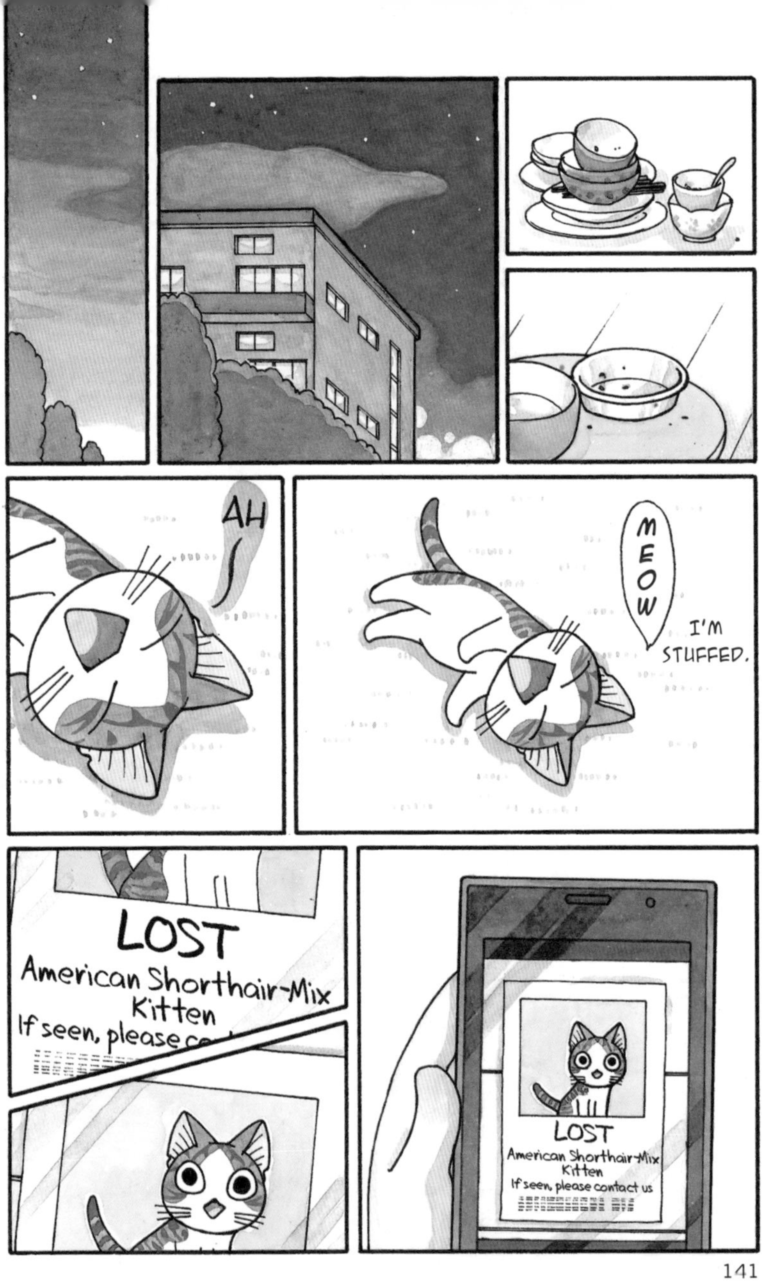

AH
MEOW
I'M STUFFED.
LOST
American Shorthair-Mix Kitten
If seen, please co
LOST
American Shorthair-Mix Kitten
If seen, please contact us

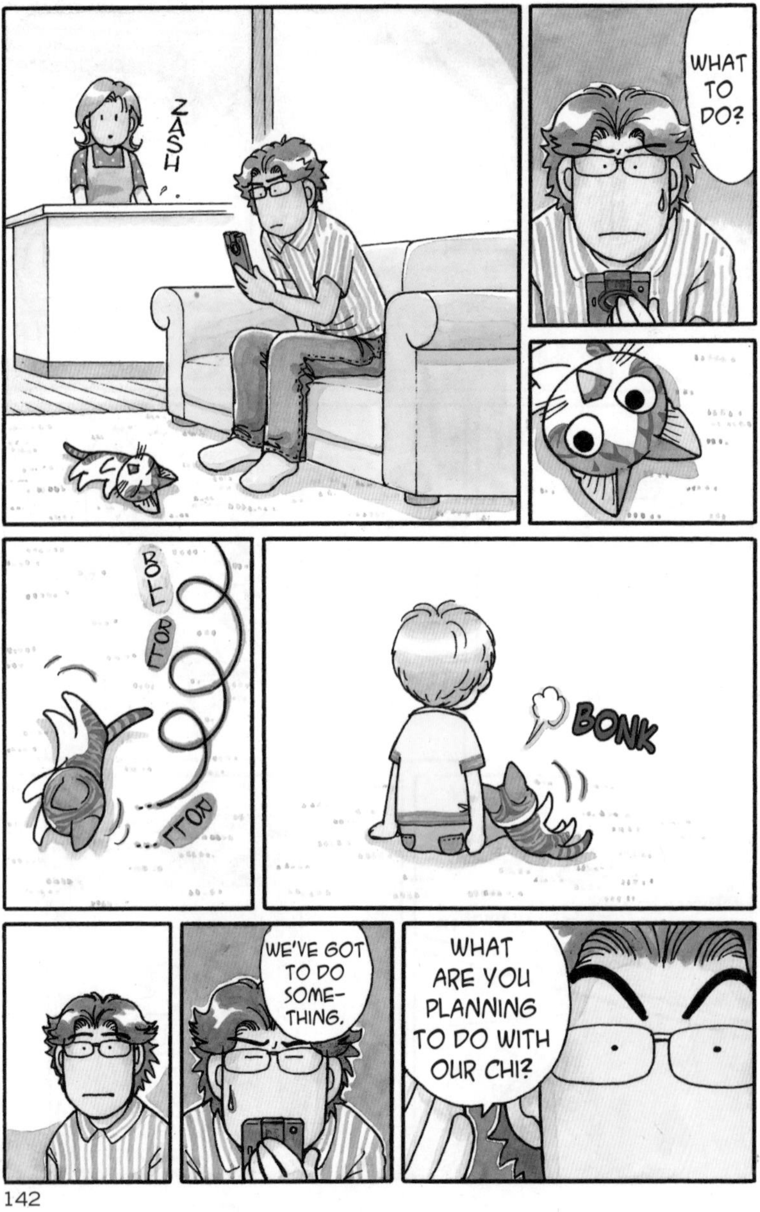
ZASH
WHAT TO DO?
ROLL ROLL ROLL
BONK
WE'VE GOT TO DO SOME-THING.
WHAT ARE YOU PLANNING TO DO WITH OUR CHI?

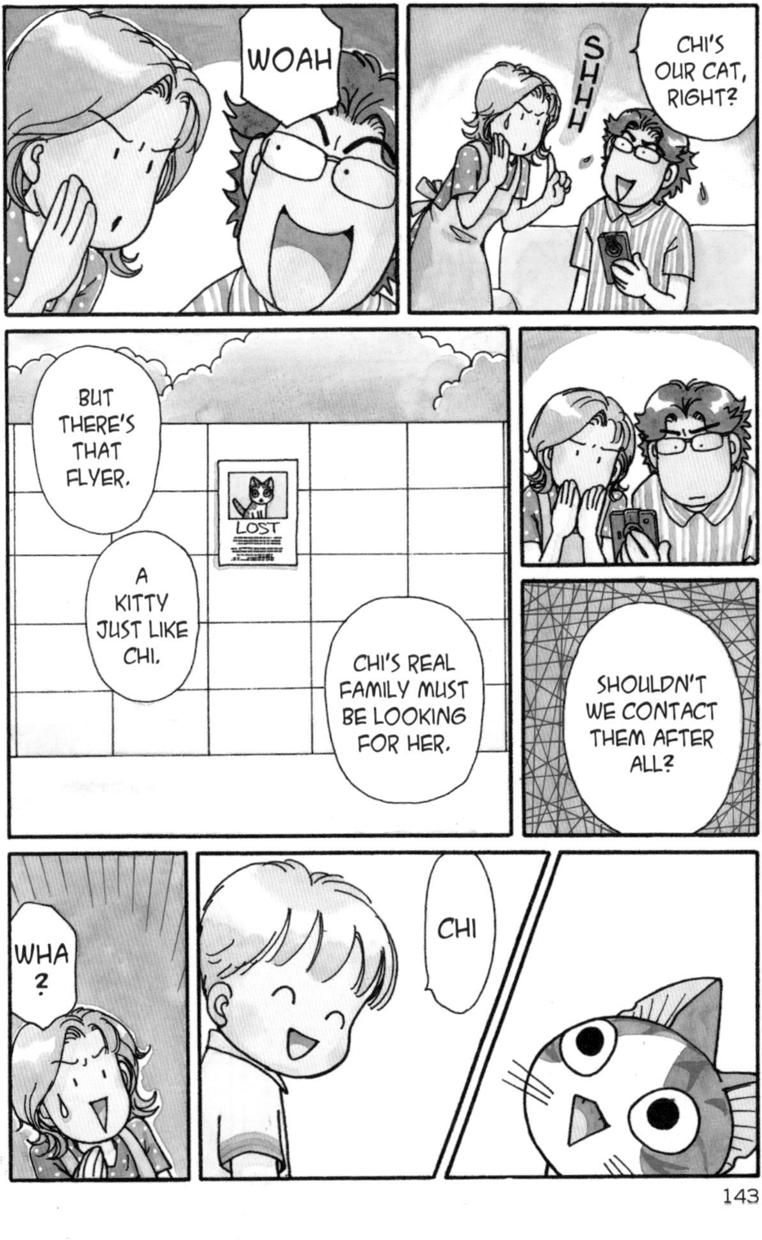
WOAH
SHHH
CHI'S OUR CAT, RIGHT?
BUT THERE'S THAT FLYER.
LOST
A KITTY JUST LIKE CHI.
CHI'S REAL FAMILY MUST BE LOOKING FOR HER.
SHOULDN'T WE CONTACT THEM AFTER ALL?
WHA ?
CHI

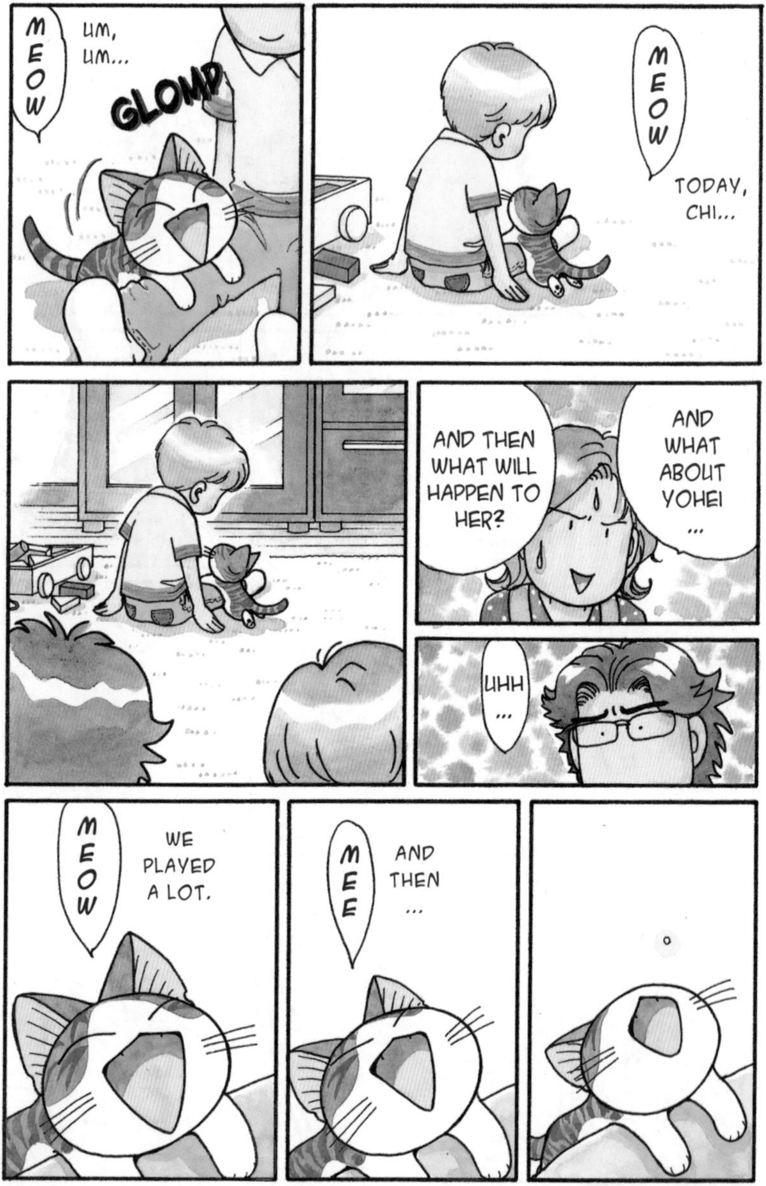
MEOW
UM, UM...
GLOMP
MEOW
TODAY, CHI...
AND THEN WHAT WILL HAPPEN TO HER?
AND WHAT ABOUT YOHEI ...
UHH ...
MEOW
WE PLAYED A LOT.
MEE
AND THEN ...

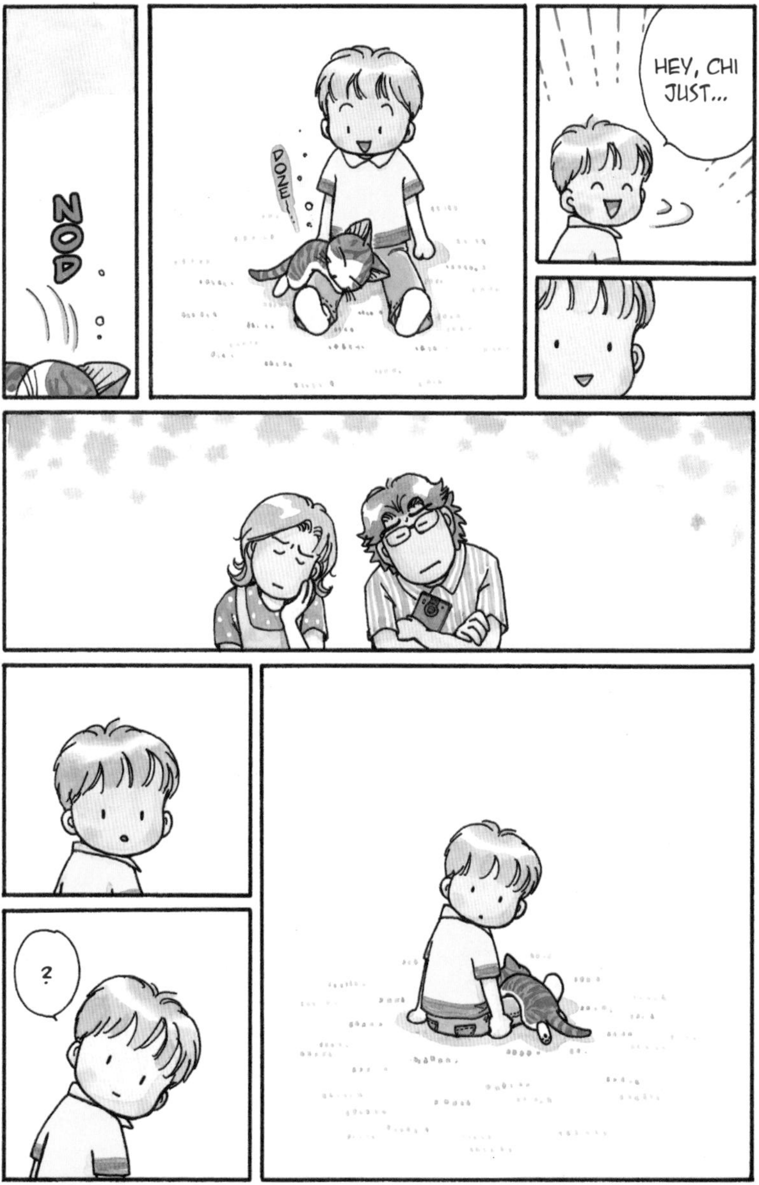
NOD
DOZE...
HEY, CHI JUST...
?

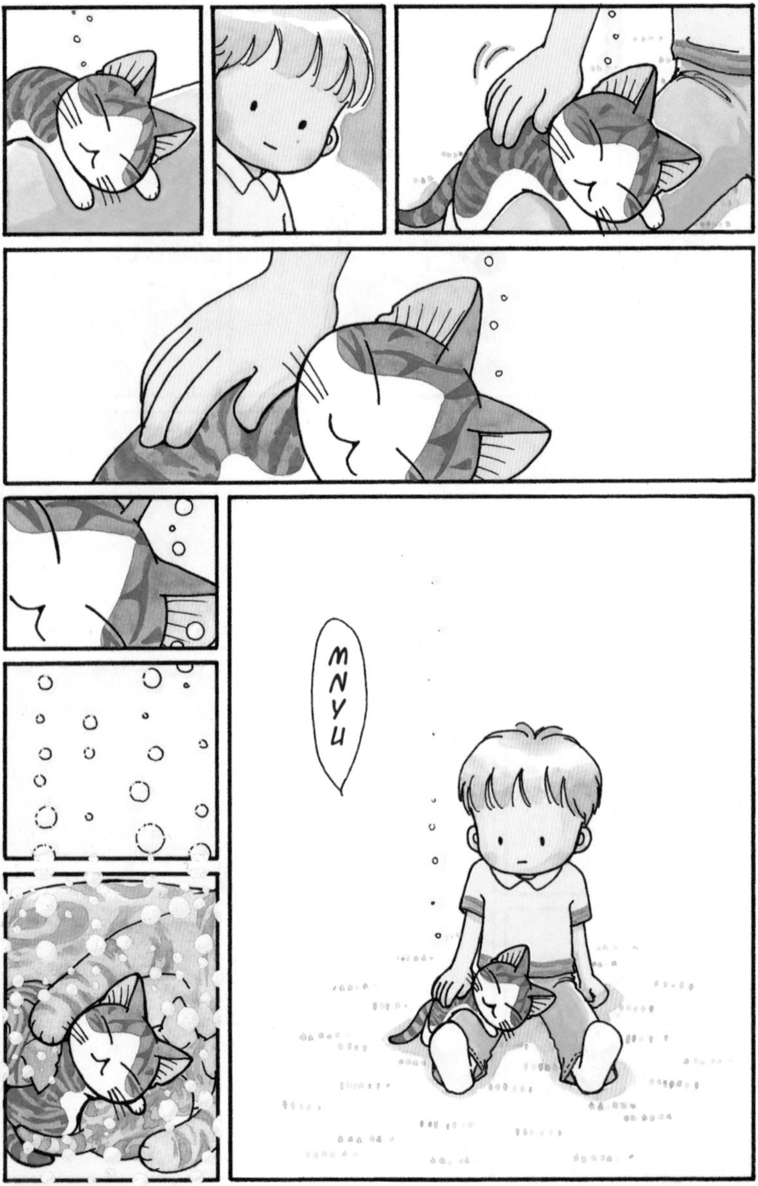
MNYU

the end

Chi's Sweet Extras

Message Cards: Cut out and give to friends!

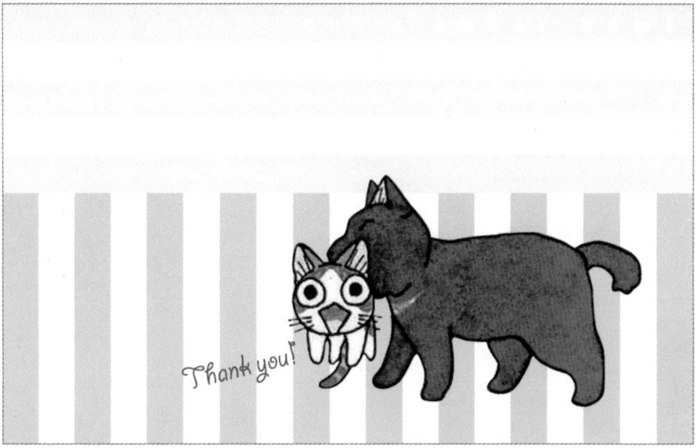
Thank you!

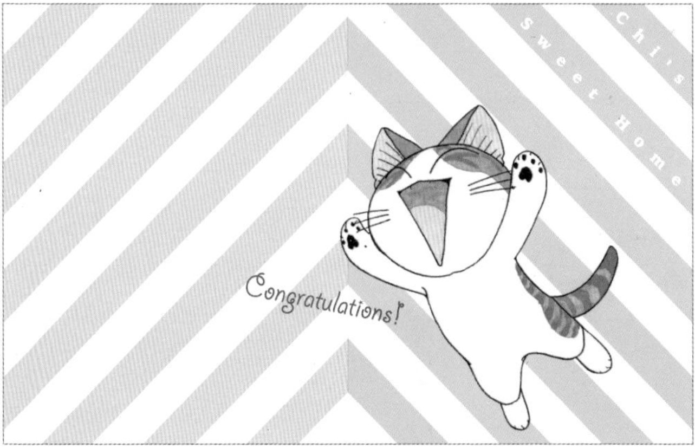
Chi's Sweet Home
Congratulations!

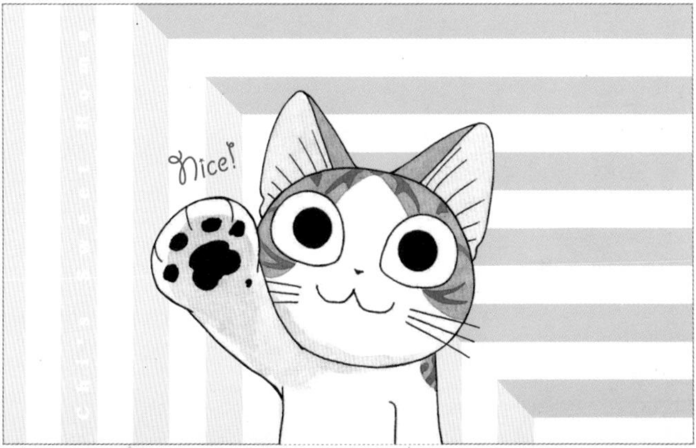
Nice!

Chi and Cocchi Spinning Fan

★ Cut out images

★ Tape both to a stick (like a chopstick)

★ Spin it between your hands!

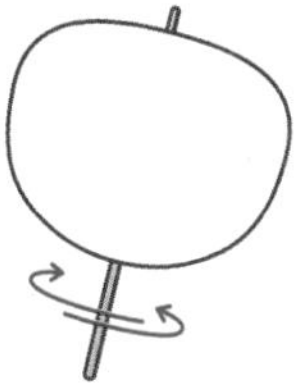

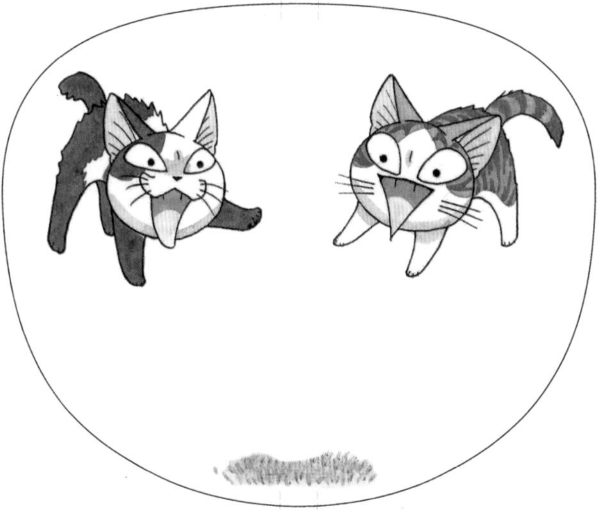

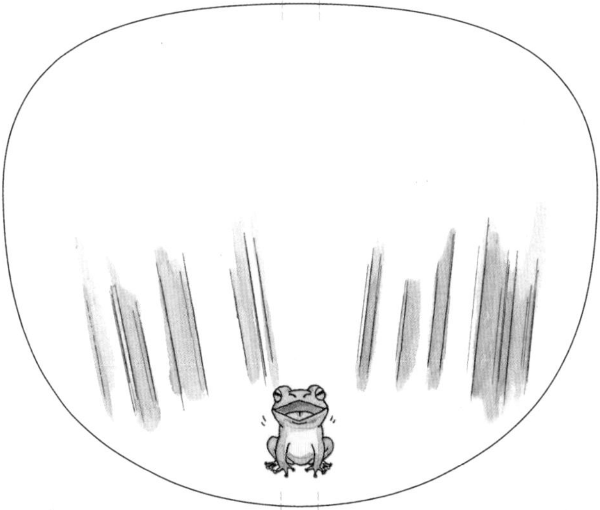

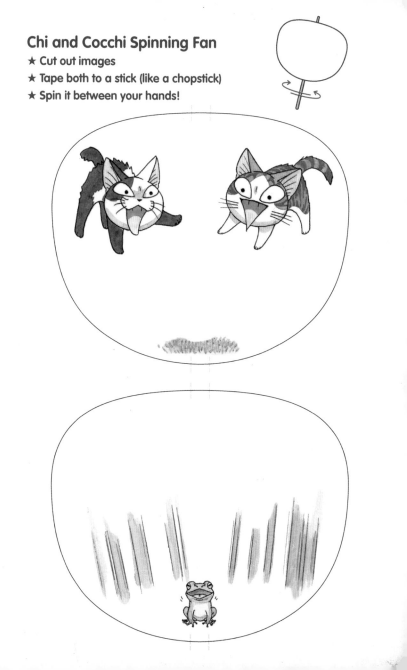

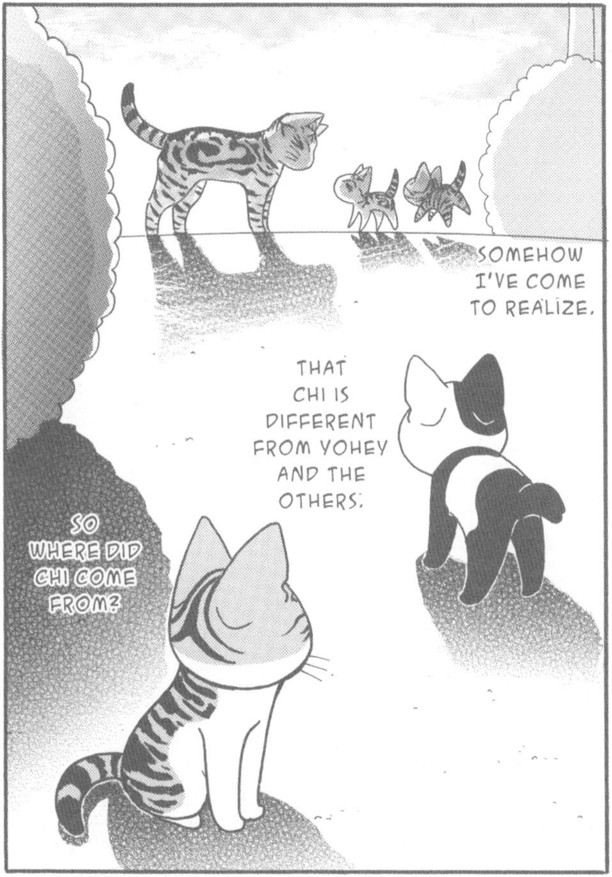
SOMEHOW I'VE COME TO REALIZE.
THAT CHI IS DIFFERENT FROM YOHEY AND THE OTHERS.
SO WHERE DID CHI COME FROM?

Chi's Sweet Home volume 11
goes on sale

FALL 2014!!

Chi's Sweet Home, volume 10

Translation - Ed Chavez
Production - Grace Lu
Hiroko Mizuno
Anthony Quintessenza

First published in Japan in 2013 by Kodansha, Ltd., Tokyo
Publication for this English edition arranged through Kodansha, Ltd., Tokyo
English language version produced by Vertical, Inc.

Translation provided by Vertical, Inc., 2013
Published by Vertical, Inc., New York

Originally published in Japanese as *Chiizu Suiito Houmu* by Kodansha, Ltd., 2011-2012
Chiizu Suiito Houmu first serialized in *Morning*, Kodansha, Ltd., 2004-

ISBN: 978-1-935654-69-8

Manufactured in China

First Edition

Vertical, Inc.
451 Park Avenue South, 7th Floor
New York, NY 10016
www.vertical-inc.com

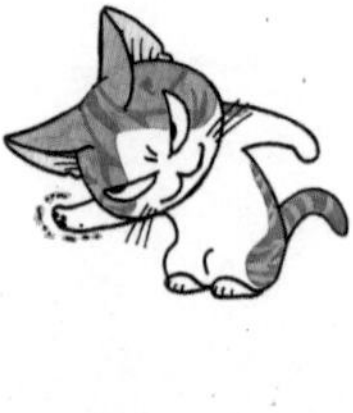

Special thanks to: K. Kitamoto